Expats IN BRUSSELS

2000

2ND EDITION

Editors
Claire de Crayencour and Anne-Claire de Liedekerke
Drawings: Philippine de Laroussilhe

FOREWORD

The Brussels-Capital Region is situated at the crossroads of Germanic and Latin influences. The Region has always been a meeting point in Europe. Since the world exhibition in 1958, Brussels has continuously reinforced its international role. Since 1960, European institutions as well as many other international organisations established head offices in Brussels. The city boasts the greatest number of international correspondents and is also one of the most important congress and diplomatic centres.

Such is the image of our city for people who do not know Brussels. Those who visit Brussels know that our Region is open and wants to stay that way. It wants to be the capital city for all Europeans, a city that's good both to be in and to work in, and where everyone feels at home.

Brussels seduces by its gastronomy, its folklore, its green spaces, its variety of education and so many other elements which can not be said in a few words.

I'm therefore delighted with the edition of this guide, which will help you discover the various aspects that make Brussels what it is and will continue to be: a human-sized city that you only think you are looking at with your eyes but that you finally end up loving with your heart.

Jacques Simonet
Minister-President of the Government
of the Brussels-Capital Region

Introduction

Brussels was born at the crossroads of the Latin and Germanic cultures. Ever since she was founded she has been a land of migration. Invaded many times during her history, she is accustomed to living side by side with people from a whole variety of backgrounds, and assimilating them. Haven't we all, at some time been Roman, Burgundian, Spanish, Austrian, French, Dutch... ? Today the presence of the European Union and NATO as well as a whole host of official delegations and foreign companies, means that, more than ever, many different nationalities and cultures live side-by-side in Brussels.

If you belong to Brussels by adoption you will soon belong to Brussels with your heart and soul. This kaleidoscope city will win you over.

Any initiative which helps our capital to become better known and which makes it easier for expatriates to participate in the cultural and social life of Brussels, must receive our support. A guide like this one is a true « open Sesame ». It will give you access to green Brussels, the Brussels of the blues, the Brussels of laughter and the Brussels of dancing. A city where folklore is alive and well and traditions live on.

A city of the arts : whether it be the culinary arts or dramatic arts, the 7th art (cinema) or the 8th (comic strips). We worship comic strips as a cult! From her administrative district to the buzzing quaysides of her sea port, via her « Kaberdouches » smelling of authentic beers, and her markets echoing with earthy humour, Brussels is a microcosm which is well worth getting to know and it is up to us, her political representatives, to make her better known.

François-Xavier de Donnea
Minister of State
Mayor of Brussels

CONTENTS

EMERGENCIES

Fire Brigade	100
Emergency Medical Services	100
Police	101
Gendarmerie	101
Child Help Line	103
Red Cross - Belgium	105
Confidential help line - Tele Accueil	107
Child Focus	110
AIDS	078 / 15 15 15
Alcoholics anonymous	239 14 15
Blood bank	829 00 00
Car accidents (24 hours)	078 / 15 20 00
Help line in English	648 40 14
Help line in German	768 21 21
Anti Poison Centre	070 / 245 245
Burns Centre	268 62 00
Suicide Prevention	649 65 55
Ambulance	649 11 22
Out of hours doctors	513 02 02
Out of hours dentists	426 10 26
Out of hours pharmacy	0900 / 10500
Out of hours vets	538 16 99
Animal Ambulance	426 12 46
Touring Assistance	233 22 11
Water accidents	739 52 11
Gas	512 05 06 / 274 34 54
Lost or stolen bank cards	070 / 34 43 44

Brussels prefix: 02
From abroad : 00 32 2

SERVICES

Telephone out of order	0800 / 33700 (French)
	0800 / 22 700 (Dutch)
	0800 / 55 700 (English)
Telephone complaints	0800 / 33900 (French)
	0800 / 22900 (Dutch)
	0800 / 55900 (English)
National information	1307 (French)
	1405 (English)
	1207 (Dutch)
	1407 (German)
International information	1304 (French)
	1405 (English)
	1204 (Dutch)
	1404 (German)
Speaking clock	1300 (French)
	1200 (Dutch)
Weather	0900 / 27003

WELCOME TO BRUSSELS, THE CAPITAL OF EUROPE

Brussels
19 communes
2 languages
1 million inhabitants

The European Union
15 countries
11 official languages
375 millions inhabitants

Ganshoren
1083

Bruxelles
1020

Berchem-Ste-Agathe
1082

Jette
1090

Saint-Josse
1030

Evere
1140

Schaerbeek
1030

Koekelberg
1081

1080
Molenbeek-St-Jean

Bruxelles
1000

Woluwé-
St-Lambert
1200

Anderlecht
1070

Etterbeek
1040

Woluwé-St-Pierre
1150

St-Gilles
1060

Forest
1190

Ixelles
1050

Auderghem
1160

Uccle
1180

Watermael-
Boitsfort
1170

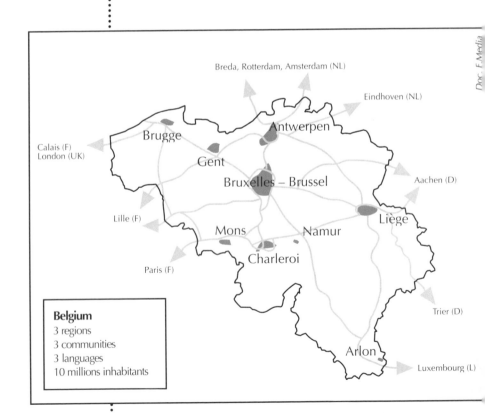

Breda, Rotterdam, Amsterdam (NL)

Eindhoven (NL)

Calais (F)
London (UK)

Brugge

Antwerpen

Gent

Aachen (D)

Bruxelles – Brussel

Lille (F)

Liège

Mons

Namur

Paris (F)

Charleroi

Trier (D)

Belgium
3 regions
3 communities
3 languages
10 millions inhabitants

Arlon

Luxembourg (L)

Doc. F.Media

Welcome Addresses

Intended for foreigners moving to Brussels, they offer an efficient and free service.

Bureau de liaison Bruxelles-Europe
Avenue d'Auderghem, 63
1040 Brussels
✆ 02 / 280 00 80
fax 02 / 280 03 86
An office particularly well equipped to reply to administrative questions of interest to Brussels' expatriates (housing law, schools...).
This office was set up by the Brussels Capital Region to fulfil a dual function: to promote the image of Brussels amongst the European Institutions and to make locals aware of Brussels' role in Europe.
In concrete terms, this office provides help to expats coming to live in Brussels and offers particularly well written, detailed documentation on all administrative matters.....etc

European Union Welcome office
Administrative address:
Rue de la Loi 200
(GUIM 0/77)
1049 Brussels
✆ 02 / 296 63 00
from 9 a.m to 5 p.m (4 p.m. on Fridays)
Entrance: rue du Commerce 91
Rue de Beaulieu, 5
1170 Brussels
✆ 02 / 295 62 80 – 295 03 80
Exclusively for European civil servants.

Info Point
Rond Point Schuman, 12
1040 Brussels
✆ 02 / 295 66 28
Centre for general documentation on the activities of the Commission, on working, on Europe ... from a political, legal or commercial aspect.
All the information is free and is produced in all Community languages.

TIB (Office de Tourisme Information Bruxelles)
Hôtel de Ville de Bruxelles
Grand Place
1000 Brussels
✆ 02 / 513 89 40
Every day from 9 a.m. to 6 p.m. Closed on 25 December, 1 January and every Sunday from November to March. There you will find information on cultural activities, hotels and restaurants in Brussels. You will also find books, including a reasonably comprehensive tourist guide on the capital, with maps and themed walks.

The Federal State on the Internet
http://belgium.fgov.be
Service fédéral d'information (SFI/FVD):
✆ 02 / 287 41 11
fax 02 / 287 41 00

OPT (Office de Promotion du Tourisme de Belgique)
Rue du Marché aux Herbes, 63
1000 Brussels
© 02 / 504 03 90
From 9 a.m. to 7 p.m. (6 p.m. in winter).
Broad range of information on Brussels: maps, brochures, leaflets
on museums and exhibitions, calendar of events ...

VGGT (Vlaams Commissariaat-Generaal voor Toerisme)
Rue du Marché-aux-Herbes, 61
1000 Brussels
© 02 / 504 03 00
fax 02 / 503 88 03
Dutch-speaking equivalent of the OPT. Information about Belgium:
brochures, maps, leaflets on museums, festivals, exhibitions etc...

Brussels Welcome Open Door
Rue de Tabora, 6
1000 Brussels (Bourse)
© 02 / 511 81 78
fax 02 / 502 76 96
e-mail: bapo@skynet.be
Open Monday to Saturday from 10 a.m. to 6 p.m.
A welcome centre which is open to all, Belgians and expats alike.
Information Centre for social, cultural and religious matters.
Books, magazines, publications on churches, religions, immigration.

Community Help Service (CHS)
Rue Saint-Georges, 102
1050 Brussels
© 02 / 647 67 80
fax 02 / 646 72 73
Help line: 02 / 648 40 14
e-mail: chs@compuserve.com
The CHS is a centre which provides information, guidance and treatment in
a crisis for the English-speaking community in Belgium. Treatment for
social, psychological and family problems. They produce a calendar
packed with invaluable information.

ADMINISTRATIVE FORMALITIES AND SETTLING IN

Before You Arrive

Registering

Getting Connected

Insurance

Car

Before You Arrive

Countries of the European Economic Area : Norway, Liechtenstein, Iceland

Spouse's employment, please see pg. 65

For Everyone

- **Go to the Belgian Embassy** in your home country, who will tell you about the formalities required for your move to Belgium.
- **School certificates**
- **Medical documents** and vaccination cards for every member of the family.
- **Medical certificates** for follow-up treatment or reimbursement.
- **Vaccinations required for cats and dogs :** rabies, Carré sickness, Leptos Provis. All certificates must be issued by an approved veterinarian and legalised, signed and stamped by the veterinarians' inspectorate in the country of origin
- **A statement from your insurers** recording the dates of any car accidents you may have had. If you have had no accident within the last six years, this will significantly reduce your insurance premiums.
- **The papers for your imported vehicle** (see below, under 'Importing, registration and customs clearance', p. 23 – "importation")

For Nationals of European Union Member States or nationals of the European Economic Area

- Your **national identity card** will entitle you to work and settle in Belgium.
- **Marriage certificate and birth certificates** translated by a certified translator.

For Nationals of countries not members of the European Union

- Any future resident wishing to stay for more than three months in Belgium with student, employee, self-employed or pensioner status, must first apply in the country of origin for a **" temporary residence permit "** (A.S.P./V.V.V.) to a Belgian diplomatic or consular post competent for his regular place of residence abroad. In the case of a stay of more than 3 months, this means a visa.
- The issue of a " temporary residence permit " (A.S.P./V.V.V.) will, without exception, be subject to the granting by the competent Belgian authorities of a **work permit** or "**professional card**" .

Permit A : valid for all employers and all professions for an unlimited period.
Permit B : valid for one employer and one profession for a renewable period of one year.
Permit C : specific to certain types of profession.

- In support of this application, he or she will need to produce a **certificate of good conduct** (police certificate) issued by the competent authorities of the last country of residence and a medical certificate issued by a doctor recognised by the Embassy or Consulate. These documents must be translated by a certified translator.
- **Marriage certificate** and **birth certificates** translated by a certified translator and legalised by the Belgian diplomatic or consular authorities in the country of origin.

Registering in your commune

Foreigners staying in Belgium for longer than three months are classed as "residents". As such they must conform with various formalities with regard to permits for both themselves and their spouses and / or child(ren).

European Union Nationals or Nationals of the European Economic Area (Norway, Iceland and Liechtenstein).

- Hold a **valid passport** or **identity card of the country of origin**.
- **Register in person** with the communal authority of the intended place of residence within eight working days of entering the country. Three passport photos are needed and a modest fee is charged (+_ 200 to 800 bef, +_4.9 to 19.8 euro) A registration certificate (**temporary permit**) **valid for three months** is issued by the Commune at the time of registration.
- **Provide proof of subsistence means.** A form (" Annex 19b " to be completed by your employer) may be obtained for proof of employment.

In the case of a one year or longer stay, the commune authorities will also deliver an application for residence. A number of documents have to be produced within a period of three months and the registration certificate is extended for a further three month period. If a residence permit is granted, the commune will issue a residence card valid for five years and will enter the alien's name in the population register.

Some members of the family living with the resident are also covered by the simplified procedures, irrespective of their nationality. They must produce :

- **Passport or identity card**
- **Documents proving their marital or parental link** with the resident, translated by a certified translator (please see " Before you arrive " pg 12).

Non-European Union Nationals

The future resident himself / herself :

In the country of origin.
Please see § " Before you arrive" pg 12.

On arriving in Belgium
Within 3 working days of arriving in Belgium go to the population or aliens department of the commune of residence with the following documents :
• **Valid passport** with temporary residence permit (A.S.P. / V.V.V.) (obtained before you arrive)
• **Work permit**, professional card (or exemption from work permit or traineeship permit for trainees)
• **3 passport photos**
• approximately 250 bef (6.2 euro) (varies depending on the commune)

The commune will then issue a **Certificate of Registration in the Register of Aliens** (C.I.R.E.). The C.I.R.E. is valid for one year and may be extended, unless the A.S.P. / V.V.V. stipulates a limit on the length of stay. This document gives the holder the right to travel unrestricted through all Schengen countries, for a maximum of three months.

Family Reunification

The spouse and children of the resident granted a residence permit in Belgium must provide proof of their marital or parental link with the resident and live in the same place of residence.
The spouse and children must present themselves within three working days of their arrival in Belgium at the communal authorities of their place of residence and apply for registration.
The commune will issue a receipt of their application to reunite the family. If this application is granted, they will be issued with a registration certificate valid for one year.

Documents to be produced :
• Documents required for entering Belgium : **valid national passport**, possibly including a visa, if your country is subject to this requirement.
• In the case of the spouse : **marriage certificate** and **birth certificate** translated by a certified translator ;
• In the case of the children : **birth certificate** with filiation translated by a certified translator
• **3 passport photos** of each member of the family
• Between **200 and 300 bef** (between 4.9 and 7.4 euro) per person (varies depending on the commune.)

Students:
Registering in your commune:
please see pg 126.

For further information on administrative formalities and the conditions for access to the territory of Belgium please refer to the detailed documents from the **Brussels-Europe Liaison Office** on which this chapter was based :
Avenue d'Auderghem, 63 à 1040 Brussels, ℡ 02 / 280 00 80 • fax 02 / 280 03 86 • e-mail: blbe@skynet.be

The 19 communes: commune administration

Anderlecht 1070
Place du Conseil, 1
✆ 02/558 08 00 • fax 02/524 36 14
étrangers: ✆ 02 / 558 09 43

Koekelberg 1081
Place H. Vanhuffel, 6
✆ 02/412 14 11 • fax 02/414 10 71
étrangers: ✆ 02 / 412 14 05

Auderghem 1160
Rue E. Idiers, 12
✆ 02/676 48 11 • fax 02/676 48 89
étrangers: ✆ 02 / 676 48 94

Molenbeek-Saint-Jean 1080
Rue Comte de Flandre, 20
✆ 02/412 36 62• fax 02/412 36 36
étrangers: ✆ 02 / 412 36 72

Berchem-Sainte-Agathe 1082
Avenue du Roi Albert, 33
✆ 02/464 04 11 • fax 02/464 04 91
étrangers: ✆ 02 / 464 04 74

Saint-Gilles 1060
Place Van Meenen, 39
✆ 02/536 02 11 • fax 02/536 02 02
étrangers: ✆ 02 / 536 02 53

Bruxelles-ville 1000
Bld Anspach, 6
✆ 02/279 22 11• fax 02/279 36 11
étrangers: ✆ 02 / 279 35 20

Saint-Josse-ten-Noode 1210
Avenue de l'Astronomie, 13
✆ 02/220 26 11• fax 02/220 27 35
étrangers: ✆ 02 / 220 26 28

Etterbeek 1040
Avenue d'Auderghem, 113-117
✆ 02/627 21 11 • fax 02/627 23 50
étrangers: ✆ 02 / 627 28 25

Schaerbeek 1030
Place Colignon
✆ 02/243 86 11 • fax 02/215 43 91
étrangers: ✆ 02 / 243 88 12

Evere 1140
Square Hoedemaekers, 10
✆ 02/247 62 62 • fax 02/241 07 51
étrangers: ✆ 02 / 247 62 58

Uccle 1180
Place J. Van Der Elst, 29
✆ 02/348 65 11 • fax 02/343 59 49
étrangers: ✆ 02 / 348 67 70

Forest 1190
Rue du Curé, 2
✆ 02/370 22 11 • fax 02/370 23 23
étrangers: ✆ 02 / 370 22 82

Watermael-Boitsfort 1170
Place A. Gilson, 1
✆ 02/674 74 11 • fax 02/675 70 29
étrangers: ✆ 02 / 674 74 23

Ganshoren 1083
Avenue Charles Quint, 140
✆ 02/465 12 77 • fax 02/465 89 04

Woluwé-Saint-Lambert 1200
Avenue Paul Hymans, 2
✆ 02/761 27 11 • fax 02/772 25 67
étrangers: ✆ 02 / 761 27 08

Ixelles 1050
Chaussée d'Ixelles, 168
✆ 02/511 90 84 • fax 02/513 62 28

Woluwé-Saint-Pierre 1150
Avenue C. Thielemans, 93
✆ 02/773 05 11 • fax 02/773 18 18
étrangers: ✆ 02 / 773 05 49

Jette 1090
Rue H. Werrie, 18-20
✆ 02/423 12 11 • fax 02/425 24 61
étrangers: ✆ 02 / 423 12 53

Around Brussels	
Zaventem (Sterrebeek)	✆ 02 / 720 02 54
Kraainem	✆ 02 / 720 48 87
Wezembeek-Oppem	✆ 02 / 783 12 11
Tervuren	✆ 02 / 769 20 11
Overijse	✆ 02 / 687 60 40
Sterrebeek	✆ 02 / 720 02 87
La Hulpe	✆ 02 / 652 05 78
Hoeilaart	✆ 02 / 657 90 50
Rixensart	✆ 02 / 652 01 10
Lasne	✆ 02 / 633 18 17
Braine-l'Alleud	✆ 02 / 386 05 11
Sint-Pieters-Leeuw	✆ 02 / 371 22 11
Dilbeek	✆ 02 / 467 21 11
Wemmel	✆ 02 / 462 05 00
Grimbergen	✆ 02 / 260 12 11
Sint-Genesius-Rode	✆ 02 / 380 20 40
Linkebeek	✆ 02 / 380 62 15
Waterloo	✆ 02 / 352 98 11

Ministry of Foreign Affairs	✆ 02 / 352 98 11
Ministry of Home Affairs, Office for Foreigners	✆ 02 / 205 54 11
Ministry of Brussels-Capital	
Operator	✆ 02 / 518 17 11
Economy & Employment Services,	
Immigration Services	✆ 02 / 204 18 85

et us welcome you to your new home in Belgium with our finest Telecom offer.

o receive the Belgacom information kit, specially prepared for you, all us now, 24 hours a day, on +32 (0) 2 208 14 89

When you arrive in a new country, ere are all sorts of new things to pe with, including a new Telecom ompany. The Belgacom information t tells you everything you need know about Belgium's national lecom operator.
How to become a customer.

- International calling discounts and other benefits from the Belgacom Club.
- All about mobile phones.
- How the Belgacom Calling Card works.
- E-mail and Internet access.

To receive your information kit, call 208 14 89 and we'll contact you later to welcome you and make sure everything went smoothly with your installation. As you can see, chocolates are not the only thing we do well in Belgium.

Code : 0011

BELGACOM
The reliable solution

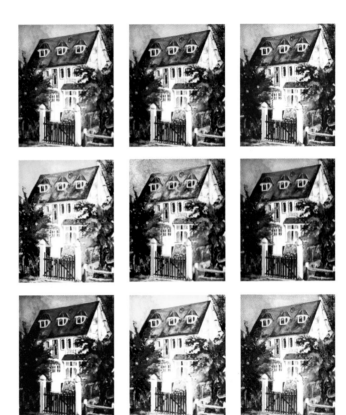

Getting Connected

Make sure the utilities are connected a few days before you move in. You will need to show proof of your identity if staff are to call on you at home. Remember to ensure that all bills have been settled by the previous occupants, and to ask where the meters are!

Water

Compagnie Intercommunale Bruxelloise des Eaux (CIBE) Rue aux Laines, 70 1000 Brussels
✆ *02 / 518 81 11*
fax 02 / 518 83 06
info@cibe.be

If you want to change the customer name without having the water cut off, a form is available from the CIBE. It will be up to you to get the meter read and to enter the figures on the said form. It will need to be signed by you AND by the previous tenant or the landlord. These two signatures will serve to guarantee the meter reading beyond which the water consumed will be charged to you. **If the water has been cut off:** you will need to get reconnected. Make an appointment at least 48 hours ahead for your connection. There is a 900 bef call out charge. You will need to show proof of your identity.

The annual charge for water connection is 840 bef. Water bills are issued annually. The rate of VAT on water is 6%.

Note: The hardness of the water varies from commune to commune. If you want to have a water softener installed, make sure you get written authorisation from your landlord.

Gas and Electricity

The 19 Brussels communes are served by two authorities:

Electrabel Interlec-Interga
Chaussée d'Ixelles, 133 1050 Brussels
✆ *02 / 549 41 11*
fax 02 / 549 46 61
Anderlecht (electricity), Auderghem, Berchem-Ste-Agathe, Etterbeek, Forest, Ixelles (gas), Koekelberg, Molenbeek-St-Jean, Uccle, Watermael-Boitsfort, Woluwe-St-Lambert, Woluwe-St-Pierre.

Sibelgaz-Sibelgas
Quai des Usines, 16 1000 Brussels
✆ *02 / 274 31 11*
fax 02 / 274 36 93
Anderlecht (gas), Brussels-Ville, Evere, Ganshoren, Ixelles (electricity), Jette, Saint-Gilles, Saint-Josse-ten-Noode, Schaerbeek.

> **Emergency number for leaks:**
> ✆ *739 52 11*

Procedure

- Telephone to make an appointment a week in advance. You will be asked to give exact details: the full address, exact floor (level, left or right, front or back). Connections are made between the hours of 8 a.m. and 3 p.m.
- Statement of the opening of a meter, provided by the commune.
- Photocopy of front and back of your identity card or your passport.
- You must be present in person, or give a proxy (a simple sheet of paper signed by you will suffice) to an adult to sign for the opening of the meter.
- Bills are issued monthly.

Emergency number if you detect a gas leak:
✆ 512 05 06 (Interga)
✆ 274 34 54 (Sibelgaz)
Electricity in Belgium:
220 Volts / 50 cycles

Telephone

Fixed telephone

For connecting to a network there is only one company : Belgacom. For the connection of one of more telephone lines:
Go to the nearest Belgacom telephone shop with proof of your identity: the connection will be made within 5 days unless the wiring needs to be changed. There is a connection charge of 2,200 bef plus VAT.

Consult the yellow pages section B 4788
Connection charge: 2,662 bef (66.1 euro) plus VAT.
Call out charge for connection : 1573 bef (39.1 euro).
Basic line rental : 1,114 bef (27.6 euro) payable every 6 months.

Once your line is installed you can choose your service provider. There are currently two operators for fixed telephones : **Belgacom** and **Mobistar.** Other companies are expected to enter this market in the very near future.

USEFUL TO KNOW:
- VAT has to be added to all the basic rates: 21% for gas and electricity, 6% for water.
- The water, gas and electricity meters are read only once a year, and your bill is readjusted annually in line with your consumption. Your first bills will correspond to estimates based on the consumption of the previous occupant. Be aware that the readjustments may be sizeable if their family profile was very different to yours!
- The supply companies listed above do not handle repairs or maintenance: it is up to you to quickly find a plumber and an electrician.
- If you have problems with your drains, call your commune: an efficient service can help you.
- Get your electricity meter set by Electrabel to identify consumption during the night (10 p.m. to 7 a.m.), which is half as expensive as during the day (two-hourly residential rate).

Mobile phones

A number of operators compete in Belgium: **Proximus (Belgacom), Mobistar** and **Orange.**

Billing: You will receive a breakdown of all international calls (date, time, country dialled, number dialled and number of units). In the case of domestic, local and long-distance calls, you will be shown only the total number of units charged.

Every telephone line you rent entitles you to one free insertion in the **telephone directory.** You will be given a copy when you are connected. Telephone directories are supplied free of charge and delivered to your home once a year.

To reduce the cost of your international calls:

Belgacom offers two packages: Belgacom Club and Belgacom Club Favori
Mobistar's rates are generally attractive.

Other companies offering reductions on international calls:

AT&T	✆ 0800 / 186 37
Econophone	✆ 0800 / 201 45
Global One	✆ 02 / 626 06 00
InTouch	✆ 0800 / 951 00
MCI	✆ 0800 / 100 12
Telenet	✆ 0800 / 660 00
Unisource	✆ 0800 / 135 04
Worldcom	✆ 0800 / 408 00

Internet:
http://www.expatsinbrussels.com

Internet

There are a number of providers in Belgium.

Compuserve	✆ 02/713 13 70
Euronet	✆ 02/717 17 17
Infonie	✆ 02/478 12 34
Online Internet	✆ 09/244 11 01
Ping	✆ 070/23 37 72
Wanadoo	✆ 0800 /13 400
Skynet	✆ 02/706 11 11
Turbo Line	✆ 0800/ 933 20
	(planned)
Uunet	✆ 0800 / 23 233
Internet by cable	
TVD	✆ 02/240 08 99
	✆ 02/240 08 88
Brutélé	✆ 02/511 65 43

If you want to protect your children from some unsavoury sites :
http://www.netnanny.com
http://www.cyberpatrol.com

To compare rates and services:

Belgacom	✆ 0800 / 33 800 (FR)
	✆ 0800 / 55 800 (EN)
	✆ 0800 / 22 800 (NL)
	✆ 0800 / 44 800 (DE)
	✆ 02 / 208 14 89
	(multilingual)
Mobistar	✆ 0800 / 21595

Mobile phones

Proximus	✆ 0800 / 15211
Mobistar	✆ 0800 / 95959
Orange	✆ 0800 / 20486

If the TV breaks down in the middle of the big game :
TV Express
☎ 0800 / 13137
every day from 8 a.m. to 10 p.m.

Belgian TV Standard : PAL

Note:
All users, even those without cable, must pay an annual TV and radio licence fee:
Service
Radio-TV-Redevance
Place Solvay
1030 Brussels
☎ 207 74 11
from 8.30 a.m. to 12 noon and from 1 p.m. to 4 p.m.

Television

Cable television gives you access to a large number of Belgian and foreign television channels. A payment is made for this service.

Every commune offers one cable television company which has the exclusive rights for the communes it serves.

TVD
Avenue Chazal, 140
1030 Brussels
☎ 02 / 240 08 08
fax 02 / 240 08 01
Berchem-Ste -Agathe, Etterbeek, Forest, Ganshoren, Jette, Koekelberg, Schaerbeek

Coditel
Rue des deux Églises, 26
1000 Brussels
☎ 02 / 226 52 52
fax 02 / 219 77 25
Anderlecht, Brussels-Ville, Uccle, Molenbeek-St-Jean, Saint-Josse-ten-Noode, Watermael-Boitsfort.

Brutélé
Rue de Naples, 29
1050 Brussels
☎ 02 / 511 65 43
fax 02 / 512 88 04
Ixelles, Woluwe-St-Pierre, Evere, Saint Gilles, Auderghem.

Wolu TV
Avenue Georges Henri, 399
1200 Brussels
☎ 02 / 736 77 89
fax 02 / 733 37 88
Woluwe-St-Lambert

Prices vary slightly from company to company:
Box installation cost: approximately 1,700 bef.
Connection cost: either approximately 2,000 bef, entitling you to 3 months' subscription, or approximately 1,000 bef with no free subscription.
Subscription cost: approximately 5,000 bef per year.

Privately owned television:
Canal+ offers films, documentaries, sport and children's programmes.
Access via cable.
Subscription: 1,095 bef per month.

Insurance

Home

Overall insurance:
- Covers fire, water damage, broken windows, civil liability for the building and certain natural disasters. Optional: theft.
- This overall insurance has to be taken out by both the tenant and the landlord. Each side's insurance, although bearing the same name, covers different risks. The landlord's covers risks inherent in the building (such as built-in inside pipes, storm damage to the roof, etc.), while the tenant's covers the tenant's risks (such as outside pipes, overflowing bathtub, etc.).

Tip: Take out insurance with your landlord's insurance company and under the same contract including a clause relinquishing the right of recourse against the tenant. This will greatly simplify matters in the event of any accident.

Personal

Family civil liability:
- Not compulsory, but recommended for everyone, even those living alone.
- Indemnifies you for any damage to third parties caused by you, your children, your pets or any person dependent upon you, up to a sizeable amount.

Domestic staff:
- Compulsory regardless of the status (legal or otherwise) of the person working in your home.
- Applies to any person working in your home in a domestic capacity, even part-time: au pair, cleaning lady, gardener, domestic staff, etc.

Health

Sickness insurance: the 'Mutuelle' (mutual association):
In Belgium, sickness insurance is compulsory for employees and for the self-employed alike, and is part of the legal requirement to belong to the social security scheme.

In the case of **employees,** contributions are paid by the employer and deducted at source from salary. The **self-employed** also have to pay into a social security fund for the self-employed.

The payment of these contributions enables you to join a mutual association, which will intervene in the reimbursement of medical and hospitalisation costs in line with the appropriate scales.

Useful fact:
Any portion of the premium not used will be reimbursed in full, so even if you are planning to move house shortly, you needn't have any qualms about paying your full premium.

One useful address might be:
Partena
Mutual association
✆ 02 / 549 76 02
http://www.partenamut.be
Social security for the self-employed.
✆ 02 / 549 74 40

Insurance Companies:
Consult the yellow pages, section B 6150

You can also save money by dealing directly with your insurer!
CGU
Expatriate Division
Av. Hermann Debroux, 54
1160 Bruxelles
✆ *02 / 676 65 99*
fax 02 / 676 69 99
mark.cryans@be.cu.com

Some big insurance companies have a 'mutuelle' department.

Complementary 'minor risks' insurance will put the self-employed person at the same rate of reimbursement as an employed person.

You are free to choose your own mutual association.

The insurance companies offer supplementary cover packages.

Hospitalisation insurance
Covers the costs above the reimbursements made by the mutual association, including the cost of a single room.

Individual accident insurance
Lump sum (amount chosen by the insured person) in the event of an accident. Covers death and/or permanent invalidity and/or temporary incapacity and/or medical expenses.

Car
The no-claims bonus system is applied, whereby the insurance premium increases or decreases depending on the accidents you have had in the past.

Civil Liability - Motor
Compulsory.

'Omnium'
Optional. Large no-claims bonuses can be obtained if you have not had any accidents within the last six years. Covers material damage to the insured vehicle, whether or not the driver was in the wrong. Covers theft, fire, broken windows and damage caused by the forces of nature.

Legal Defence
Not compulsory, but recommended. Covers lawyers' fees and court costs in Belgium and abroad in the event of liability being disputed (this is becoming more and more common among individuals and insurance companies).

The Broker

Consult the yellow pages, section B 6152
To help you, he will research the insurance best suited to your particular needs. He will advise you and help you in the event of an accident. He will represent you and deal with the big insurance companies on your behalf.

One useful address:
Gestinsure
Rue Gachard, 37
1050 Brussels
✆ *02 / 649 59 33*
✆ *02 / 646 20 42*

Car

Importing, Registration and Customs Clearance

Cars must be registered in Belgium within 6 months of your registration in your commune. No tax is payable provided that:
- the car is used;
- you were already the owner before you moved to Belgium;
- the car was purchased at least 6 months before you imported it.
- It must pass the Belgian M.O.T.

Registration conditions:
- You have registered in your commune.
- The car must meet Belgian standards (certificate of conformity issued by the manufacturer).
- It must be insured with a Belgian insurance company (compulsory civil liability - motor).

Procedure
- Ask your insurance company for a belgian registration application form.
- Get your vehicle cleared through customs:
  Tour et Taxis
  Rue Picard, 1-3 (counter 57)
  1000 Brussels
  ✆ *02 / 421 38 28*
  (Open from 8 a.m. to 11.30 a.m. and 1 p.m. to 3.30 p.m.).
A custom's stamp and a "705" sticker will be fixed to the application form.

- Send the following documents to the D.I.V. (Direction des Immatriculations des Véhicules):
  - registration application form properly completed by the customs and with the insurance sticker attached.
  - The M.O.T. certificate.
  - 2.500 bef worth of fiscal stamps (62.1 euro).

D.I.V.
Rue de la Loi, 155
1045 Brussels
✆ *02 / 287 31 11*
fax 02 / 287 43 80
from 9 a.m. to 1 p.m.

You will receive one number plate within a few days. It is your property and may be transferred from one vehicle to another.

Anyone holding a registration number must pay an **annual road tax**, according to the size of the vehicle's engine.

When you leave Belgium, you should return your number plate to the D.I.V.

Note: If your vehicle is no longer on the road, remember to return the number plates so that you are not paying the road tax unnecessarily.

For those not resident in Belgium, a provisional ('Transit') 6 month number plate can be obtained from the Ministry of Communications. In this case, the import formalities need not be completed. If you are staying in Belgium for over 6 months, you must import the vehicle.

Driving Licence

Anyone over 18 years old who holds a valid driving licence is authorised to drive a vehicle in Belgium.

For Nationals of European Union Member States:
Belgium has signed exchange agreements for driving licences with most non-EU member states. Nationals of these countries must go to the "driving licence" department in their commune to exchange their national licence for a Belgian licence, as soon as they register with their commune.

For Nationals of countries not members of the European Union:
If you come from a non-EU Member State, you should use an international driving licence when you drive in Belgium (see page 12). This is valid only for one year, and so you need to exchange it for a European one via your commune, (police or administration), depending on the commune.

Procedure:
- Provide a translation of your national driving licence in French or Dutch by a certified translator;
- Bring proof of six months' residence in the country which issued the licence at the time it was delivered.

Holders of special residence permits issued by the Ministry of Foreign Affairs are not required to exchange their licences

Insurance

See above, 'Insurance', p. 21.

Vehicle assistance and accidents

See 'Transport', p. 148.

Note that the validity of licences issued by certain countries is not recognised in Belgium. If this is the case with your licence, you will need to sit a theory test and a practical test in order to obtain a European licence, although you will not need to take lessons.
Information:
- "Foreign driving licence" departments of the Communes (Please see pg 15 and 16)
- Ministry for Communication- "Driving Licence" department
  rue de la Loi, 155
  ✆ *02 / 287 44 36 and 34*, from 9 a.m. to 4 p.m.

ACCOMMODATION

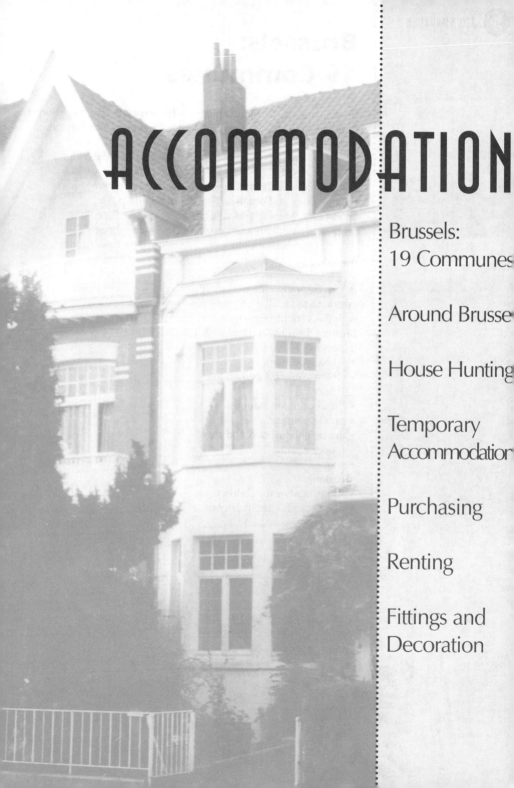

Brussels: 19 Communes

Brussels has the great advantage of being a capital city in which it is relatively easy to find somewhere to live.

The choice is wide and varied, ranging from studio flats to apartments, houses, and villas; properties may be bought or rented, furnished or unfurnished.

Before deciding where to settle, take time to familiarise yourself with the various districts in Brussels, bearing in mind such factors as:
- where you work.
- where your children go to school.
- the airport and stations.
- public transport.
- the neighbourhood and surrounding area.
- shops.
- parking.
- sports centres for children.
- noise (careful about aircraft noise).

The **Brussels-Capital region** is made up of 19 communes.

You will find the telephone numbers of the various commune administrations p. 15 and p. 16.

The map on page 8 will show you where the various communes are.

Thumbnail portraits of some of the Communes:

Auderghem 1160
Area: 900 hectares.
Population: 29,200.
Many parks + Forêt de
Soignes.
Club du Château Sainte-
Anne.
Brussels Japanese School.
Commune administration:
✆ 676 48 11

Brussels-Ville 1000
Area: 3,292 hectares.
Population: 136,000.
The charm of historic
Brussels at the heart of the
commune.
The royal estates, Heysel and
planetarium in the North.
The Bois de la Cambre and
the luxury shopping district of
Avenue Louise in the South.
Commune administration:
✆ 279 22 11

Etterbeek 1040
Area: 315 hectares.
Population: 44,000.
Close to the European Union
buildings.
Close to the Forêt de Soignes
and Woluwe Park.
British Junior Academy.
City International School.
Prinses Juliana Dutch school.
Commune administration:
✆ 627 21 11

Ixelles 1050
Area: 634 hectares.
Population: 73,000.
Many shops: Place Flagey,
Porte de Namur, Avenue de
la Toison d'Or.
The charm of the district
around the Abbaye de la
Cambre and the Ixelles lakes.
Brussels English Primary
School (BEPS).
Commune administration:
✆ 511 90 84

Saint-Gilles 1060
Area: 252 hectares.
Population: 43,000.
Gare du Midi station, the ter-
minus for the Thalys and
Eurostar trains.
Close to the Forest Park.
Commune administration:
✆ 536 02 11

Uccle 1180
Area: 2,290 hectares.
Population: 75,000.
Many houses with gardens.
Shopping centres.
Forêt de Soignes and many
parks including Wolvendael.
European School I.
French School.
Commune administration:
✆ 348 65 11

Watermael-Boitsfort 1170
Area: 1,293 hectares.
Population: 25,000.
The charm of a 'village'
atmosphere.
Shopping at Place Keym.
International School of
Brussels (ISB).
Commune administration:
✆ 674 74 11

Woluwe-Saint-Lambert 1200
Area: 723 hectares.
Population: 50,000.
Many small parks.
Shopping centres including
the Woluwe Shopping Center.
European School II.
Commune administration:
✆ 761 27 11

Woluwe-Saint-Pierre 1150
Area: 885 hectares.
Population: 38,000.
A very green commune: 60
hectares of it is covered by
the Forêt de Soignes,
Woluwe Park and the
Mellaerts lakes.
Many embassies.
Commune administration:
✆ 773 05 11

Around Brussels

You may also prefer to live out of town. Many outlying areas are very pleasant and offer the twin bonuses of closeness to Brussels and a quieter pace of life in a rural environment.

Commuting into town is relatively easy (although the morning rush hour into Brussels on weekdays should be avoided if possible!), but do remember that you will find virtually everything you need locally: shops, sports centres and schools.

The districts popular with foreign communities are from Brussels to Wavre, Brussels-Waterloo and Brussels-Louvain. Ask your estate agent or have a chat with compatriots who have already settled in.

Ecoles: v. p. 118

Foreign schools outside Brussels:

Bierges
Le Verseau International School
Braine- l'Alleud
Montessori House Belgium
Limal
Beps 2-Limal
Rhode-St-Genèse
International Christian Academy
Montessori School Brussels (Finnish-English)
Brussels Scandinavian School
Sterrebeek
Brussels American School (BAS)
Tervuren
International Montessori School
British School of Brussels (BSB)
Vossem
British Primary School
Waterloo
St John's International School
The Children's Academy
European Montessori School
Reine Astrid School (Scandinavian)
Wezembeek-Oppem
Deutsche Schule Brüssel

House Hunting

As you walk around the districts you like the look of, watch out for the '**A louer'/'Te huur**' ('For rent') and '**A vendre/'Te koop**' ('For sale') notices. These will give you a phone number to call, or the name of an estate agency which can provide more details.

Estate agencies

One solution is to consult several agencies. However, one agency can just as easily look through other ones in order to find you the property you are looking for.
You will never have to pay them: their fees are exclusively payable by the owner.
Choose your estate agent in light of the price bracket, the district, and whether you wish to buy or to rent. The best recommendation is by word of mouth!

Here are some useful addresses:

Ferco
Brusselsesteenweg, 615
3090 Overijse
✆ *02 / 657 04 12*
fax 02 / 657 28 67
mail@ferco.be

Immobilière Le Lion
Av. Franklin Roosevelt, 123, bte 37
1050 Brussels
✆ *02 / 672 71 11*
fax 02 / 672 67 17
http://www.immo-lelion.be
info@immo-lelion.be

Housing Service IGC
Boulevard Saint Michel, 51
1040 Brussels
✆ *02 / 732 99 20*
fax 02 / 732 91 39
http://www.housing-service.be
info@housing-service.be

Rosu &Chassart
Avenue Louise, 391
1000 Brussels
✆ *02 / 639 60 30*
fax 02 / 647 01 47
a.ddechassart@euronet.be

OP
Avenue Emile DeMot, 19-21
1050 Brussels
✆ *02 / 626 08 26*
fax 02 / 626 08 38
http://www.op1875.be

Victoire Properties
Avenue de Tervuren, 418
1150 Brussels
✆ *02 / 771 12 40 (locations)*
✆ *02 / 772 15 30 (ventes)*
fax 02 / 772 33 76
http://www.publisite.be/victoire
victoire@skynet.be

To find out more:
UPI (Union Professionnelle des Immobiliers)
Avenue Albert, 29
1190 Bruxelles
✆ *02 / 344 57 52*
Can supply a list of estate agents specialising in sale or rental.

Refer to the
"Useful addresses",
p. 205

Relocation Agencies

These agencies work preferably independently of any property interest, and will guide you in your move, even before you arrive in Belgium. A questionnaire will enable them to look for the kind of property you want, even before they have met you. They will help you with the administrative formalities, obtaining a work permit and visas, utilities,connections, and even the translation of certain official documents. With them, you almost won't need us at all - but watch their prices!

The quality of the service they offer does not depend on the size of the agency. Some of the agencies mentioned below are run by only one person, others have a few dozen employees. Your choice should depend on the kind of service which best suits you. The larger agencies also provide "expatriates' administration management" or 'business set up".

Here are some addresses:

Art of Living
Avenue Ernest Solvay, 59
1310 La Hulpe
✆   02 / 653 00 37
fax 02 / 653 24 41
art.of.living@skynet.be
Contact: Virginie Limauge

P.R.S. Europe
(Professional Relocation Services)
Bosdellestraat, 120 Box 1
1933 Sterrebeek
✆   02 / 785 09 85
fax 02/ 785 09 99
nsepulchre@prseurope.com
http://www.prseurope.com
Contact: Nicolas Sepulchre

Brussels Relocation
Boulevard Henri Rolin , 3
1410 Waterloo
✆   02 / 353 21 01
fax 02 / 353 06 42
Contact: Catherine Mulders
http://www.brussels.relocation.com
brussels.relocation@skynet.be

BRA Belgian Relocation Assistance
Tramlaan, 279
1933 Sterrebeek
✆   02 / 784 34 24
fax 02 / 784 26 96
be.home@skynet.be

Europ Assistance
Relocationsettler International
Rue du Bosquet, 75
1060 Brussels
✆   02 / 533 78 10
fax 02 / 534 66 66

Meeting Tops
Place Dumont, 2
1150 Brussels
✆   02 / 775 94 56
fax 02 / 775 94 57

Corporate Relocation
Avenue Guillaume Macau, 5
1050 Brussels
✆   02 / 646 05 86
fax 02/ 646 06 82

Contact: Marit Borchardt
F.R.S.Foreign Service Relocation
Melkstraat, 91
1830 Machelen
✆ 02 / 02/ 253 20 05
fax 02/ 252 61 16
pdm@frs-relocation.com
Contact: Patrick De Maere

Management Relocations
Chemin de Dadelane, 4
1380 Lasne
✆ 02 / 633 36 21
fax 02/ 633 30 27
mgtreloc@skynet.be
http://www.mgtrelocations.com
Contact: Cathy Roggemans

Map Relocations
Brusselsesteenweg, 410D
3090 Overijse
✆ 02 / 658 80 80
fax 02/ 657 50 33
info@map-relocations.com

Y. Timmermans
Rue de Vieusart, 10
1325 Chaumont-Gistoux
✆ 02 / 010/ 68 01 88
fax 010/ 68 07 99
Contact: Yolande Timmermans

Cabinet Solutions
Chaussée de Bruxelles, 9
7000 Mons
✆ 065 / 84 74 05
fax 065 / 84 70 17
4s@pronet.be
Contact: Sadi Schoonbroodt

Intro B
Avenue Maurice, 31
1050 Brussels
✆ 02 / 648 64 93
fax 02/ 646 41 62
Contact: Johanna Tent

BRC Belgian Relocation Association
Molenweg, 47
2930 Braasschaat
✆ 03 / 605 06 50
fax 03/ 605 05 50
brc.viv@village.uunet.be

Vickman Relocation center
Stationstraat, 26/8
1930 Zaventem
✆ 02 / 725 77 79
fax 02/ 725 91 61
info@vickman.be

Well Relocation
Rue Robert Jones, 72
1180 Brussels
✆ 075 / 23 25 41
Contact: Isabelle Dubois

Property advertisements in various newspapers

- Dailies:
  Le Soir (Fridays),
  La Libre Belgique (Thursdays);
- Weeklies:
  Vlan (Wednesdays),
  The Bulletin (Thursdays);
- Monthlies:
  L'Evènement immobilier,
  L'Eventail.

Temporary Accommodation

Hotels

Hotel prices tend to be lower than in London, Paris or Rome, and there is a particularly wide choice.
For further information before you arrive in Brussels, call one of these two offices and ask them for their recommendations.

Office National Belge du Tourisme
(publishes a guide)
✆ 02 / 504 03 90

Office du Tourisme de Bruxelles
✆ 02 / 513 89 40

Or in bookshops:
Bruxelles, le guide autrement
Published by Editions Autrement.
Le Petit Futé – Bruxelles
Published by Nouvelles Editions de l'Université.
Un Grand Week-End à Bruxelles, Published by Hachette.

> **Useful to know:** there is a free hotel reservation service available from the BTR (Belgique Tourisme Réservations) on
> ✆ 513 74 84
> *from 9 a.m. to 6 p.m.*

Here is an interesting arrangement for single people: rooms with a family
For the addresses of families renting out a room in their home, look in the small ads published by:
• *l'UE* ✆ 02 / 296 63 00 – fax 02 / 296 09 06
• *The Universities:*
  ULB ✆ 02 / 650 85 00 – 02 / 650 21 56 *(after 4 p.m.)*
  UCL ✆ 02 / 764 41 20 – 02 / 764 41 29
• The *Vlan,* a Brussels weekly free sheet issued on Wednesdays. (Also on sale in bookshops).
• One association in Brussels also gives information on a *'Bed and Breakfast'* type of arrangement at reasonable prices:
Bed and Brussels
rue Gustave Biot, 2
1050 Brussels
✆ 02 / 646 07 37
fax 02 / 644 01 14
http://www.BnB-Brussels.be
BnBru@ibm.net

IN TOUCH
Telecom
The Innovator Operator

070·777·777

rom today, make your international calls at interzonal rates.

5 BEF per minute off-peak, 7 BEF per minute during peak hours (VAT incl.).

iks to InTouch's PhoneTone, you can now make cheap international calls. With no subscription or contract needed, can call all the countries of the European Community, Switzerland, the USA, Canada and Hong Kong* at interzonal 3. Hurry up and try it!   *The list is provisional. Other Countries will soon be added.

ial the PhoneTone number: 070 / 777.777. **2** Wait for the dial tone. Then dial your required rnational number (00 ...). **3** End by pressing the gate button (#) or wait 4 seconds. You now call iterzonal rates: 3.5 BEF per minute off-peak, 7 BEF per minute during peak hours. **4** These calls appear on your normal telephone bill, listed under 070. You start paying once you hear the dial tone. qually advantageous for calls from your mobile phone.

● **7** ●

THE PHONETONE
GTS · IN TOUCH

FOR FURTHER INFORMATION, CALL 0800/88 101 FREE.
MaxFax On Demand 0800/88.170 WWW.INTOUCH.BE

Serviced Apartments

This is a very pleasant scheme, for it allows you to benefit from all the services you would get in a hotel, such as cleaning, bed-linen, etc.

Here are a few addresses: if you want to find out more refer to the « **Useful addresses** » section at the back of the guide.

Apparthotel Citadines Toison d'Or
Avenue de la Toison d'Or, 61-63
1060 Brussels
✆ 02 / 543 53 53
fax 02 / 543 53 00
http://www.citadines.be
bruxelles@citadines.com

Arcotrade
rue du page, 11-13
1050 Brussels
✆ 02 / 538 35 85
fax : 02/ 538 36 11
*http://www.expatsinbrussels.com/
    arcotrade*

New Continental
33,rue Defacqz
1050 Brussels
✆ 02 / 536 10 00
fax 02 / 536 10 15
info@ncf.be

New Yorker
403,avenue Louise
1050 Brussels
✆ 02 / 649.90.05
fax 02 / 640 30 76

Ixel Invest
Rue Souveraine, 40
1050 Brussels
✆ 02 / 511 90 49
✆ 02 / 513 41 65
fax 02 / 511 20 29

Alfa Louise Hotel
212,Avenue Louise
1050 Brussels
✆ 02 / 644 29 29
fax 02 / 644 18 78
alfa.louise@alfahotels.com

Estate &Concept
Brussels
✆ 02 / 732.00.00
fax 02 / 732 00 01
e-concept@skynet.be

Purchasing

You will find a list of notaries in the Gold Pages' phonebook A, under *"Professions libérales"* (blue margin page 50) Please note that the **Notaires Federation** will answer most queries about their various functions free of charge: purchase, loans, marriage, death, etc... ✆ 02 / 505 08 11 *http://www.notaire.be* Wednesday only from 10 a.m. to 12 noon and from 2 p.m. to 4 p.m.

The purchaser does not pay any commission to the agency.

The purchase occurs in two stages: the provisional sales agreement ('compromis') and the sale proper, some 6 weeks to 4 months later.

Deposit
The two sides normally agree on a deposit of 10% of the selling price. But this is not obligatory. However, do be careful if the vendor asks you for a large deposit. You should be aware that, in the event of a lawsuit, it would be very difficult to get it back.

Sale Contract
This is always conducted before a **notary.** Choose your own, because it is hard for one notary to represent the interests of both parties. It will not cost you any more: the fees are simply divided between the two notaries.

Sale Agreement
Is used for the settlement of the incidentals, and is irrevocable. You may agree it privately with the vendor, but it is only sensible to have it checked over by your notary before you sign anything.

A written **offer** countersigned by the vendor within the deadline is equivalent to a sale.

An **option** granted by the vendor and taken up by the purchaser within the deadline is equivalent to a sale.

Loan
A sale agreement is irrevocable. Therefore, if you have not yet obtained your loan, be sure to get a "subject-to-loan" suspension clause added to the sale agreement in case you are not granted the loan.

Taxes
On purchase of a building, you automatically have to pay 12.5% in taxes. The law provides that the purchaser generally has four months within which to pay, starting from the date of the notarised deed. In addition, as soon as the notarised deed has been signed, the purchaser has to bear all taxes relating to the building, because he now owns it. *Property tax:* payable annually, calculated on the rateable value. *Occupation tax:* a communal tax payable annually.

Latent Defect
If the vendor includes a clause relinquishing responsibility in the event of a latent defect, you are advised to have the property surveyed before you sign the contract. You are entitled not to accept this clause.

Watch out for the promise to buy: it irrevocably binds you to buy the property, but it is not binding upon the vendor. So be careful and don't take it for granted that the deal is done.

Renting

If you rent a property **'furnished'**, this will include not only the furniture, but also the kitchen utensils, crockery and bed covers. It will not normally include sheets, towels, kitchen-towels, etc. Ask for an inventory; this will offer you protection in the event of a dispute.

If you rent « unfurnished » you should be aware that the majority of decent apartments include kitchen appliances but that curtains, curtain rails, carpets and light fixtures (ceiling lamps, wall lamps etc) are not usually included.

Leases
- A lease generally runs for *9 years,* and is renewable under certain conditions (see table below).
- Short-term contracts: The new legislation provides that a short-term contract (maximum 3 years) can now be renewed only once, and under the same conditions.
- The « diplomatic clause » no longer really exists as this regulation has now been applied to all tenants : the lease can always be terminated provided 3 months' notice is given.

How to terminate an ordinary lease before the normal expiry date			
When ?	Reason	Notice	Amount payable to the other party
By the tenant			
1 st 9 years			
• during 1 st year	none	3 months	3 months rent
• during 2nd year	none	3 months	2 months rent
• during 3rd year	none	3 months	1 month rent
• any time after 3rd year	none	3 months	none
3-year extension	none	3 months	none
By the landlord			
1st 9 years			
• any time during the lease	occupation in person or by close relative	6 months	none
• any time other than 1st year	major work in several apartments in the building	6 months	none
• at end of 3rd year	none	6 months	9 months rent
• at end of 3rd year	major work in the apartment	6 months	none
• at end of 6th year	none	6 months	6 months rent
• at end of 6th year	major work in the apartment	6 months	none
• at expiry of contract	none	6 months	none
3-year extension			
• any time during the lease	occupation in person or by family	6 months	none
• any time during the lease	major work in several apartments in the building	6 months	none
• at the end of a 3 year period	none	6 months	none

Source: Budget & Droits nr. 133, june 1997.

Tenant and Landlord: Who Pays What?

Payable by the Tenant

- the salary of the managing agent, maintenance of the caretaker's premises and the maintenance of the lift
- Private consumption (water, gas, electricity, heating, telephone), including the charges and the meter costs.
- Consumption of the communal areas; taxes affecting the enjoyment of the property (refuse disposal, commune taxes, motor power, etc.).
- Maintenance of communal areas and equipment (lift, lobby windows, staircases, etc.); caretaking costs.
- Occupant's insurance (e.g. insurance against theft); chimney-sweeping.
- Replacement of fuses, plugs, bulbs, repairs following a short-circuit.
- Cleaning and maintenance of gutters and pipes (lagging); maintenance of the septic tank, cleaning of pavements.
- Cleaning of inside paintwork (in communal areas); maintenance and repair to mail-boxes, bells and intercom systems (aside from normal wear and tear).
- Maintenance of burners and taps on a gas installation.

Payable by the Landlord

- Repairs of the caretaker's flat. Reparing the lift.
- Bank charges, withholding tax on income from immovable assets, and property tax.
- Fire insurance for the building and recourse of third parties; civil liability management insurance; purchase, maintenance or rental of fire extinguishers.
- Purchase of communal material (lawnmower, floor polisher, etc.); communal planted areas; repairs to the roof; renewal of sanitary installations.
- Replacement and major maintenance work on heating system (annual maintenance is payable by the tenant).
- Renewal of paintwork in the lobby area, on the facades, the entrance door, and outside woodwork after normal wear and tear.
- Renewal of wallpaper and wall coverings after normal wear and tear; repairs to balconies.
- Repairs to guttering, piping, cornices, cleaning out of wells, maintenance and repair to outside pavements.
- Maintenance of the facade, upkeep of gas piping, replacement of outdated electrical installations.
- Maintenance and repair of tanks; replacement of floor coverings or tiles.

NOTE!
Even though some repairs are payable by the landlord, it is nevertheless for the tenant to establish what needs to be done and to notify the landlord accordingly.

With the help of Budget & Droits nr. 128, august 1996

Inventory of Fixtures ('Etat des lieux')

This should be drawn up in the first month of occupation (within the first two weeks in the case of a lease for less than one year), at the initiative of the landlord.

In the absence of this inventory, the landlord can, in principle, not claim anything from the tenant by way of any damage he or she may cause.
If the inventory is drawn up by an expert (choose your own or agree this with the landlord), the costs will need to be shared between the landlord and the tenant.

It is important to be vigilant when the inventory is drawn up, and to make sure that it records any defect or fault which may exist. It will be your protection when the lease is terminated, at which point a fresh inventory will be drawn up and compared against the first one.

Registering the Lease:

Once you have signed your lease, you have 4 months to register it. An unregistered lease has no legal value and cannot be invoked against a third party. To register your lease, contact:

*Bureau du Receveur de
l'Enregistrement
Rue de la Régence, 54
1000 Brussels
✆   02 / 509 46 11
fax 02 / 509 46 58*
Open every working day from 8 a.m. to 12 noon
Make sure to take with you 1,000 bef, 2 x 200 bef in fiscal stamps, the original and 2 copies of your lease.

Tenant's Guarantee

May not exceed 3 months rent. Must be lodged in a bank account opened in the name of the tenant and may not be released except with the agreement of both parties.

Interest earned on the guarantee will be the property of the tenant when he leaves the property.

The guarantee is used to cover any damage which the tenant may cause to the rented property or failure to abide by the rental termination clauses. You should never pay cash in hand.

Normally, you will be given the guarantee back at the end of your lease, after the final inventory.

Indexing of the Rent

Rents are index-linked every year depending on the evolution of the index.
For information on the various indices applicable for indexing purposes, call the answering machine at the Ministry of Economic Affairs:
✆ 02 / 206.56.41

Disputes

In the event of a dispute, you will need to refer to a magistrate.

For further details:

Office national des Locataires
3 rue du Congrès
1000 Brussels
✆ *02 / 218 75 30*
fax 02 / 218 75 43

UPI (Union Professionnelle des Immobiliers)
Av. Albert, 29
1190 Brussels
✆ *02 / 344 57 52*
upi-vib@skynet.be

They will provide you with a list of estate agents for purchase or rental.

Fédération Bruxelloise des Unions de Locataires
✆ *02 / 201 03 60*
febul@misc.irisnet.be

A word of advice:
If you have any pets, remember to secure the landlord's agreement in the lease contract.

The current situation of the rental market in Brussels allows the tenant to negotiate a lower rent or to ask the landlord to carry out certain work (which must be listed in the annex to the lease contract).

Some landlords are less respectful of the law than others; so be sure that everything you do is strictly official and legal.

CD-Rom of the streets of Belgium

Belgian leader in cartography
✆ *02 / 216 91 00*

Moving In

---

10 rules for moving in successfully:

1. All your belongings are insured for their replacement value.
2. The water and electricity are on.
3. Show the removals team around the whole house first ; you may even want to put signs on each door with the name of the room in a language which is understood by the team (English is spoken in most removals companies).
4. The removals team comprises no more than 4 people. If there are more you will find it difficult to cope.
5. Take the time to explain exactly what you want.
6. Plan to have your children looked after.
7. Provide something to eat and drink. If you offer a drink to the members of the team this will be much appreciated.
8. Make sure that EVERYTHING is unpacked and that crates, boxes and paper are cleared away before the removals men leave.
9. Make a note of any damage, ask for the team leader's signature and do not sign the removals receipt without adding in front of your signature the following words: « sous réserve de vérification de perte ou de dégâts » (subject to checking for loss or damage).
10. Don't forget a tip (approximately 500 bef for each team member)

The names of a few removals companies:

Gosselin World Wide Moving
✆ 02 / 360 55 00
http://www.gosselin.be

Trans Euro World Wide
✆ 02 / 253 25 50
http://www.transeuro.be

Allied Arthur Pierre
✆ 02 / 689 27 11
http://www.alliedintl.com

Fittings and Decoration

Cleaner **De Geest**

For your carpets, tapistries, curtains, drapes,...
High quality service
☎ 02 / 512 59 78

For designing your building work you will find a list of **Architects** in the Yellow Pages (Section A), blue margin, p. 1 If you are having outside major works or alterations carried out, you may need planning permission. Contact the technical service at your commune, or:
Centre urbain de Bruxelles
☎ 02 / 512 86 19
from 9.30 a.m. to 12.30 p.m. and from 1.30 p.m. to 6 p.m.

For carrying out your building work you will find the list of **Building Contractors** in the Yellow Pages section B « Contractors – House building» (6192)

Decoration
You may wish to call on a decorator, do it yourself or opt for an intermediate solution involving working with a decorating shop where you will find a wide selection, advice and someone to help you translate your ideas into reality.

We have chosen a few addresses but we advise you to refer to the « **Useful Addresses** » section at the back of this guide if you would like to find out more.

Interior Design

Les Petites Heures du Matin
Chaussée de Waterloo, 1197
1180 Brussels
☎ 02 / 375 35 91
fax 02 / 375 49 31
http://www
Open from 9.30 a.m. to 6.30 p.m. Both decorators and shop, it offers a superb choice of fabrics and wallpapers. A team of painters, paper hangers, picture framers, carpenters and carpet-fitters provides a top-quality service. The whole range of furniture, light fittings, sofas and 'objets' is in an elegant, traditional, setting.

Nicole Cooremans
Rue de la Concorde, 62
1050 Brussels
by appointment
☎ 02 / 511 31 86
A talented woman of taste and style who has been brilliantly combining the traditional with the modern for 30 years, which has earned her the accolade of «By appointment to the Royal Court of Belgium»..

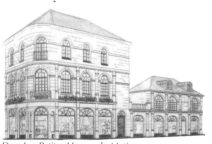
Doc. Les Petites Heures du Matin

Les Petites Heures du Matin

DÉCORATION

1197 Chaussée de Waterloo – 1180 Bruxelles

•

02 / 375 35 91

THE BEST IN BRUSSELS INFORMATION

BRUSSELS, YOURS TO DISCOVER.

THE "GUIDE & MAP"
**the whole of
Brussels in under
100 pages**

THE "GOURMET"
**your essential guide
to good food**

BRUSSELS,
YOURS TO DISCOVER.

300,-BEF - 7,5€

Tourist Passport

THE TOURIST
PASSPORT
*discounts at
your favourite
locations*

Best Of
BRUXELLES

April
May
June
July

BRUSSELS,
YOURS TO DISCOVER.

Main events in The Capital of Europe until
Principales manifestations culturelles à Bruxelles jusqu'au

THE BEST OF
*The diary of
events selected
by TIB.*

TiB

TOURIST AND INFORMATION OFFICE OF BRUSSELS
Town Hall - Grand-Place / Grote Markt - 1000 Brussels
TEL. ++32/2/513 89 40 / FAX ++32/2/514 45 38
e-mail : tourism.brussels@tib.be

Why in the world should you change Banks?

Because Citibank offers you the global access you desire with the control you deserve

Open your Citibank Account to access your bank:

Anytime: 7d/7 and 24h/24 via CitiPhone, Internet Banking and Citicard Banking Centers

Anywhere: via ATMs around the world

Anyhow: by opening a Citibank Account

Free of charge: if the combined monthly average balance of all your Citibank accounts exceeds 200 000 BEF.*

http: // www. citibank. be
Citiphone 02/626.50.50
24h / 7 days

Find out the special privileges offered to Expatriates and Pan-European Executives

Citibank has tailored its products and services to meet the special needs of Expatriates and Pan-European Executives

* you also earn 1% interest p.a. on your checking or current account (credited monthly)

To receive your free expatriate banking guide, mail attached coupon to:
Citibank Belgium, Expatriate Marketing/Roger Van den Broeck,
263g Bld Général Jacques, 1050 Brussels, or fax t o: 02/626.56.24

Name   First name

Street   N°

Postal code   City   Telephone   Fax

EIB99

La compagnie des Cotonnades
rue François Libert, 9
1410 Waterloo
☎ 02 / 353 18 59
fax 02 / 353 16 62
Open Mondays from 2 p.m. to 6 p.m. and Tuesday to Saturday from 10 a.m. to 6.30 p.m.
A team of four energetic young women who are bursting with ideas for designing charming rooms from delicate, subtle coordinates.

fabrics. A wide choice of trimmings. They take care of the sewing and fitting and will cover armchairs and sofas in coordinating fabrics.

Les Tissus du Chien Vert
(with le chien du chien and les puces du chien)
Rue du Chien vert, 2
1080 Brussels
☎ 02 / 411 54 34
A mine of extraordinary and exclusivce fabrics which, very reasonably priced.

Fabrics

Most fabric shops will also make up curtains etc.

KA International
Chaussée de Waterloo, 1359
1180 Brussels
☎ 02 / 374 66 82
fax 02 / 372 02 39
and
Boulevard de Waterloo, 3
1000 Brussels
☎ 02 / 514 71 17
fax 02 / 514 71 14
Very good value for money. A wide range of exclusive fabrics. A collection of sofas, wrought iron accessories, throws and lampshades in the fabric of your choice.

Les Tissus du Sablon
rue Joseph Stevens, 34
1150 Brussels
☎ / fax 02 / 502 48 60
and
rue van der Elst, 2
1950 Kraainem
☎ 02 / 784 38 64
fax 02 / 784 38 71
A superb collection of top quality stylish Egyptian cotton

Belgian Interior Design guides published by:

- *L'Evénement* magazine
  ☎ 02 / 333 07 00
  fax 02 / 332 05 98
  evenement@mm.be

- *Déco idées*
  the Belgian interior design magazine
  ☎ 02 / 333 32 11
  fax 02 / 333 32 10

Rue Blaes and rue Haute below the Sablon are teeming with good addresses and treasures just waiting to be found if you like a good rummage around. Please see the « **Grenier d'Igor** », near place de la Chapelle and « **New de Wolf** «, rue Blaes for furniture and Christmas decorations.

See also: antique shops, salerooms, flea markets, p. 172 to 188

Doc. Richoux

Furniture

Antiques & Design Center
place de la Chapelle, 6
1000 Brussels
✆ 02 / 511 86 85
2000 m2 of antique pine furniture.

La Savonnerie
Rue Edith Cavell, 102
1180 Brussels
✆ 02 / 36 30 87
Closed on Mondays.
A good address for antiques and interior design. They will search for the things you need.

Bathrooms

Facq
Facq in Ixelles, Boitsfort, Saint-Gilles, Laeken, Waterloo and Zaventem :
The largest showroom in Belgium is in Zaventem. You will find a huge choice of bathroom fittings and accessories. Catalogue on request
✆ 02 / 719 87 00

Baden Baden
rue Haute, 78-84
1000 Brussels
✆ 02 / 548 96 96
fax 02/ 548 96 91
A fine choice of antique bathtubs and toilets.

Kitchens

Liedsen
Very beautiful made to measure kitchens.
✆ 016 / 44 01 64

Ambiance Cuisine
Chaussée de Waterloo, 1138
1180 Brussels
✆ 02 / 375 24 36
fax 02 / 375 39 74

Light fittings

Luminaires Richoux
Avenue de l'Armée, 8
1040 Brussels
✆ 02 / 734 79 28
A huge choice to suit every room and every lifestyle. A professional service offers restoration of light fittings and made to measure lampshades.

Sophie Cappelle
Chemin du Bois Magonette, 4b
1380 Ohain
✆ 02 / 653 41 78
Open on Thursdays from 9 a.m. to 7 p.m. and by appointment on other days. A wide choice of all kinds of lamps.

Projet & Création
rue Neerveld, 57
1200 Brussels
Murielle Francqui creates unique pieces for you in the colours of your choice.

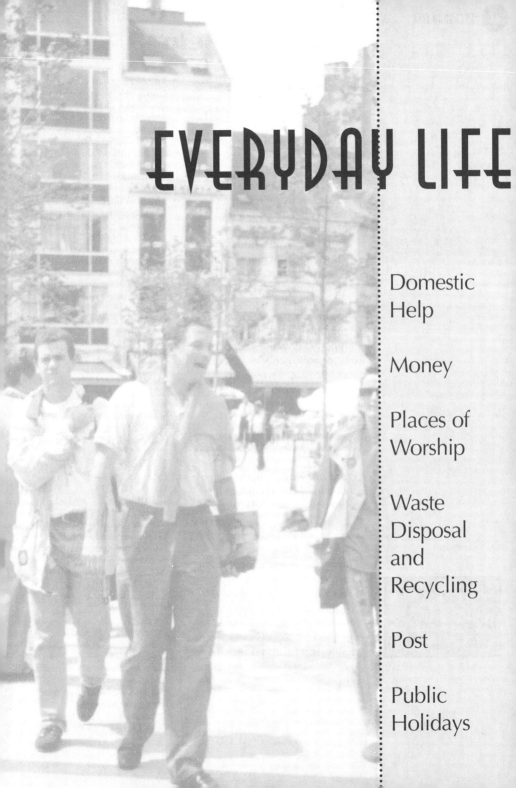

EVERYDAY LIFE

Domestic Help

Legality

- It is possible, although difficult, to find someone of Belgian nationality to help you with your household tasks.
- You should be aware that there are, living legally in Belgium, nationals of the Member States of the European Union, and nationals of other countries holding a residence document.
- Employing someone who is living illegally in Belgium can mean very stiff fines. You are running the risk of being reported (this does happen!) or of police checks in various public places where any person you employ is likely to be.

Looking for Help

Word of mouth between neighbours, friends and compatriots is often the system that works the best, and any references can be checked immediately.

Placing an advertisement in the newspaper:
Situations wanted: read these advertisements regularly.
Situations vacant: you should stipulate very precisely what you require, otherwise you are liable to be inundated with replies from people who are totally unsuitable.

Check references and residence status

- **Le Soir:** appears on Wednesdays (copy must be received by midday on Tuesday) and on Saturdays (copy to be received by Thursday midday).
  ✆ *02 / 225 55 00*
  fax 02 / 225 59 06
  Rue Royale, 120
  1000 Brussels
  annonces: tel@lesoir.be
- **The Bulletin:** deadline midday on Monday for publication on Thursday.
  fax 02 / 374 02 87
  (have your credit card handy)
  Chaussée de Waterloo, 1038
  1180 Brussels
- **Telegraaf:** Dutch newspaper whose Brussels headquarters is located at
  Boulevard de la Woluwe, 42
  1200 Brussels
  ✆ *02 / 762 60 20*
- **Le Ligueur:** monthly journal of the 'Ligue des Familles'.
  Rue du Trône, 127
  1050 Brussels
  ✆ *02 / 507 72 11*
  Subscription only.
  For a copy of the grid required for your insertion, contact *Promedit*
  ✆ *02 / 626 00 43*
  To subscribe to the Ligueur, contact *Ligue des Familles*
  Rue du Trône, 127
  1050 Brussels
  ✆ *02 / 507 72 11*
- **Vlan:** An advertisement in the Vlan, distributed throughout Brussels on Wednesdays (copy to be received one week in advance) will automatically appear in the 'Vlan Plus' issued on the Saturday and on sale in newsagents.
  ✆ *02 / 730 35 35*
  fax 02 / 730 35 96
  (have your credit card handy)
  Avenue Léon Grosjean, 92
  1140 Brussels
  enclosing a crossed cheque.
  http://www.vlan.be
- **La Voix du Nord:** (North of France newspaper)
  on Saturday and Sunday
  ✆ *+33-3 / 20 15 81 89*

Money

Money Matters

Belgian Franc (bef) and Exchange Rates

The Belgian franc is divided into 100 centimes.
The denominations are:
Coins: 0,50 bef,1 bef, 5 bef, 20 bef, 50 bef;
Notes: 100 bef, 200 bef, 500 bef, 1,000 bef, 2,000 bef, 10,000 bef.
The exchange rate parities between the Belgian franc and the other currencies in the Euro were fixed in January 1999.
The parities between the Belgian franc and other currencies are subject to fluctuation.
Belgian daily newspapers publish the exchange rates. Your bank will also be able to give you them.

How to Pay ?

In cash: If necessary, ask for a bill or a till slip as proof of purchase.
By cheque: These will be provided by your bank or your financial institution. Eurocheques are the most widely accepted form of cheque in Belgium, as in the rest of the European Union. Most retailers will ask you to show your Eurocheque card when you pay.

Transfer (bank or giro): This form of payment is handy for settling your bills by inter-account transfer. It enables you to keep track of your payments very easily. Paper transfer forms are supplied by your bank. You can make transfers by telephone or via your PC.
Eurocheque card: Issued by the banks, this is the necessary complement to your Eurocheques and also serves as a Mister Cash-Bancontact and Proton card.
Mister Cash-Bancontact card: Allows you to make payments in many outlets: is generally accepted in all department stores, at filling stations and most shops. It also serves as a Eurocheque card.
Proton card: This new card allows you to make small purchases very easily, and you can reload it with money at cash dispensers or at your bank. It is generally combined with the Eurocheque card.
Credit cards: Issued via banks, these are widely accepted in Belgium and the rest of the European Union.
Cash dispensers (Bancontact-Mister Cash): Widely distributed throughout the entire country. They allow you to withdraw money using your Bancontact, Mister Cash and credit cards, as well as reloading your Proton card.

1 €	= 40,33BEF
	= 6,55 FRF
	= 2,20 NLG
	= 1,96 DEM
	= 1936,27 ITL
	= 200,48 PTE
	= 13,76 ATS
	= 166,38 ESP
	= 40,33 LUF
	= 0,78 IEP
	= 5,94 FIM

Euro Info line
0800 / 12002

Banks and Financial Institutions

Money Changing Office

Money changing offices in the Gare du Midi (South station) (open daily from 6.30 a.m. to 10.30 p.m.), Gare du Nord (North station) (open daily from 7 a.m. to 10 p.m.) accept foreign currency, Visa, Eurocard and Mastercard credit cards, as well as Travellers Cheques. They take a commission of 30 bef per transaction.

Tip: Avoid changing money in the money changers around the Grand Place: they take 10% on each transaction!

If your credit card is lost or stolen:
CARD STOP:
070/344 344

Opening hours:
9 a.m. to 1 p.m. and 2 p.m. to 4 p.m., Monday to Friday. Some banks are open on Saturday mornings from 9 a.m. to 12 noon.

The Belgian financial institutions are subject to strict control by the Banking Commission and have a reputation for reliability. However, do make enquiries before making your choice and depositing your money.
• Savings accounts.
• Deposit accounts.
• Nominal accounts.

Your bank will be able to advise you on managing your finances, although it will not take any responsibility for this.

The management of your assets by the bank is known as 'private banking'.

Private Banking:
Private Banking is practised in Belgium by banks, stock brokers, fund managers or financial brokers. It is a profession which is carefully regulated and controlled. Here are some addresses:

Artesia
Avenue de Tervuren, 268
1150 Brussels
✆ *02 / 779 10 10*

Bearbull
Chaussée de Waterloo, 880
1000 Brussels
✆ *02 / 373 00 20*

Mees Pierson
Desguinlei, 50
2018 Anvers
✆ *03 / 240 08 88*

BBL
Cours St Michel, 60
1040 Brussels
✆ *0800 / 993 99*

Degroof
Rue de l'Industrie, 44
1040 Brussels
✆ *02 / 287 91 11*

For further information :

A.B.G.C.
(Belgian Association of Fund Managers and Investment Advisers)
✆ *02/ 373 00 20*
fax 02/ 374 76 41

ABMB
(Belgian Association of Stock Exchange Members)
✆ *02 / 509 13 91*
fax 02 / 509 13 42

Belgian Banks Association:
✆ *02 / 507 69 70*
fax 02 / 507 69 79

Please also visit our website: http://www.expatsinbrussels.com

Taxation

VAT: value-added tax is levied on almost all goods and services sold in Belgium at the rate of 21%. The rate falls to 6% on essentials and on property renovation work on buildings over 15 years old.
VAT is generally included in the selling price of commercial articles. However, practice varies when it comes to work or services provided. Always ask first.

Excise: petrol, alcohol, tobacco and a few other products are subject to this form of taxation, and is included in the prices.

Withholding tax on income from immovable assets: if you own a building in Belgium, you will have to pay an annual charge on its rateable income.

Income from work: salary, fees, emoluments, directors' percentages of profits, tips, etc. are all subject to taxation and specific taxation (social security) on a progressive, no-ceiling basis. In this respect, Belgium is one of the most heavily penalised countries. However, officials of the European Union are not subject to Belgian taxation, and expatriates working for foreign companies established in Belgium are entitled to a favourable exemption scheme for a limited period. Consult a tax adviser or a tax lawyer, or ask your employer if it is a foreign company.

Other income:
Income from shares: subject to Property Tax at 25% or 15% (discretionary).
Income from financial deposits or investments: subject to withholding tax at 15% (discretionary).
Capital profits (losses): non-taxable and non-deductible. In this respect, Belgium is regarded by many people as a tax haven for those holding capital.

Places of Worship

Belgium is a mainly Catholic country, and therefore the vast majority of the churches in and around Brussels are Catholic ones. They are open to all, parishioners and non-parishioners alike. Mass is usually held in French or in Dutch. The times of services are posted outside or inside the churches. Some churches offer masses specifically for children or of a more musical kind. Ask for details.

For further information:
Cultes des communautés chrétiennes belges et d'origine étrangère
Bruxelles Accueil Porte Ouverte
Rue Tabora, 6
1000 Bruxelles
✆ 511 81 78

In German

Protestant
Deutschsprachig
Evangelische Gemeinde
Avenue Salomé, 7
1150 Brussels
✆ 02 / 762 37 37
Sundays at 10.30 a.m.

Catholic
Katholische Gemeinde
Deutsche Sprache
Rue A. Fauchille, 3a
1150 Brussels
✆ 02 / 735 57 77
Mass at St Jean l'Evangéliste,
Tervuren
Sunday at 11 a.m.

In Danish

Église Luthérienne Danoise
Den Danske Kirke i Bruxelles
Avenue Delleur, 31-33
1170 Brussels
✆ 02 / 673 31 18
at the Botanique church
Boulevard Bischoffsheim, 40
1000 Brussels
1st and 3rd Sunday of the
month at 5 p.m. 2nd Sunday at
9 a.m.

In Norwegian

Den Norske Kirke i Brussel
Chaussée de Charleroi, 2
1420 Braine-l'Alleud
✆ 02 / 385 17 44
The 1st Sunday of the month at
5 p.m.

In English

Anglicans
Pro-Cathedral of the Holy
Trinity
Rue Capitaine Crespel, 29
1050 Brussels
✆ 02 / 511 71 83
Sundays 8.30 a.m.,
10.30 a.m. and 7 p.m.

St Paul's
à Sint Paulus Kerk
Dorpstraat, 707 A
3061 Leefdaal
✆ 02 / 767 34 35
Sunday at 10.30 a.m.
at the
British School
Leuvensesteenweg, 19
3080 Tervuren
On Sundays

Protestants
International Protestant
Church
Kattenberg, 19
1170 Brussels
✆ 02 / 673 05 81
alongside the ISB
Sundays 10.30 a.m.

Perfectly tuned management: music to your portfolio's ears

Our constant quest for performance enables us to offer our clients the benefit of optimum returns on their portfolios. We remain totally independent of other players in the financial markets, a principle practised by Bearbull for more than 25 years. To hear how perfectly we can tune in to your personal objectives, *call us on 02/373.00.20 or write to us at Bearbull (Belgium) sa, Chaussée de Waterloo 880, B-1000 Brussels.*

Bearbull
Portfolio Management

Landmarks

YOU CHOOSE YOUR BANK FOR ITS ABILITY TO TAKE CARE OF YOUR ASSETS.

Your assets are unique and belong to you and you alone. Looking after them is quite an art. You are fully entitled to expect impeccable financial, fiscal and legal expertise from your bank, whether your assets comprise transferable securities, property or works of art. Whatever the return and required duration, we respect your wish to pass on your assets to your heirs. With the strength of 175 years of experience in the management, structuring and transferring of assets, ARTESIA BANK meets all your needs. Through its fundamental philosophy of putting its clientele at the centre of all its operations, so as to have a clear idea of their situation and to set up the most appropriate strategy. Thus building a privileged relationship, based on long-term confidence. A principle which never ceases to confirm our motto: "The Art of Banking".

ARTESIA BANK

WTC · Tower 1 · Boulevard Emile Jacqmain 162-B2 · B-1000 Brussels
Tel: (02) 204 41 11 · Fax (02) 203 20 14 · http://www.artesia.be

Lutheran

All Lutheran Church
of Brussels
At the German church
Avenue Salomé, 7
1150 Brussels
2nd and 4th Sundays in the
month, from September to
June
4.30 p.m.
Contact:
Pastor G. van Hattem
℡ 03 / 233 62 50

Baptist

International Baptist Church
1970 Wezembeek-Oppem
IPCbrussels@compuserve.be

Eglise Baptiste Internationale
Lange Eikstraat, 76-78
1979 Wezembeek-Oppem
℡ 02 / 731 12 24

Waterloo Baptist Fellowship
Chaussée de Charleroi, 2
1420 Braine-l'Alleud
℡ 02 / 351 13 68

Catholic

St Anthony Parish
Oudstrijderslaan, 23-25
1950 Kraainem
℡ 02 / 720 19 70

Our Lady of Mercy Parish
St Anne Church
Place de la Sainte Alliance, 10
1180 Brussels
℡ 02 / 354 53 43

Presbyterian

St Andrew's Church
of Scotland
Chaussée de Vleurgat, 181
1050 Brussels
℡ 02 / 672 40 56
Sunday at 11 a.m.
pitkcathly@compuverse.com

Quaker

Quaker House
Square Ambiorix, 50
1000 Brussels
℡ 02 / 230 63 70
quakers@xs4all.be
Masses at 9.15 a.m. , 10.30
a.m. (for children – except
during holidays) and 12.00
noon on Sundays.
6 p.m. on Saturdays

Charismatic Community

International Christian
Fellowship
Rue des Confédérés, 114
1000 Brussels
℡ 02 / 734 38 80
In English and in French
Sundays at 2.30 p.m.

In Spanish and Italian

N.D. Immaculée
Place du Jeu de Balle
1000 Brussels
℡ 02 / 513 21 01
Sunday at 12.30 + feastdays

Mission catholique
espagnole
Rue de la Consolation, 60
1030 Brussels
℡ 02 / 242 22 58
fax 02 / 242 66 87
Saturday at 6 p.m.
and Sunday at 11 a.m.

Saint-Servais
Chaussée de Ath, 286
1030 Brussels
Mass at 5 p.m. on Sundays
(in Spanish)

Lumen vitae
Rue Washington, 186
1050 Brussels
Foyer Catholique Européen
Rue du Cornet, 51
1040 Brussels
℡ 02 / 230 39 38
fax 02 / 230 05 56
Saturdays at 6 p.m. (in
Italian) and 7 p.m. (in
Spanish)

Chapelle Saint-François
Avenue Père Damien, 29
1150 Brussels
Sundays at 11 a.m. (in
Italian)

In Swedish

Waterloo Baptist Fellowship
Chaussée de Charleroi, 2
1420 Braine-l'Alleud
℡ 02 / 351 13 68

Eglise suédoise
Chaussée de Charleroi, 2
1420 Braine-l'Alleud
℡ 02 / 387 25 19
fax 02 / 376 72 19
brussels@stut.be
Sunday at 11 a.m.

Synagogues

Beth Hilled S.
of Brussels
Avenue Kersbeek, 96
1190 Brussels
℡ 02 / 332 25 28
fax 02 / 376 72 19
cilb@skynet.be
Fridays at 8 p.m. and
Saturdays at 10.30 a.m.

Synagogue of Brussels
Administrative Office:
rue J. Dupont, 2
Place of worship:
Rue de la Régence, 32
1000 Brussels
℡ 02 / 512 43 34
fax 02 / 512 92 37
Fridays: 7 p.m.
Saturdays: 9.30 a.m.

Mosque

Mosquée de Bruxelles
Parc du Cinquantenaire, 14
1000 Brussels
℡ 02 / 735 21 73
fax 02 / 735 30 71

Waste Disposal and Recycling

Les Petits Riens
rue Américaine, 101
1050 Brussels
℗ 537 30 26

Terre
℗ 071 / 52 35 10
℗ 04 / 240 58 67

Armée du Salut
℗ 02 / 217 61 36

Emmaüs
℗ 02 / 523 80 45

Permanent containers.
La Déchetterie
Rue du Rupel,
near the "Pont
(bridge) van Praet"
in Brussels.
A number of skips
all intended for
different products.
Open to all.

Household Waste and Paper

There are usually two collections a week. Rubbish should be bagged up and left on the pavement in front of the house no earlier than 6 p.m. the evening before the collection.

Selective Recycling:

Organised by Bruxelles Propreté for all 'communes'.
Yellow bags (2 per month): paper.
Blue bags (1 per week): metal, tetrapaks, plastics, glass (bottles go into your nearest glass skip). Take care with sharp glass or metal objects!
Normal grey bag (2 per week): unsorted household waste.

Every January, a special collection is organised for your **Christmas trees.**
Out-of-date **telephone directories** are collected after the new ones are distributed.

Textiles (clothing, etc.)

Regular collections are organised by **Les Petits Riens** or by **Terre,** depending on the district. A plastic bag, showing when it will be collected, will be put through your letterbox.

Food

Food Bank
Rue de Glasgow, 116
1070 Brussels
℗ 522 97 00
If you have any left-over food and don't know what to do with it, call the Food Bank. It will notify the various associations who will call round and collect the food from you and then distribute it.

Household Chemical Waste

Bruxelles Propreté handles the collection of these materials, via mobile or stationary 'green corners' located in various public places. Ring Bruxelles Propreté to find out times and locations. These items can also be collected, by arrangement and against payment.
Some department stores offer used battery disposal facilities. Most chemists will take back out-of-date medicines.

Larger Items

Bruxelles Propreté **Doorstep collection** is available on request and by appointment, every weekday and on Saturday mornings. The first cubic metre is removed free of charge once every six months.

Rental of skips
✆ 0800 / 981 81

Communal skips:
once or twice a year, you can dispose of your heavy items here on presentation of your identity card.

For more information:
Bruxelles Propreté
✆ 0800 / 981 81

Have you thought about composting and cutting your household waste by 75% ? If you would like to receive a free copy of the « Guide du compost facile» in Brussels, call
✆ 02 / 775 75 75

Bag/colour	what for	what not for	tips
Yellow bags	newspapers, magasines books, exercise books publicity leaflets envelopes phone books	greasy, dirty paper plastic paper stickers carbon paper wall paper	fold boxes cardboard must be tied up.
Blue bags	tins jars plastic bottles aerosols foil trays drink cartons glass	dirty containers plastic trays wrapping "frigolite" plastic bags poisonous products syringes	compress plastic bottles push in metal tops do not box up different packaging
Glass containers	all glass items	mirrors, lights, pyrex, china, neon crockery.	take out corks and empty.

Post

Price of stamps

For Europe we would advise you to use « Prior » stickers, available free at post offices otherwise it will take your letters 3 weeks to arrive !

Post Offices are open from 9 a.m. until 4 p.m. or 6 p.m. from Monday to Friday.

The post office behind the Woluwé Shopping Center is open until 7 p.m. on Fridays and until 12 noon on Saturday mornings.

The one in the Gare du Midi is **open 24 hours a day**

The one in the Monnaie Centre (bld Anspach) is open **until 7 p.m. on weekdays** and **from 10 a.m. until 3 p.m. on Saturdays**.

For letters under 20 gr	Prioritaire (first class)	non prioritaire (second class)
Within Belgium	17 bef	17 bef
Within the EU	21 bef	19 bef
Rest of Europe	30 bef	21 bef
Rest of the World	34 bef	23 bef
price on 1st August 99		

Express Couriers

Taxi Post
✆ 02 / 240 84 10
250 bef for a parcel weighing less than 10kg to any commune in Brussels.

City Bike Express
✆ 02 / 648 95 10
National and International service.

Public Holidays

	Public Holidays	School holidays
All Saints	1st November	01/11/99 - 05/11/99
Armistice	11th November	
Dynasty Festival	15th November	
Christmas	25th December	27/12/19 - 7/1/2000
New Year	1st January	
Carnival		6/3/2000-10/3/2000
Easter Monday	24th April2000	10/4/2000-21/4/2000
Labour Day	1st May	
Ascension	1st June 2000	
Whitsun	11th June2000	
Assumption	15th August	

F°	C°
32°	0°
50°	10°
60°	16°
212°	100°

Clocks change:
    31 october 99 (you gain an hour: at 3 a.m. belgian time, it's 2 a.m. again)
    26 march 2000 (you lose an hour: at 2 a.m. belgian time, it's 3 a.m.)

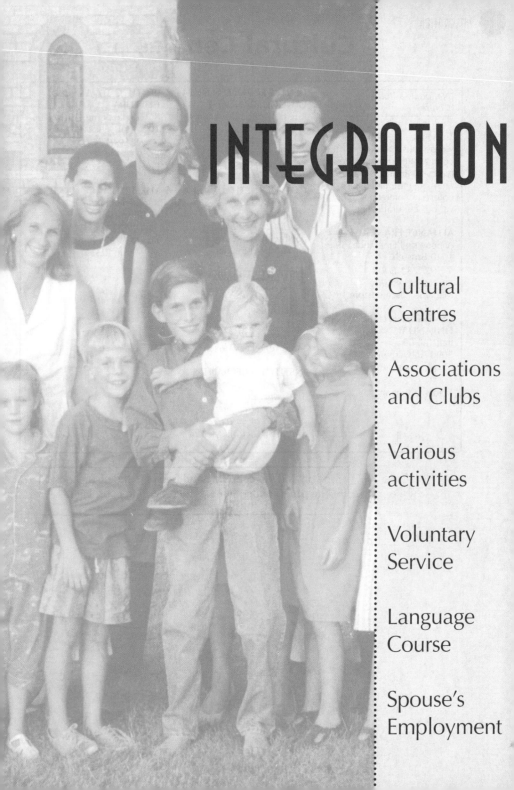

INTEGRATION

Cultural
Centres

Associations
and Clubs

Various
activities

Voluntary
Service

Language
Course

Spouse's
Employment

Cultural Centres

National Cultural
Centres

These are official bodies whose role is to promote the culture of the country they represent among Belgians. They organise language courses, conferences and various cultural events.

ALLIANCE FRANCAISE
Avenue de l'Emeraude, 59
1040 Brussels
✆ 02/ 732 11 03
fax 02/736 47 00
Madame Pascale Fabre

**CENTRE CULTUREL
FINLANDAIS**
Italielei, 69
2000 Antwerpen
✆ 03 / 231 87 51
fax 03 / 227 27 47
Madame Johanna Lindstedt

**CENTRE EUROPEEN DE LA
LANGUE FRANCAISE**
Rue d'Arlon, 24
1000 Brussels
✆ 02 / 502 46 49
fax 02 / 502 33 77
Madame Pascale Fabre

GOETHE INSTITUT
Rue Belliard, 58
1040 Brussels
fax 02/ 230 77 25
goethe.library@euronet.be
Dr Bernhard Beutler

**INSTITUT CULTUREL
DANOIS**
Rue du Cornet, 22
1040 Brussels
✆ 02 / 230 73 26
fax 02 / 230 55 65
Mme Lone Leth Larsen

INSTITUTO CERVANTES
Avenue de Tervuren, 64
1040 Brussels
✆ 02 / 737 01 90
fax 02 / 735 44 04
Sra Maria Victoria Morera

**ISTITUTO ITALIANO DI
CULTURA**
Rue de Livourne, 38
1000 Brussels
✆ 02/ 538 77 04
fax 02 / 534 62 92
Prof. Giuseppe Xausa

THE BRITISH COUNCIL
Rue de la charité, 15
1040 Brussels
✆ 02/ 227 08 42
fax 02 / 227 08 49
Mr Martin Rose

You will find the **consulates' addresses** in the phonebook (white pages) under "Ambassades - section consulaire"

Associations and Clubs

Essential reading:

The Bulletin apart from its weekly magasine and bi-annual "New Comer", it also publishes a guide/directory (*Expats Directory*) which includes a full list of associations (particularly English-speaking ones). Ackroyd Publications - Chaussée de Waterloo 1038 - 1180 Brussels
✆ 02 / 373 99 09 - fax 02 / 375 98 22 - e.mail: Ackroyd@innet.be

Qui Italia, , monthly news and culture for the Italian community.
136 rue Franklin – 1000 Brussels – ✆ 02/ 742 27 29 – fax 02 / 735 85 20

El Sol de Belgica, the Spanish magazine of the capital of Europe. Monthly
12A Boulevard Clovis – 1000 Brussels – ✆ 02 / 732 19 80 – fax 02 / 732 23 92
e.mail: elsoldebelgica@hotmail.com

Der Kontact
120 rue Royale – 1000 Brussels – ✆ 02 / 219 12 58– fax 02 / 219 23 35
Magazine in German.
e.mail: msr@mail.dma.be

Brüssel-Rundschau, bi-monthly news magazine in German.
Rue Amadée Lynen – 1210 Brussels – ✆ 02/ 219 29 19 – fax 02 / 219 92 00
e.mail: bruesselrunschau@euronet.be

Annual publications
Agenda española is published every year which includes a list of the Spanish associations in Belgium. Further information from El Sol de Belgica.

Amici in Citta, , practical information for Italians living in Brussels. On sale in bookshops.

Brussels Pass, concise, practical information for English speakers.

Brüssel-Paß, the same for German speakers.

Most of the national and international associations publish a newsletter for their members.

Den Danske, Danish publication - ✆ 02 / 376 66 35

Parlööri, Finnish publication - ✆ 02 / 673 73 57

Bladet, Swedish publication - ✆ 02 / 354 06 98

Associations and national clubs

Asia

Asia Pacific Women's Association
Avenue des Erables, 13
1640 Rhode St Genèse
Carmel Chong
✆ 02 / 354 78 03
For diplomats' wives.

Australia

Australia Society
Deborah Watson
✆ 02 / 648 47 95
eric.watson@compuserve.com

Austria

Austrian Association in Belgium
Eva Van Gool
✆ 02 / 375 86 15

Canada

Canadian Women's Club of Belgium
Linda Edgar
✆ 02 / 731 49 82
Linda Adcock
✆ 02 / 647 42 89
Meetings, evening events, family activities.

China

Belgium Hong Kong Society
Av. de Tervuren , 188a
1150 Brussels
✆ 02 / 775 00 88
fax 02 / 770 09 80
Secretary: Muriel Albert

Denmark

Danish Association in Belgium
Trosdreef, 18
1190 Brussels
Finn Haming
✆ 02 / 376 66 35
fax 02 / 376 69 91
ddfb@ddfb.be
Publication: *Den Danske Forening i Belgien*

Dansk Contact
Mette Jespen
✆ 02 / 358 458 01
Danish family club
See also "Scandinavia"

Finland

Suomi Klubi a.s.b.l.
✆ 02 / 673 73 57
fax 02 / 660 76 43
http://www.suomi-klubi.com
Mme Hanna Wagner
Publication: *Parlööri*
See also "Scandinavia"

Association Belgique –Finlande
Rue Cervantes, 4 Bte 4
1190 Brussels
✆ 02 / 344 46 25

France

Accueil des Françaises
Rue Marie Depage, 53
1180 Brussels
Claude Ribon
✆ 02 / 347 02 17
fax 02 / 345 16 04
accueil@ping.be

Union des Français de l'Etranger
Chssée de Roodebeek, 140
1200 Brussels
Mme Roussot
✆ 02 / 771 08 55
Friendly, apolitical theme meetings.

Germany

Deutsche in Brüssel
Mme Doris Wendel
✆ 02 / 354 23 87

Great Britain

Brussels British Unity Association
✆ 02/ 344 68 77
Barbara Blackwell
Association which groups together some 36 sports, cultural, artistic and social clubs etc.

British and Commonwealth Women' Club
Rue au Bois, 509
1150 Brussels
✆ 02 / 772 53 13
http://www.Xpat.com
Janet Martin
publication: *passeport magazine*

Royal Belgo British Union
Michael P. Ingham
✆ 02 / 672 18 09
fax 02 / 675 75 03

Iceland

Islandfeladir i Belgien
rue au Bois, 258
1150 Brussels
✆ 02 / 779 58 88
fax 02 / 286 18 00
Mrs Jenny Davidsdottir
See also "Scandinavia"

India

European-Indian Association
Bharat Darshan
191 Av. de Roodebeek
1030 Brussels
✆ 02 / 734 00 54

Ireland

Irish Club of Belgium
Rue Archimède, 67
1000 Brussels
✆ 02 / 742 27 37
fax 02 / 742 27 37
icb@skynet.be

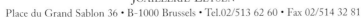

The art of cleaning.

LE TEINTURIER   DE VERVERIJ

Rue de l'Hôpital 37-41
1000 Bruxelles

02 / 512 59 78

For over 150 years,
the cleaning specialist for
clothes, carpets, armchairs and curtains.

Les Nocturnes du Sablon

Each year in November
25, 26, 27 November 1999
23, 24, 25 November 2000

Information: 02 / 502 16 31

EMPORIO ARMANI

Place du Grand Sablon 37
Bruxelles 1000 Brussels
Tel.: 02/551.04.04

Ouvert tous les jours de 10h30 à 19h00	Daily opened from 10:30 to 19:00
y compris le dimanche de 11h00 à 18h00	including Sunday from 11:00 to 18:00
Fermé le mardi	Closed on Tuesday

Les Tissus du Sablon

ALL YOUR SOFT FURNISHING NEEDS:
MAKING UP, FINISHING TOUCHES, INTERIOR DESIGN ADVICE
Sablon: 34 rue Joseph Stevenstraat • 1000 Brussels
Tel. 02 / 502 48 60 – 502 48 26 • Fax 02 / 502 48 60
Place Dumon: rue Van der Elst, 2 • 1950 Kraainem
Tel. 02 / 784 38 64 • Fax 02 / 784 38 71

We enjoy putting a smile on your face

WELCOME

We work hard at keeping a smile on our clients faces, that is how we like to do business.

At CGU, our aim is at all times to provide the optimum of advice and the ultimate in service, sure, in the knowledge, that your satisfaction is our satisfaction. Through our determination to make the transition into a new way of life as easy as possible, we have grown to be recognized as the insurer most capable of meeting the individual specific needs of the expatriate.

Our range of home, car and personal insurance policies ensure that you and your family have the best and most competitive cover possible.

An insurer dedicated to the expatriate community...
What a refreshing thought.

CGU | **Expatriates Division**

CGU, the assurance of satisfaction

By dealing direct with CGU, you save valuable time and you also receive the best possible rates.
To receive our welcome pack simply contact us by phone, fax or email ;

CGU / Expatriates Division
Avenue Herrmann-Debroux 54 • 1160 Brussels
tel : 02/676.65.99 • fax : 02/676.69.99
e-mail : mark.cryans@be.cu.com

Italy

There are a huge number of Italian associations organised according to region or special interests. For information call the Italian Cultural Institute.
✆ 02 / 538 77 04

Japan

Association Belgo-Japonaise
Avenue Louise 287 bte 7
1050 Brussels
✆ 02 / 644 13 33
fax 02 / 644 23 60

Japan Club EU
Mme Dicorrado
✆ 02 / 299 41 67
fax 02 / 299 10 33
daniela.dicorrado-andreoni@dg1.cec.be

New Zealand

New Zealanders in Belgium
✆ 02 / 771 19 49

Norway

Den Norske Forening i Belgia
Mr Gunnar Borch
✆ 02 / 305 31 92
fax 02 / 726 47 09

Norsk-Flamsk Forening
Mr Karel Bouving
✆ 03 / 366 28 54
fax 03 / 366 28 54
See also "Scandinavia"

Scandinavia

Antwerpse Kring voor Scandinavie
Isabella Brandstraat, 47
2018 Antwerpen
✆ 03/ 248 49 50
fax 03/ 248 49 47
Erwin de Boel

Cercle Nordique
Rue Franz Merjay, 159
1050 Brussels
✆ 02/ 344 53 50
fax 02/ 244 87 92
Mr Ian Larsen

South Africa

South African Women Club
Brussels: Katya Barnes
✆ 02 / 688 02 02
Anvers: Debbie Smith
✆ 03 / 385 17 56

Spain

There are a huge number of Spanish associations organised according to region or special interests. For information call the Spanish Cultural Institute
✆ 02 / 737 01 90

Sweden

Svenska Klubben
Château d'Argenteuil
Square d'Argenteuil, 5
1410 Waterloo
✆ 02 / 354 06 98
fax 02 / 354 06 98
Mme Elisabeth Stael von Holstein
Publication: *Bladet*

SWEA (Swedish Women's Educational Association International Inc.)
Avenue W. Churchill, 216
1050 Brussels
✆ 02/ 346 53 29
Mme Christina Malaise

Société Belgo-Suédoise
Rue du Luxembourg, 3
1000 Brussels
✆ 02 / 501 53 81
fax 02 / 501 53 82
Mme Catharina Verhaegen

Svensk Samling i Antwerpen
✆ 03/ 789 12 02
fax 03/ 789 12 02
See also "Scandinavia"

USA

American Women's Club of Brussels
Avenue des Erables, 1
1640 Rhode St Genèse
✆ 02/ 358 47 53
awcbbelgium@compuserve.com

American-Belgian Association of Brussels
Guillemine de Vaubernier
Place Blijkaerts, 13
1050 Brussels
✆ 02 / 646 53 30
fax 02/ 646 53 30

American Club of Antwerp
(Men)
✆ 02 / 660 54 68
Email: dstarr@directpub.com

American Club of Brussels
✆ 02 / 203 63 61
fax 02 / 203 22 37
american.club@usa.net
For both private individuals and companies. Organises social and professional activities. More than 25 nationalities represented. A place to meet, relax and make contacts.

International associations and clubs

Alloquium
Palais d'Egmont
Place du Petit Sablon, 8
1000 Brussels
✆ 02 / 501 48 70
Association for the wives of
Belgian diplomats

**Association Femmes
d'Europe**
Avenue de Beaulieu, 1
1160 Brussels
✆ 02 / 660 56 96
✆ 02 / 675 48 19
Phone lines staffed from 9.30
a.m. to 12 noon.
Charitable association for all
nationalities. More than 1,000
members, over many national
groups. Fund raising through
the organisation of cultural
events, bridge tournaments,
conferences and dinners.
Sponsorship required.

**BCT
(Brussels Childbirth Trust)**
✆ 02 / 215 33 77
A self-help group for English
speaking families in
Belgium. Information on
pregnancy, childbirth and
young children. Meetings
and discussions. Ante-natal
classes. See § «"Children" p.

Brussels Contact
✆ 02 / 733 93 65
Monique
✆ 010 / 22 91 49
Elizabeth
✆ 02 / 231 11 96
International friendship group
for adults over 40.

Cercle Polyglotte
✆ 02 / 216 47 63
Roger Malavez
For anyone who would like
to practise a language they
can already speak and make
contact with people who
speak the same language.

Meetings on Wednesday
evenings at tables organised
according to language.

Club Montgomery
✆ 02 / 734 63 50
International women's club:
lunch, conferences, variety of
courses and avtivities, mini-
trips. Sponsor necessary.

**Club International du
Château Sainte-Anne**
Rue du Vieux Moulin, 103
1160 Brussels
✆ 02 / 660 29 00

Focus Career Services
Rue Lesbroussart, 23
1050 Brussels
✆ 02 / 646 65 30
fax 02 / 646 96 02
Mrs Luchner
See "Spouse's employment"
pg 66.

FRIENDS a.s.b.l.
✆ 02 / 784 37 60
✆ 02 / 767 26 05
Ms Rosemary Pallett
Young, informal, international
social club which aims to
foster friendship regardless of
nationality, social status or
age.

**International Christian
Women's Club**
✆ 02 / 376 78 15
Cathy Delhaye

**STUDS (Spouses Trailing
Under Duress Successfully)**
Dan Gamber
✆ 02/ 736 24 73
dan-gamber@compuserve.com
Group for the husbands and
partners of women who have
moved to Belgium for professional reasons. Meets every
Friday from 10.00 a.m. to 12
noon at the Pain Quotidien,
6 avenue de Hinnisdael in
Stockel.

Women of Color in Belgium
✆ 02 / 673 55 56
Renée Williams

**International Study group
(I.S.G.)**
Avenue de Messidor 336/3
1180 Brussels
Felicitas Donker
✆ 02 / 375 39 98
fax 02 / 375 40 11
Meets once a month during
the day in an intellectually
stimulating environment.
International ladies' club
restricted to 135 members.

Welcome To Belgium
Prieuré de Val Duchesse
Avenue Val Duchesse, 1
1160 Brussels
✆ 673 59 53
(Monday to Thursday from
9.30 a.m. to 12 noon).
The goals of this association
are to create friendship links
between foreigners and
Belgians and to discover
Belgium in all its aspects.
The 3 sections:
Welcome Brussels et
Welcome Week-End
reserved for the wives of
members of the Diplomatic
Corps, the wives of
European Union civil ser-
vants as well as civi-lian and
military members of NATO
and the OEU.
Welcome Mons, reserved for
the wives of SHAPE officials
and incorporated members.
Sponsorship required.

**Women's International Club
of Brussels**
Rue J. Vanderlinden, 1
1180 Brussels
Gerda Van Leeuwen
✆ 02 / 770 59 43
fax 02 / 770 59 43

Various activities

Special interest social groups

Depending upon your own tastes and skills, you can find the course to suit you in Brussels. Many are run by cultural centres, academies, schools and foreigners' associations. Here are some courses run for Belgians and foreigners alike.

Art and Culture

Brussels Historical Association
✆ 010/ 84 43 70
Lionel Bishop
Branch of the same association in England. Visits, conferences and discussions.

Art Perspectives International
✆ 02 / 771 30 55
Contact Elise Pinkow, info
Sandee Johnson
✆ 02 / 731 64 59
Group of dedicated expat artists which has grown to include the Belgian community, the EU and beyond.

**Arabel
(Art et Accueil en Belgique)**
Rue Voot, 9
1150 Brussels
✆ 770 15 27
(from 9 a.m. to 12 noon, everyday except Wednesdays).
Conferences, exhibitions, tours, trips in Belgium and abroad.
Inscription: 1,000 bef. Charges for activities. Sponsorship required.

Arcadia
✆ 534 38 19
Guided walking visits in and around Brussels every Sunday morning. À la carte programs with guides and lecturers.

Lundis de Drouot
Le Club de l'Art
Rue Defacqz, 78/80
1060 Brussels
✆ 02 / 537 50 78
e.mail: jeudisdedrouot@wanadoo.fr
jeudisdedrouot@wanadoo.fr
Courses-conferences. Visits. Trips.

Artisanat

Decorative and Fine Arts Societies
Maureen Barnett
✆ 02 / 736 66 66

BFAS (Belgian Flower Arrangement Society)
Kortrijksesteenweg, 834
9000 Gand
✆ 09 / 222 77 07
The Belgian branch of an international association.
Flower arranging competitions with foreign delegations. Monthly meetings and an annual trip.
Sponsorship required.

Centre Crousse
Rue au Bois , 11
1150 Brussels
✆ 771 83 59
An extensive programme for adults: water-colours, painting, yoga, floral art, miniature workshop, patchwork, sewing, lace-making, decoration, cookery, painting on silk, painting on porcelain, bridge, basket-weaving, etc. English spoken.

Ateliers de la rue Voot
Rue Voot, 9
1150 Bruxelles
✆ 762 48 93
A wide programme for adults: sculpture, calligraphy, photography, ceramics, painting, drawing, etc.

Singing

British Choral of Brussels
✆ 02 / 653 64 11

Brussels Choral Society
✆ 02 / 735 07 44

Carols for Christmas
✆ 02 / 219 07 89
For adults and children. Concert at the beginning of December.

Chœur d'enfants de la Monnaie
✆ 02 / 229 12 00

Chapelle des Minimes
Adult choir. Bach cantatas.
Patrick Minet
✆ 02 / 345 83 45

Theatre

American Theatre Company
✆ 02 / 660 85 78

Brussels Shakespeare Society
✆ 02 / 660 99 28

English Comedy Club
✆ 02 / 514 10 68

Irish Theatre group
✆ 02 / 688 04 37

Brussels Youth Theatre Society
✆ 02 / 675 54 64
Workshop for children aged 8 to 14 years. On Saturday mornings at the British School in Tervuren.

Sports

Brussels Hash House Harriers
✆ 02 / 734 45 60 - 771 88 33
Jogging every saturday afternoon. Informal english-speaking group.

Voluntary Service

The voluntary service sector is not very highly developed in Belgium, and does not generally require any particular qualifications.

A few addresses for those wishing to give up some of their time for others, while making new friends.

You could also offer to work as a volunteer at a local hospital, school or parish.

Entraide et Amitiés
Rue de la Charité, 43
1040 Brussels
✆ 02 / 223 21 41
entraide-amitie@skynet.be
Allows you to help a sick person at home, or to become a volunteer in a clinic or rest home.

Amnesty International
Rue Berckmans , 9
1060 Brussels
✆ 02 / 538 81 77
aibf@aibf.be
English speakers should contact:Heather Clarke
✆ 02 / 736 25 53
Regular writing of letters to the authorities in countries violating Human Rights.

Ligue belge de Défense des Droits de l'homme
Rue de l'Enseignement, 91
1000 Brussels
✆ 02 / 209 62 80
ldh@linkline.be
To ensure that the application of the laws respects the spirit of the Universal Declaration on Human Rights.

Croix Rouge de Belgique
Chaussée de Vleurgat , 94
1050 Brussels
✆ 02 / 645 47 27
Training programmes twice a year.

American Red Cross
✆ 02 / 361 00 79
✆ 065 / 44 40 08 (evenings)
Solidarity actions: running classes in first aid, raising young people's awareness of blood donation, protecting life and health, helping the disabled, visiting the sick, the elderly or those living alone, etc.

Médecins sans Frontières
Rue Dupré, 94
1090 Brussels
✆ 02 / 474 74 74
zoom@msf.be
Telling those around you about the work of MSF and raising their awareness (12 regional bases).

Want to know more?

Association pour le Volontariat
Rue Royale , 11
1000 Brussels
✆ 02 / 219 53 70
Centralises all voluntary work opportunities.

Télé Service
Rue du Boulet, 24
1000 Brussels
✆ 02 / 548 98 00
This association publishes a brochure listing over 200 voluntary associations.

Groot Eiland
Groot Eilandstraat, 84
1000 Bruxelles
✆ 02 / 502 66 00
Information about dutch associations in need of volunteers.

Centre national de Coopération au Développement
Quai du Commerce , 9
1000 Brussels
✆ 02 / 223 49 19
Participation in the 11 11 11 operation, organised every November for the benefit of concrete projects in various parts of the Third World.

Community Help Service (C.H.S.), rue St Georges, 102
1050 Brussels
✆ 02 / 647 67 80
All volunteers for the "Help line" or other services are given a six week training course.

Informations und Beratüngsstelle Deutschsprachige (I.B.S.)
✆ 02 / 768 21 21
German-speaking equivalent of the CHS
Training sessions begin in September

Malte Assistance
Active in a number of fields, this organisation really needs volunteers.
General information:
✆ 02 / 252 30 72
Volunteer training:
Norbert de Schaetzen
✆ 012 / 23 71 31

La Fontaine
Showers and care for the homeless.
Aloyse de Saint-Marcq
✆ 02 / 512 74 11

Service Social juif
Rue Ducpétiaux 68
1060 Brussels
✆ 02 / 538 81 80
Administrative, psychological and social aid for foreigners of all nationalities.

United Fund of Belgium
Av. de Tervuren 270-272
1150 Brussels
✆ 02 / 761 49 50

Language Courses

Here are some addresses. If you would like to find out more please refer to the **"Useful addresses"** section at the back of the guide.

French

Fondation 9
Avenue Louise, 412
1050 Brussels
✆ 02 / 640 21 92
fax 02/ 640 22 01
A foundation set up under the auspices of the ULB (Université Libre de Bruxelles), the city of Brussels and the CCIB (Chambre de Commerce et d'Industrie de Bruxelles). French conversation classes. Intensive immersion courses 7 days a week.

Active French School
Brusselsesteenweg, 416
3090 Overijse
✆ 02 / 657 20 44
French courses for adults and children.

Centre d'étude du Français – Washington School
Chaussée de Vleurgat, 275
1050 Brussels
✆ 02 / 344 15 15

Dutch

For information on Dutch language courses in the Brussels communes:
✆ 02 / 648 20 30

Cultureel Centrum « Den Blank»
Begijnhof, 11
3090 Overijse
✆ 02 / 687 59 59
fax 02 / 687 42 90
info@denblank.be
Beginners, advanced and conversation classes specially designed for expats.

Centrum Basiseducatie
Nieuwstraat, 5
1830 Machelen
✆ 02 / 252 51 50
fax 02/ 252 40 31
Courses designed for different purpo-ses: reading, writing, help with school work for children, Information technology, Internet, topical issues, art appreciation through visits to museums or exhibitions.
Courses for adults organised in Machelen, Vilvoorde, Grimbergen, Zaventem, Tervuren, Overijse and Hoeilaart.

GLSP Volwassenonderwijs
Brusselsesteenweg, 106
3080 Tervuren
✆ 02 / 767 04 30
fax 02 / 767 04 30
Free courses, registration fee 400 bef. One department in Tervuren and another in Hoeilaart.

The cultural centres organise language courses.
See pg 54

Most communes organise language courses.
See pg 15 and 16

Essential reading: 'Le guide des langues' published by IDJ, 195 bef.
✆ 02 / 772 70 20

De Rand
Witherendreef, 1
3090 Overijse
6 bureaux
Sint-Genesius-Rhode
✆ 02 / 381 14 51
Overijse
✆ 02 / 657 31 79
Wezembeek-Oppem
✆ 02 / 731 43 31
Kraainem
✆ 02 / 721 28 06
Linkebeek
✆ 02 / 380 77 51
Wemmel
✆ 02 / 460 73 24
Dutch courses for adults.

European Languages

Aria d'Italia
Avenue Paul Deschanel, 27
1030 Brussels
✆ 02 / 241 69 11
Courses in Italian language and culture

Ceran
Avenue du Château, 146
4900 Spa
✆ 087 / 79 11 22
Various total-immersion language courses.

CLL
Passage de la Vecquée , 17
1200 Brussels
✆ 02 / 764 22 93
Programme of immersion for adults and children.

Centre de culture européenne
Avenue des Cerisiers, 128
1200 Brussels
✆ 02 / 734 06 99
fax 02 / 736 91 92
Courses, seminars, lectures and guided tours in various European languages.

Nedelands Taal Instituut
Rue de l'Association, 56
1000 Brussels
✆ 02 / 219 03 27
fax 02/ 219 54 61
Individual or group lessons for adults and teenagers. Various languages.

Call International
Boulevard de la Cense, 41
1410 Waterloo
✆ 02 / 353 13 00
fax 02/ 353 08 09
Avenue d'Auderghem , 277
1040 Brussels
✆ 02 / 644 95 95
fax 02 / 644 94 95
Specialised in accelerated language courses.

Other world languages

Liren International Institute
Rue du Beau- Site, 13 bte 15
1000 Brussels
✆ 02 / 646 27 69
fax 02 / 646 27 56
All the main languages of Europe, Scandinavia, Eastern Europeand Asia plus Arabic.

Clearly not moved by Gosselin

The items you treasure most deserve the greatest attention when you move. They are treated with the utmost care by those meticulous men sent by Gosselin, who wrap them in that specific Gosselin paper and move them in accordance with the Gosselin master plan specially drawn up for you. Gosselin World Wide Moving has over 65 years' experience in VIP treatment. Their service is so impeccable that you will be moved when you see their specialists at work.

GOSSELIN WORLD WIDE MOVING N.V.

We Know How To Move People

Keesinglaan 28 • 2100 Antwerp • Belgium • Tel. +32 3 360 55 00 • +32 2 772 34 87 • Fax +32 3 360 55 79
E-mail: Comm@Gosselin.be • Internet: WWW: http://www.gosselin.be

Avec le soutien de la
Région de Bruxelles-Capitale

Met de steun van het
Brussels Hoofstedelijk Gewest

Spouse's employment

For E.U. nationals there is no problem. Your identity card is all you need to live and work in Belgium (please see « administrative formalities pg 12)

For non E.U. nationals obtaining a work permit is a very long and difficult process. The difficulties are so great and so many applications are rejected that we would advise you to entrust the task of obtaining a work permit to the professionals. There are lawyers who specialise in this area.

The company your spouse works for may wish to help you find work and may call upon a firm of specialists. Net Expat (see box), will take up the matter with you. They will carry out the formalities for obtaining a work permit, revise your CV and adapt it to Belgian standards, make you aware of some cultural differences, train you to perform at your best during interviews and look for suitable work for you even if you cannot speak a word of French or Dutch. They take you through the steps pro-actively from A to Z in a tried and tested way with an exceptionally high success rate.

For anyone who is attempting this obstacle course on their own,, Focus (see box) can help you. It is an association of highly efficient volunteers. You can find resources, services, help and advice whether your aim is to pursue a professional career in Belgium, stay in contact with the world of work or develop your skills by following a training programme. There are so many members of such high quality that you will find a real network of contacts which will certainly be useful professionally.
You could also call on the temping agencies if you have the right profile and you do not require a work permit. Some have a section for expatriates.

Randstad Interim
Place Stéphanie, 20/9
1050 Brussels
✆ 02 / 511 53 53
fax 02 / 511 97 72
info@randstad.be

Interlabor Interim
Place de Brouckère
1000 Brussels
✆ 02 / 229 14 00
fax 02 / 223 29 09

Net Expat : For successful expatriations
Net Expat is a company which has developed a unique range of services in Europe
to help expatriate spouses pursue their professional careers.
With offices in Brussels, London and Paris, Net Expat, through its range of six programmes, offers various levels of support adapted to the professional profile of each
spouse..
Net Expat is a multidisciplinary team with a vast experience of the international
environment, in-depth knowledge of the expat world, Human Resources and the
Belgian employment market.
All their programmes are entirely free of charge for the expats and are paid for by
the « expatriating» companies.

Do not hesitate to contact them for any further information :
NET EXPAT S.A.
Avenue Louise 149/24
1050 Brussels
✆ 02 / 358 62 28
fax 02 / 358 62 29
http://www.netexpat.com
info@netexpat.com

Focus Career Services
Founded in 1989, Focus is a non profit-making organisation whose aim is to meet
the needs of professionals of all nationalities living in Belgium and looking for a
career. Focus offers a wide range of programmes and services to help these professionals find work, take up a career again, form their own company, gain the self-
confidence needed to look for alternatives or build up their own professional network.
Besides its professional development and information technology training programmes, Focus has a library of more than 1000 books and provides personal
advice services to help define career objectives and develop a plan to achieve
them. With offices in Brussels, London and Paris, Focus now has over 400 highly
qualified and motivated members, representing over 40 different nationalities. If
you wish to succeed in a working environment which is becoming more and more
international and mobile, becoming a member of Focus will allow you to achieve
your career objectives.

FOCUS CAREER SERVICES
Rue Lesbroussart, 23
1050 Brussels
✆ 02 / 646 65 30
fax 02 / 646 96 02
http: www.focusbelgium.org
focus@focusbelgium.org

GOING OUT AND HAVING FUN

Breakfast

Going out
at night

Cafés, concert
cafés, theatre
cafés and jazz
clubs

All-night shop

Restaurants
open till late

Breakfast

Le Pain Quotidien
Ideal for a sociable breakfast
round the table.
Chaussée de Waterloo, 515
1180 Brussels
℗ 02 / 343 33 59
Open at 8.00 a.m.

Place du Grand Sablon, 4
1000 Brussels
℗ 02 / 513 51 54
Open at 7.30 a.m.

Rue des Tongres, 71-73
1040 Brussels
℗ 02 / 733 38 97
Open at 7.30 a.m.

Avenue de Hinnisdael
1150 Brussels
℗ 02 / 772 70 66
Open at 7.30 a.m.

Parvis St Pierre, 16
1180 Brussels
℗ 02 / 344 04 14
Open at 7.30 a.m.

Avenue Louise, 124
1050 Brussels
℗ 02 / 646 49 83
Open at 7.30 a.m.

Going Out at Night

Where to Go?

Places full of atmosphere in
Brussels between 8 p.m.
and 1 a.m.
The greatest concentration of
trendy cafes and clubs is to be
found around the Grand Place
and the Bourse.
On a nice evening, the Sablon is
a lively and very pleasant district.

Some suggestions:

Typical Brussels Cafés

La Mort Subite
Rue Montagne aux
Herbes potagères, 7
1000 Brussels
℗ 02 / 513 13 18
Beer tasting.

Le Corbeau
Rue St Michel, 18-20
1000 Brussels
℗ 02 / 219 52 46
bo137416@skynet.be
Specializes in "knights"
(1 litre glasses).

Ultieme Hallucinatie
Rue Royale, 316
1000 Brussels
✆ 02 / 217 06 14

Foreign Cafés

Rick's
Avenue Louise, 344
1050 Brussels
✆ 02 / 647 75 30
Popular with American businessmen.

Conway's
Avenue de la Toison d'Or, 10
1050 Brussels
✆ 02 / 511 26 68
American restaurant and bar.

Monkey Business
Rue Defacqz, 30
1050 Brussels
✆ 02 / 538 69 34
American restaurant and bar

Kitty O'Sheas
Boulevard Charlemagne, 42
1000 Brussels
✆ 02 / 230 78 75
fax 02 / 230 74 02
Sunday brunch from 11.30 a.m.
to 3 p.m. One of the best Irish pubs
in Brussels. Folk music session every
Wednesday evening.
Avenue Louise
1000 Brussels
✆ 02 / 648 85 56
fax 02 / 649 63 41

James Joyce
Rue Archimède, 34
1000 Brussels
✆ 02 / 230 98 94
Open every day from 11 a.m.
to 2 p.m.
An authentic Irish pub.

The Bank
Rue du Bailli, 79
1050 Brussels
✆ 02 / 537 52 65
Irish pub with a lively atmosphere
of rock and Celtic music.

El Corazon de Lila
Rue Général Leman, 123
1040 Brussels
✆ 02 / 736 13 64
Café espagnol.

Concert-cafés, theatre-cafés, cabaret and jazz clubs

Le Jardin de ma sœur
Rue du Grand Hospice, 54
1000 Brussels
✆ 02 / 217 65 82
A bistro with a difference which
turns into a « theatre-café » some
evenings. Shows on Wednesdays
and Thursdays at 8.30 p.m., Fridays
and Saturdays at 10.00 p.m. Price
of seats: 350 bef (adults) , 300 bef
(OAPs) and 250 bef (students)

L'atelier de la Dolce Vita
Rue Middelbourg, 13
1170 Brussels
✆ 02 / 672 02 63
resto@dolcevitaboitsfort.com
http://www.cyclone.be/dolcevit/
Dinner with shows on Mondays,
« Literary Tuesdays » with poetry,
story-telling and theatre at 8 p.m.,
« musical evenings » on
Wednesdays at 8.30 p.m., « apéritif-
concerts » on Sundays at noon and
« poetry tea-time » on Sundays at
4 p.m. followed by a discussion.

Halloween
Rue des Grands Carmes, 10
1000 Brussels
✆ 02 / 514 12 56
fax 02 / 511 66 91
Halloween.belgium@skynet.be
http://www.cinemaniacs.be/Halloween
A brasserie with shows and entertainment in a unique atmosphere.

Espace Sambe
Rue de Stassart, 29
1050 Brussels
✆ 02 / 511 04 19
espacesambe@ping.be
A cultural brasserie run by a dynamic, creative couple offering light snacks, concerts, plays and exhibitions.

Beurschouwburg
Rue Orts, 22
1000 Brussels
✆ 02 / 513 82 90
fax 02/ 511 73 15
beurs@innet.be
http://beursschouwburg.vgc.be
Open from Thursday to Saturday from 7 p.m. until 2 a.m.
A bar with jazz concerts, experimental rock, techno or South-American music.

La Tentation
Le café du Centre
Galego
Rue de Laeken, 28
1000 Brussels
✆ 02 / 223 22 75
fax 02/ 219 07 00
Traditional music from all 4 corners of the world, from Portugal to England via Ireland or Russia. Free concerts every Friday from 8 p.m. for members, the annual membership fee is 200 bef!

Sounds
Rue de la Tulipe, 28
1050 Brussels
✆ 02 / 218 40 86
A little café-concert for lovers of jazz and tango

Grain d'Orge
Chaussée de Wavre, 142
1050 Brussels
✆ 02 / 511 26 47
Free blues and rock concerts every Friday at 9.30 p.m.

Do Brazil
Rue de la Caserne
1000 Brussels
✆ 02 / 513 50 28
Exotic food and drink in a beautiful vaulted cellar setting, to the wild sound of Brazilian music.

La Movida
Rue Saint-Géry, 3
1000 Brussels
✆ 02 / 502 02 84
Open from 8 p.m., closed on Mondays.
Tapas every day and flamenco at weekends. Mostly Spanish-speaking crowd.

Nightclubs

Discotheques tend to open at about 11 p.m., but things don't usually starting hotting up until about 1 a.m.
Entrance fees vary from 200 bef to 500 bef

Magasin 4
Rue Blaes, 4
1000 Brussels
✆ 02 / 223 34 74
Open on Fridays and Saturdays from 9 p.m. Weekdays according to the programme. Ground floor bar. Upstairs : weekend concerts alternating hardcore, funk, alternative rock and experimental music.

Mirano
Chaussée de Louvain, 38
1210 Brussels
✆ 02 / 227 39 70
Open Saturdays. THE place to see and be seen in Brussels.

Le Garage
Rue Duquesnoy, 16
1000 Brussels
Thursday, Friday, Saturday and Sunday. The latest sounds plus oldies but goodies. Popular with gays.

Fuse
Rue Blaes, 208
1000 Brussels
✆ 02 / 511 97 89
Open on Saturdays.
Themed evenings and concerts.
Techno music.

Jeux d'Hiver
Bois de la Cambre
1050 Brussels
Thursday, Friday and Saturday.
Very 'preppy.'

La Doudingue
Clos Lamartine, 5
1420 Braine-l'Alleud
✆ 02 / 384 02 81
Young crowd, themed evenings.

if you forget your key in the middle of the night:
AA Express 2000
✆ 02 / 640 88 11

To read:
- The chapter «Sortir Mode d'emploi» in *Un Grand week-end à Brussels*, Hachette.
- *Le Petit Futé – Bruxelles*, Editions de l'Université.

White Nights

Pioneer of the sleepless night. Sweets, cigarettes, alcohol, videos, photocopies, etc....

Place du Châtelain, 43
1050 Brussels
✆ 02 / 640 22 20

Avenue Brugmann, 359
1180 Brussels
✆ 02 / 343 35 56

Chaussée de Waterloo, 792
1180 Brussels
✆ 02 / 374 86 85

Rue Ernest Allard, 34
1000 Brussels
✆ 02 / 502 44 42

Square Montgomery
Avenue de Tervuren, 189
1040 Brussels
✆ 02 / 733 93 37

Rue du Lombard, 8
1000 Brussels
✆ 02 / 514 32 52

Open from 5 p.m. or 6 p.m. until 1 a.m., 2 a.m. or even 3 a.m.! It's safer to call them first.

Restaurants

La Maison du Cygne
Grand Place, 9
1000 Brussels
✆ 02 / 511 82 44
Closed Saturday lunchtime and
Sundays. Recognised as one of the
gastronomic jewels in the Belgian
crown. Delicious food served in
the refined setting of a typical
XVIIIth century Brussels house.

Au Vieux Fusil
Chaussée de St-Job, 676
1180 Brussels
✆ 02 / 375 88 50
Closed Saturday lunchtime and
Sundays.
A charming little restaurant with a
terrace shaded by a splendid oak
tree and serving excellent food.

Le Loft
Rue Simonis, 21
1060 Brussels
✆ 02 / 534 43 33
The trendy restaurant right now.
Loft-style (soho district, New York).

Restaurants open until late

Le Corbier
Rue des Minimes, 51
1000 Brussels
✆ 02 / 513 51 95
Open from 7 p.m. until 1 a.m. except
Sundays. Dining room with a log fire,
hidden away in an authentic XVIIIth
century candlelit cellar.

Vert de Jade
Chaussée de Boendael, 372
1050 Brussels
✆ 02 / 649 86 77
Open from 12 noon until 3 p.m.
and from 6.30 p.m. until midnight
(1 a.m. at weekends)
recipes inspired by Vietnamese,
Thai or Japanese traditions.

Cap de Nuit
Pl. de la vieille Halle aux blés, 28
1000 Brussels
✆ 02 / 512 93 42
fax 02 / 512 93 42
From 6 p.m. until dawn. Relaxed
atmosphere, non-stop food, ideal
after a concert or the theatre.

Le Saxe Café
Bld de Waterloo, 49
1000 Brussels
✆ 02 / 511 50 90
fax 02 / 512 26 53
Café/restaurant featuring two styles
of food: classic, refined French and
light, delicate Thai. Musical entertainment with a New Orleans band
(Tuesdays) and an Olivier Saxe trib-
ute concert....

Rugantino
Boulevard Anspach, 184-186
1000 Brussels
✆ 02 / 511 21 95
Ideal for a dinner down town,
maybe after the cinema or theatre.
Open until midnight.

Le Falstaff
Rue Henri Maus, 25
1000 Brussels
✆ 02 / 511 98 77
Open all night...

CHILDREN

Having a baby

This chapter was totally reworked and improved by **Dr Linda Cairns.**

Linda Cairns moved to Brussels as an expat with a one-year-old son. Her second son was born here and both children are now attending a local commune school. Shortly after her move, she took on the role of editor for the BCT, a position she held for nearly four years. "As well as experiencing life with children in Brussels first-hand through my own family, as editor I have benefited from a wealth of contacts with BCT members" explains Linda.

Many thanks to her.

Getting ready

If this is your first baby, you will probably be eager to read out about what is happening to you and find out some idea of what to expect over the next nine months.

There are plenty of informative books on the subject of pregnancy and childbirth and if you need foreign-language books why not go to one of the bookshops in Brussels (listed under "Shopping) or order over the Internet.

Having a Baby in Belgium is a useful little book (available from the CHS – see box) which can help you with specific information about the system here; it also has a helpful English-French-Dutch glossary of vocabulary you probably don't yet know!

There are regular information evenings called "Having a Baby in Belgium" run by the Brussels Childbirth Trust (BTC). This organisation also offers pre-natal classes to help you prepare for the birth of your baby.

Choosing where to have your baby

When deciding where to have your baby, you normally need to choose the consultant (gynaecologist) that you wish to provide your pre-natal care and deliver the baby. Your choice of consultant will then dictate which hospital or clinic you go to.

To find a consultant:

* you could enquire at your nearest hospital (listed under "Health")

* ask your GP

* join a group for pregnant women and new mothers (see Making Friends below) and talk to the other members.

* the BCT provides an information service on gynaecologists and other specialists.

It is possible to have a home birth in Belgium. Here are two organisations that provide support:

Having a Baby in Belgium is published by the Community Health Service (CHS). It is available from them at
rue St George, 102
1050 Brussels
℗ 02 / 647 67 80
by mail order (400 BEF+ 50 BEF postage) or call for information on stockists.
The CHS also publishes the invaluable "Expatriate Calendar" which is crammed with useful information.

- **Bolle Buik** (English, French and Dutch) Prenatal check-ups; home births and support during labour and immediate post-natal care at home for hospital or polyclinic deliveries. Also has own birth centre, a homely alternative to hospital.
  Contact: Leen Massy
  ✆ 02 / 759 30 48
  Hilde Vandendriessche
  ✆ 016 / 40 67 76
  Benedicte Vansina
  ✆ 016 / 47 17 32

- **Centrale des Accoucheuses** "Midwives" (English and French) Prenatal care for pregnancy problems, home deliveries, and postnatal nursing care for mother and baby.
  ✆ 02 / 344 27 40

Help with your new baby

Office de la Naissance et de l'Enfance, **ONE** (French-speaking) and **Kind en Gezin** (Dutch-speaking) provide baby clinics, health visitors, advice on parenthood, lists of baby minders.

La **Ligue des Familles**, French-speaking; concerned with all aspects of family life. Membership costs 1250 BEF/year. Weekly newsletter.
✆ 02 / 507 72 11

The Dutch-speaking equivalent organisation is **Bond van Grote en van Jonge Gezinnen.**
✆ 02 / 507 88 11

If you want information or help with breast-feeding you can contact one of the BCT's breast-feeding counsellors; or contact La Leche League which publishes information in a number of languages.

Making friends

It was once said that the biggest favour you can do for a pregnant woman is introduce her to another pregnant woman in the same street. You probably will want to meet other mothers-to-be to share experiences and make friends for yourself and ultimately playmates for your child.

- Local mother and baby groups – Enquire at **Ligue des Familles**, ✆ 02 / 507 72 39 (Anne Jaumotte) to see if there is a mother and baby group in your area.

- **La Leche League** holds informal discussion meetings for expectant mothers and new mothers with their babies.

- The **BCT** organises "Bumps and Babies" groups for mothers who are pregnant or have a small baby. They are held on Tuesday afternoons at Imagine, Wezembeek-Oppem and at other times in some of the 12 BCT local sub-groups spread over Brussels.

- For other ideas see **Organised activities for parents and young children p. 113.**

BCT, Imagine
77 Ch. de Malines
1970 Wezembeek
✆ 02 / 215 33 77

La Ligue des Familles
Secrétariat général
127 Rue du Trône
1050 Brussels
✆ 02 / 507 72 11

Bond van Grote en van Jonge Gezinnen
125 Rue du Trône
1050 Brussels
✆ 02 / 507 88 11

ONE
✆ 02 / 539 39 79

Kind en Gezin
✆ 02 / 513 19 97

La Leche League
Karen Maxwell
✆ 02 / 219 00 76

Child-care arrangements

Au Pairs

Rates and employment conditions:
An au pair must:
- have her own room;
- be given board and laundry facilities;
- be paid from 3.000 to 4.000 bef per week in pocket money;
- have 1 or 2 days off every week;
- work 5 to 6 hours per day;
- basically look after children and minor domestic tasks;
- participate in the life of the family and eat meals with the family;
- be given time to follow courses;
- be covered by your family civil liability insurance or a 'domestic staff' insurance policy;
- be covered by sickness insurance (Form E 111 for the EU)

Finding your Au Pair

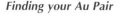
The small ads

Consult the chapter on 'Domestic help', p. 44. This will give you information on the small ads. If you are looking for an au pair, we would recommend the following:

- ***Le Telegraaf*** (Hollande)
  Avenue de l'Horizon, 6
  1150 Brussels
  ✆ *02 / 762 60 20*

- ***The Bulletin***
  Chaussée de Waterloo, 1038
  1180 Brussels
  ✆ *02 / 373 99 09*

- *Le Ligueur*
  Rue du Trône, 127
  1050 Brussels
  ✆ *02 / 507 72 11*
  ✆ *02 / 507 72 23*

- ***La Voix du Nord***
  (Nord de la France)
  ✆ *+33-3-20 15 81 89*

Agencies

Useful to know:
Au Pair Club
✆ *02 / 767 33 91* (Catherine)
✆ *02 / 687 66 87* (Liz)
Monthly meetings for English-speaking au pairs of all nationalities to help them to integrate.
Meet at the
Irish Club
67 rue Archimède
1040 Bruxelles

Service de la Jeunesse Féminine
Rue Faider, 29
1050 Brussels
Mme Benoît
✆ 02 / 539 35 14
On Tuesdays and Fridays from 9.30 a.m. to 2 p.m.
5,000 bef in administrative costs.

New Windrose
La Rose des Vents
Avenue P. Dejaer 21A
1060 Brussels
✆ 02 / 534 71 91
Minimum rate: 2,500 bef per week. Young women of all nationalities, aged at least 18.

The Danish Church
✆ 02 / 660 93 34
List of girls available for 1 year.

Au Pair Europa
BP 162
1060 Brussels
✆ 02 / 538 74 22
This organisation handles the presentation of the applications and provides a follow-up.
Handling fee: from 9,500 bef.

Home from Home
Spillemanstraat, 1
2140 Antwerpen
✆ 03 / 235 97 20
Recruiting agency for au pairs, member of the International Au Pair Association.

Nannies

Nannies Incorporated
Avenue de la Floride, 105
1180 Brussels
✆ 374 31 81
English agency recruiting qualified, experienced English nannies.
Rates:
- for nannies hired to care for an infant 24 hours a day, 6 days a week: between 20,000 and 24,000 bef per week.
- for nannies hired to look after children 10 to 12 hours a day, 5 days a week + 2 evenings baby-sitting: between 10,000 and 14,000 bef per week.

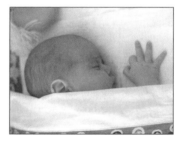

Some of the information in this chapter is taken from **'Le grand Bruxelles des enfants'**, which we recommend (if you understand some French). It contains comprehensive information on activities for children. It is on sale in bookshops for 450 bef, or may be obtained by mail for 500 bef from:
Éditions Clair de Lettre
140, avenue des Combattants
1332 Genval

Here's an original idea for all you theatre and cinema fans.
Special theatre and cinema service:
Le Rideau de Bruxelles, Le Théâtre de la Vie, Le Public, the Varia and National theatres and the association 'Les Petits Déjeuners du Cinéma' have teamed up with the Ligue des Familles to offer a baby-sitting service.
When you book your tickets (ideally 5 days ahead), mention that you want to use this service.
Price for the evening: 120 bef per hour.
Ligue des Familles
☎ *512 57 66*
Petits Déjeuners du Cinéma
☎ *223 20 20*

Baby-sitting

Fees: Prices vary, but the rates applied by the Ligue des Familles are the most common:

- 120 bef per hour in the evening.
- 650 bef per night (8 p.m. to 7 a.m.)
- Weekend rate: 3,000 bef + accommodation and meals.

Some useful addresses:

Ligue des Familles
Rue du Trône, 127
1050 Brussels
Famiphone-Infos
and Baby Sitting
☎ *0900 / 273 71*
(members only)
To join the Ligue des Familles:
☎ *02 / 507 72 11*
from 8.30 a.m. to 4 p.m.
and Fridays until 2 p.m.

Baby Kid Sitting
Rue Paul Lauters, 5
1000 Brussels
☎ *02 / 646 46 11*
Experienced team, students training to be nursery nurses or nurses.
Price: 150 bef per hour (minimum 3 hours).
300 bef per hour + transport for a nursery nurse specialising in infants.
300 bef in agency fees.

Télé-Service
Rue du Boulet, 24
1000 Brussels
☎ *02 / 548 98 00*
Open from 1.30 p.m. to 4.30 p.m.

ULB Student Job Service
☎ *02 / 650 21 71*
from 10 a.m. to 1 p.m. and from 2 p.m. to 4 p.m.
Price: 120 bef per hour.
For one night: 120 bef per hour before midnight; 500 bef for the rest of the night.
Extra 50 bef per child per hour if there is more than one child.

UCL Student Job Service
☎ *02 / 762 11 96*
Price: 150 bef per hour for passive child minding; 200 bef per hour for active child minding.

Louvain-la-Neuve Job Service
☎ *010/ 47 24 77*
☎ *010 / 47 20 02*
Open from Monday to Friday, from 9 a.m. to 5 p.m.
Price: 120 to 150 bef per hour for passive child minding; 200 to 220 bef for active child minding.

'La Cambre' baby-sitting service
Place Flagey, 19
1050 Brussels
☎ *02 / 640 96 96*
Baby-sitting services provided by students from La Cambre.

Le C.A.R.A.M.E.L.
Rue Kelle , 85
1150 Brussels
☎ *02 / 772 66 61*
24-hour emergency cover service, our place or yours, for a minimum of 3 hours.
Price: 200 bef per hour (including transport).
Price for the night: as from 7.30 p.m. (including breakfast): 1,000 bef.

Infor Jeunes – Service Jobs
Place Dailly, 8
1030 Brussels
☎ *02 / 733 11 93*
Every day from 12 noon to 6 p.m.

Picky Club (service de nuit)
Rue Neerpede, 805
1070 Brussels
☎ *02 / 522 20 84*
Will take care of your children aged from 2 to 8 overnight.
Fees: from 6.30 p.m./ 7 p.m. to 10 a.m., 1,000 bef for the night; 100 bef per additional hour. Until 12 noon.

Care for Sick Children

Some crèches offer the services of a nursery nurse to care for your sick child at home.

It is also worth asking your commune: some of them have a 'sick children's service' which will send out a nursery nurse to your home.

Commune services

Private services

Boitsfort 1170

ASBL Action Sociale
✆ 02 / 660 58 71
from 8.30 a.m.
For children aged up to 8.
Medical statement required.

Uccle 1180

Crèche du Globe
Chaussée d'Alsemberg , 883
✆ 02 / 376 28 17
✆ 02 / 348 68 33
For children aged up to 12.
Medical statement required.
Price: 864 bef per day and
519 bef for half a day.

Woluwé-St-Pierre 1150

Avenue du Haras, 100
✆ 02 / 773 59 29
✆ 02 / 773 59 28
For children aged up to 12.
Open from 8.30 a.m. to 4.30
p.m.; after 4.30 p.m. and at
weekends: ✆ 773 57 11
Medical statement required.

Waterloo 1410

Mr Bastenier
✆ 02 / 352 35 11
For children aged up to 12
Price: 120 bef per hour
+ 75 bef travel.

Bruxelles 1000

Baby Kid Sitting sprl
Rue Paul Lauters, 5
✆ 02 / 646 46 11
Experienced team available
within 2 hours.

Etterbeek 1040

Promotion Santé asbl
Rue de l'Étang, 131
✆ 02 / 649 38 55
From 8.30 a.m. to 7 p.m.
Nursery nurses will come to
your home.

Rhode-St-Genèse 1640

Baby Golf Club
Avenue du Golf, 44 bte 2
✆ 02 / 358 50 93
For children aged up to 12
Price: 190 bef per hour;
740 bef per half day
(5¹/₂ hours); 1,250 bef per
day (10¹/₂ hours)

Uccle 1180

Association Regina Pacis
Rue Vanderkindere, 183
✆ 02 / 347 56 19
From 7 a.m. to 8.30 a.m.
and 8 p.m. to 10 p.m.
Emergency child minding at
home from 8 a.m. to 5 p.m.
For children aged from 3
months to 12 years.
Medical statement required.
Price: 650 bef per day.

Woluwé-St-Pierre 1150

C.A.R.A.M.E.L.
Rue Kelle, 85
1150 Brussels
✆ 02 / 772 66 61
For children aged from
2 to 11. Home service.
Price: 180 bef per hour.

Dion-Valmont,
Chaumont-Gistoux
and the neighbouring
communes:

✆ 010 / 24 22 23
For children aged up to 12.
Monday to Friday, from 8 a.m.
to 6 p.m.
Statement required.
Price: 800 bef per day.

Child-minders

Child-minders work at home, in a family-style atmosphere, because they cannot take in more than 3 children under 7 (their own children under 3 included).
In principle they are monitored by the ONE.

For further details:
Fédération
des gardiennes d'enfants
(independent child-minders)
Mme Hasselvoet
✆ 02 / 523 73 64

Vie Féminine
Services Maternels et Infantiles
(trained child-minders)
rue de la Poste , 111
1030 Brussels
✆ 02 / 227 13 00

You can leave your child (aged 0 to 6) here for an hour or more. Qualified staff organise educational games or a programme of stet activities.

Les farandolines
A participative system of child-minding. Ideal for getting to know other mums and your child's little friends and good preparation for a child that will be going to a French-speaking school.
Ages: From 1 to 3 years.
Times: Two mornings a week, from 9 a.m. to 12 noon on school days.
Commitment: father or mother may be asked to attend once a month to help the staff, and the child must attend regularly.
Price: family registration fee per month: 100 bef (insurance).
Fee per child per session: 220 bef.
Free of charge on the days a parent is attending.
What to bring: nappies and a change of clothes.
Where? There are centres in almost all the Brussels communes.
For further details:
Marielle Helleputte
✆ 02 / 770 88 56

MENS' WEAR

Belvest, Baldessarini,
Bouvy, Ballantyne,
Fratelli Rossetti,
Hugo Boss Golf,
Alden, Orian, Bruphils,
Allegri, Aquascutum

BOUVY
Since 1932
Shirtmaker & Tailor

WOMENS' WEAR

Donna Karan Signature, Cortina, Margon,
Natan, I Blues, Brunello Cuccinelli, Rue Blanche,
Costas, Ramosport, Mani, Allegri, Gaby Lauton,
Eres, Kiwi, Fratelli Rossetti, Nathalie R,
Tod's, Armani Foulards, Calvin Klein Foulards,
Osprey Sacs, Ingrid Van de Wiele

BOUVY

SPORTSWEAR

Ralph Lauren, Tommy Hilfiger, Blanc Bleu,
Timberland, Nautica, Calvin Klein Jeans,
Guess, Tod's, Hogan, Cotton Belt,
Villebrequin, Mason's,
Bouvy 32, Dockers, Barleycorn

32
BOUVY

BOUVY

Av. Louise 4 Louizalaan / Av. de la Toison d'Or 52 Gulden Vlieslaan – Bruxelles 1060 Brussel Tel. 02 513 07 48 E-mail Bouvy32@skynet.be
Av. du littoral 169 Kustlaan – Knokke-le-Zoute 8300 Knokke-Zoute Tel. 050 60 25 86

KEEP UP WITH A CHANGING EUROPE

For all of three decades, from the Swinging Sixties to the Astonishing Nineties, Ackroyd Publications have been in the business of keeping their readers informed and entertained. Now more than ever, Anglophones, whatever their nationality, need an insider's knowledge of life in the Capital of Europe.

The international journalists who write regularly for **The Bulletin**, the first and best English-language newsweekly published in continental Europe, are insiders all. Week after week, The Bulletin provides close coverage of political, cultural and business events from a unique perspective.

What's On is Belgium's English-language guide to entertainment, with detailed listings of the week's happenings in the theatre, cinema, music and art, the exhibitions, the european-wide television programmes, the special events.

Passport Sabena is the-inflight magazine of Sabena, the national a Every month Passport Sabena explores the lesser-known aspects of far places and the should-be-known features of the towns and landscapes travellers miss in Belgium, Europe and in other Sabena destinations.

Twice a year, in March and in September, **Newcomer** tells visitor prospective visitors what they can look forward to during their stay in It explains the kingdom's customs and quirks, the not-to-miss events a the most valuable facts for everyday living.

AmCham, the quarterly of the American Chamber of Commerce invaluable guide to the intricacies and opportunities of the Brussels bas International business scene.

Expat Directory, an annual directory crammed with essential info addresses and contact names. A must for the expatriate living in Belgiu

ACKROYD PUBLICATIONS
News with a European accent

1038 Chaussée de Waterloo
1180 Brussels
Tel: 373.99.09- Fax: 375.98.22

Crèches

- Communal crèches run by the commune.
- Private crèches.

How it works
Whether communal or private, all crèches in Belgium are accredited by the French-speaking ONE (Office de la Naissance et de l'Enfance) or the Dutch-speaking Kind en Gezin. This means that the rules, staff qualifications and operating arrangements, are the same everywhere in the country.
Note: You should register your child even before it is born, because demand is high and places limited!

ONE – Administration centrale
Av. de la Toison d'Or, 84-86
1060 Brussels
✆ 02 / 542 12 11

Times
Reception: every day except weekends, legal holidays and generally for a period of two weeks to a month in the summer holidays.

Opening hours: generally from 7.30 a.m. to 6.30 p.m.

Cost
The financial contribution varies from 69 bef to 691 bef per day, depending on the net joint income of the married, cohabiting or single-parent household. Reductions of up to 30% are granted to parents placing more than one child in the same crèche. There are tax deductions for 80% of the care costs, but the tax deduction is limited to 345 bef per day.

For further details, ask for a child-care leaflet from:
Ministère des Finances
Brochure Gardes d'enfants
rue de la Loi, 12
1000 Brussels
✆ 02 / 210 22 11

The people in the following addresses are mostly french-speaking people. For non french-speaking people, these crèches are useful places where your child can get to know the french language. Ex-pats will also be able to meet other mothers.

More information is available at your commune as is information on family help services.

Playgroups and Nurseries

There is a wide choice of pre-school playgroup and nursery options available in Belgium: local crèches, Farandolines and Halte garderies; private playgroups; nursery schools and some Montessori schools. The places listed below provide care and activities for pre-school age children i.e. up to two and half - the age when children start state schools here.

However, many of the nurseries cater for children older than this so you don't have to move your child at 2¹/₂ if you don't want to. See also Schools in the chapter "Studying in Brussels" p.117.

Factors to think about when deciding on child-care:

• What are your future educational plans for your child? If your child will be attending the local Belgian school from 2¹/₂ years then early familiarisation with the language is a good idea.
• Length of time in Belgium? If you are on a temporary assignment here then you may wish to search out a playgroup or nursery that is similar to ones in your home country.
• What is available locally? Are you able to speak (or prepared to learn) the right language Flemish/French?
• Do you actually just need a few hours off occasionally (Try a Halte garderie) or do you want regular structured play and stimulation for your child (Try a playgroup or a Farandoline p. 82).

Brussels 1000	Etterbeek 1040	Ixelles 1050
The children's playhouse (Day-care) (run by Tri-Mission Ass) Rue du Régent ✆ 02 / 508 22 90 From 6 weeks to 10 years old Price : registration 1.000 bef per family, 125 bef hour, 500 bef half day (5 h), 900 bef per day (8 h). **English spoken.**	**Ya Ka C'éveiller** ✿ Rue du Noyer, 73 1040 Brussels ✆ 02 / 732 84 50 For children aged up to 5 From 3 p.m. to 6.30 p.m. Price: 150 bef per day; Wednesdays from 12 noon to 6.30 p.m. including meal: 300 bef; during the school holidays: 600 bef per day	**The Anglo-French Kindergarten** rue Faider , 10 ✆ 02 / 537 49 97 fax 02 / 537 49 97 Bilingual day nursery! Open every day. Ages: from 3 months to 5 years. Introduction to music, dance and physical expression. Price: 4,800 BEF per term, for 2 hours per week. **English spoken.**

✿ indicates holiday activities.

Woluwé-St-Pierre 1150

Le C.A.R.A.M.E.L.
Rue Kelle, 85
✆ 02 / 772 66 61
Open 24 hours a day, 7 days
a week. Ages: from 1 to 5.
Price: 130 bef per hour; 450
bef for 4 hours; 800 bef for
the day.

Halte Garderie
Rue Kelle, 31
✆ 02 / 772 50 95
Every morning from 9 a.m. to
12.30 p.m., except Mondays
(until 4.30 p.m.)
From 0 to 3 years.
Price: 90 bef per hour; 300
bef for the morning; 500 bef
for the day.

La P'tits Schtroumpfs
Rue Longue 161
✆ 02 / 779 07 22 (Sabine)
French speaking playgroup
Costs: 400 bef (including
food) for a morning

Uccle 1180

Crèche du Globe - Baby Halte
Chaussée d'Alsemberg, 883
✆ 02 / 376 28 17
✆ 02 / 348 68 33
Open every day from 7.30
a.m. to 5.45 p.m. From 0 to 4
years. Price: 60 bef per hour.
English spoken.

Galipette
Avenue de Floréal , 84
✆ 02 / 345 30 04
Open every weekday.
Ages: from 18 months to 3
years. 1 hour of psychomotor
activities: 300 bef; half-day:
600 bef; full day: 1,000 bef

Youplaboum
Avenue Latérale, 171
✆ 02 / 375 60 76
youplaboum@finart.be
For children aged from 18
months to 10 years. Monday to
Friday, from 9 a.m. to 5 p.m.

Woluwé-St-Lambert 1200

Les Loupiots
Rue St-Lambert, 56
✆ 02 / 772 32 72
For children aged from 18
months to 3 years
Price: 180 bef per hour or
1,000 bef per day
From 3 to 5 years:
Wednesdays and Saturdays
from 2 p.m. to 6 p.m.: 500
bef per session

Halte Garderie
Rue J.B. Timmermans, 39
✆ 02 / 736 34 35
Every morning from 9 a.m. to
12.30 p.m., except Mondays
(until 4.30 p.m.)
From 0 to 3 years.

Wavre 1300

Les Ateliers du Beaumont
Rue Sainte Anne, 152
✆ 010 / 22 77 63
For children aged from 18
months to 4 years
Tuesday to Friday from 9 a.m.
to 11.30 a.m.Price: 2,000 bef
for 5 sessions.

Limal 1300

Baby-Halte
Maison Communautaire
Résidence Saphir , 7
✆ 010 / 41 72 55
From 0 to 3 years. Every
Tuesday and Thursday, from
9 a.m. to 12 noon. 80 bef for
the first hour and 50 bef for
subsequent hours.

Little Bears Cottage
8 Rue Léon Deladrière
✆ 010 / 40 11 61
Nursery for 18 - 36 months,
Costs: Registration fee 500
bef, 500 bef half day, 900 bef
full day. Within walking
distance of BEPS 2 School.
English spoken.

La Hulpe 1310

Maison Pacific
25 Av. du Chant d'Oiseau
✆ 02 / 652 10 76 (Laurence)
From 1 - 3 years of age.
Open all day from Monday
to Friday.
English spoken.

Lasne 1380

Peter Pan
Rue des Saules 3
✆ 02 / 354 84 18
(Mrs. Maguire)
English-style homely nursery
school from 2 years
Costs: 700 bef per session
(am or p.m.)
Often has a waiting list for
mornings because it's so
popular.
English spoken.

Waterloo 1410

La Petite Ecole
Rue de la Station,96
✆ 02 / 353 03 43
Mme Amparo Garcia
Belgian nursery from 16
months - 6 years.
Monday to Friday, from 9 a.m.
to 12 noon or 3 p.m.
Psychomotor activities.
Welcomes slightly handicapped
children. Price: 500 bef for the
morning; 1,000 bef for the day.

Rhode-St-Genèse 1640

Baby Golf Club
Avenue du Golf , 44 bte 2
✆ 02 / 358 50 93
From 0 to 6 years. Monday
to Friday, from 7.30 a.m. to 6
p.m. Price: 140 bef per hour.
English spoken.

**International Christian
Academy**
Chaussée de Waterloo, 47
✆ 02 / 358 16 64
fax 02 / 358 35 24
ica@xc.org
Every day of the week.
English spoken.

BEPS early years.
Nouveau!
280 chaussée de Waterloo
✆ 02 / 358 56 06
English-style nursery school
for 2¹/₂ to 5 year-olds.
English spoken.

Wezembeek 1970

Playaway
at Imagine
chaussée de Malines 77
✆ 02 / 230 36 81 (Sally)
✆ 015 / 41 43 64 (Michelle)
English-style playgroup for
2-4 year-olds.
Costs: 12,000 - 14,000 bef
for 3-4 mornings

Brussels Childbirth Trust
✆ 02 / 242 14 63
Creche for children before
they go to school.
English spoken.

Ecoline
Avenue du Grunne 101
✆ 02 / 782 20 00
(Christine Sornasse)
French-speaking playgroup
Costs: 500 bef per half day
session Mon. - Fri 9.00-12.00
Popular with a wide mix of
nationalities.

Tervuren 3080

Jay's Cradle
Moorselstraat 264, Moorsel
✆ 02 / 767 30 39
Crèche (from 3 months) and
English-style playgroup (from
2 yrs). Costs: Crèche 350/400
bef (half day) 700 bef full
day (meals extra 50 bef)
Playgroup payable per term:
e.g. 1 session per week 6650
bef. Well established and
popular playgroup now
being run by the British
School of Brussels
English spoken.
✆ 02 / 766 04 30

Tiny Tots
Huisbergstraat 17
3078 Meerbeek
✆ 02 / 759 46 13
(Louisa Driesen-Garland)
English style playgroup 18
months - 3 years.
Costs: 480 bef morning (400
bef for 12 - 18 months 2
afternoons a week)
Small playgroup with an
emphasis on arts and music,
**English, Dutch and French
spoken.**

Mother Goose
Smisstraat 1, Vossem
✆ 02 / 767 83 60 (Katrine)
Crèche and playgroup for
under 2's
Costs: 750 bef full time (8.00

- 6.00 p.m.); 500 bef morning (8.00-12.30 p.m.);
Includes snacks and hot
lunch.
Within walking distance of
the British Primary School.
**English, French and Dutch
spoken.**

Baby Team
Hondsbergenstraat 13A
Vossem
✆ 02 / 767 16 10
(Patricia et Chantal)
Flemish speaking crèche.
French & English also spoken.
Costs: 550 bef full time (7.30 -
6.00 p.m.) 400 bef half day
(max. 5 hrs). Includes snacks
and meals.
At 2¹/₂ years children are
expected to progress to a local
school and this crèche provides valuable language preparation for the Flemish system.
Usually a waiting list.

**International Montessori
School**
Rotselaarlaan 1, Tervuren
✆ 02 / 767 63 60
(Annie Hoekstra-de Roos)
Montessori School from 18
months (**Bi-lingual
French/English**)
Costs: 144,000 bef for 3 morn-
ings for one school year.

Overijse 3090

Babyschooltje
Brusselsesteenweg 298
✆ 02 / 687 68 52
(Mevr. Callewaerts)
Flemish speaking crèche.
Costs: e.g. 2 full days: 6100
bef, 2 half days: 4100 bef per
month (becomes cheaper the
more you use it)
Very popular, has been running 20 years.

☼ *indicates holiday activities.*

Workshops and summer schools

Creative Workshops for Older Children

Only your budget and your willingness to provide a taxi service limit the number of activities that your children can do out of school hours! Here we list a selection of courses and workshops that take place after school in term time and holiday activities for the long and short school holidays.

| Etterbeek 1040 |

Atelier du Soleil ✿
Rue des Eburons, 38
✆ 02 / 230 27 83
info.turk@ping.be
From the age of 6. Every Wednesday from 1.30 p.m. to 4 p.m. Pottery, textiles, painting, folk dancing, theatre skills, etc.

Humpty Dumpty ✿
Rue van Eyck, 37
✆ 02 / 647 03 75
fax 02 / 640 65 25
humpty-dumpty@arcadis.be
Handicrafts, theatre skills, mime, sketches. Price of courses: 3,950 to 7,800 bef per week. **English spoken.**

| Auderghem 1160 |

Club Neptune ✿
Centre Sportif de la Forêt de Soignes
Rue du Concours, 15
✆ 02 / 662 20 43
fax 02 / 662 20 43
club-neptune@skynet.be
From 10 a.m. to 1 p.m.
Courses for children aged between 5 and 13 during school holidays: various sports, quad bikes, outings, etc.
English spoken

| Rhode-Saint-Genèse 1640 |

Les Ateliers de l'Art du temps
Parvis Notre-Dame, 19
✆ 02 / 358 29 65
fax 02 / 358 29 65
From the age of 5.
Wednesdays from 1.30 p.m. to 3.30 p.m. and Saturdays from 10 a.m. to 12 noon.
Jewellery, modelling clay, etc.
Price: 350 bef all in.

| Uccle 1180 |

La Ronde des Loisirs
Place du Chat Botté, 6
✆ 02 / 377 05 66
From the age of 4: musical workshop. From the age of 8: silk. painting. Price: 1,200 bef per term.

| Watermael-Boitsfort 1170 |

La Vénerie
Place A. Gilson, 3
✆ 02 / 660 49 60
fax 02 / 660 61 20
From the age of 4.
Imagination, movement, theatre skills, woodwork, etc. Wednesdays and Saturdays. Price: 6,500 bef per year.

| Wezembeek-Oppem 1970 |

Toboggan ✿
Champ des fleurs, 7
✆ & fax 02 / 731 11 96
3 to 5 year olds: psychomotor activities, cookery, music, singing, circus skills, drawing, etc. 6 to 12 year olds: theatre skills, drawing, video, cartoons, macramé, mime, etc.

| Woluwé-St-Lambert 1200 |

Les Enfants au Malou
Château Malou
Chaussée de Stockel, 45
✆ 02 / 734 42 25
3½ to 12 year olds.
Wednesday afternoons from 2 p.m. to 4 p.m. and from 4 p.m. to 6 p.m.
Music, drawing, painting, theatre skills, puppets, etc.
Multilingual.
Price: 300 bef for 2 hours of activities.

J.J.J.Y
Place du Tomberg, 6A
✆ 02 / 761 28 80
fax 02 / 772 50 41
3 to 12 year olds.
Wednesdays from 2 p.m. to 5 p.m. and Saturdays from 10 a.m. to 12 noon. Physical exercice and co-ordination, cookery, introduction to music, story-telling, etc.. Price for 10 sessions: 2,400 bef for Wednesdays and 1,200 bef for Saturdays.

Pavillon Créatif Schuman
Clos des Bouleaux, 10
✆ 02 / 770 94 65
For children from the age of 5 Wednesdays from 2 p.m. to 4 p.m. and Saturdays from 10 a.m. to 12 noon.
Ceramics, basketwork, sewing, woodwork, etc.

Alaeti
Chantiers du Temps Libre
Avenue Paul Hymans, 251
✆ & fax 02 / 772 91 12
2 1/2 à 6 ans. 2½ to 6 year olds.
Physical exercice and co-ordination and sports activities.

| Woluwé-St-Pierre 1150 |

C.A.R.A.M.E.L.
Rue Kelle, 85
✆ 02 / 772 66 61
Wednesdays, week-ends and school holidays. From 8 a.m. to 6 p.m. Price: 100 bef for the day or 5,000 bef for the week.
Excursions, computers, tennis, bicycle, puppets, photo, video...

✿ *indicates holiday activities.*

For sports workshops and summer schools please refer to § « sports »pg 189

Ateliers Créatifs du Parc Crousse
Rue au Bois, 11
✆ 02 / 770 11 24
From the age of 4.
Every Wednesday afternoon from 2 p.m. to 5 p.m. and Saturdays from 9.30 a.m. to 12 noon. Physical expression, music, cookery, modelling, languages, painting, etc.

Ateliers Créatifs du Chant d'Oiseau
Av. du Chant d'Oiseau, 29
✆ 02 / 268 49 17
✆ 02 / 771 60 66
http://perso.infonie.fr/bd.edgard
bd.edgard@infonie.be
From the age of 4: rhythmics.
From the age of 5: story-telling, puppets, handicrafts, painting.From the age of 9: ceramics, drums and guitar.
Wednesdays from 2 p.m. to 6 p.m. and Saturdays from 9.30 a.m. to 11.30 a.m.
Price: 150 bef per session.

Animation Vacances
Rue Kelle, 31
✆ & fax 02 / 772 50 95
3 to 8 year olds. From 9 a.m. to 5 p.m.
Multilingual.

Vitamômes
Rue au Bois, 369
✆ 02 / 720 87 07 (after 8 p.m.)
4 to 12 year olds:
drawing workshop.
From the age of 3: music workshop.
Wednesday afternoons and Saturday mornings.
Price: 180 bef per hour.

Créatine
Rue Longue, 6
✆ 02 / 772 95 15
fax 02 / 772 94 92
From the age of 5.
Drawing, jewellery, modelling, silk painting.
Wednesday afternoons and Saturday mornings.

Waterloo 1410

Re'Création
Rue de la Station, 16
✆ 02 / 351 21 12
fax 02 / 354 44 80
4 to 9 year olds: handicrafts on Wednesdays and Saturdays.
8 to 12 year old: pottery on Wednesdays
Price: 1,600 bef for 4 sessions.

Espace Bernier
Centre Culturel de Waterloo
Rue de la Station, 17
1410 Waterloo
✆ 02 / 354 47 66
ages 4 - 12: theatre, drawing, cartoon strips.
ages 5 - 8: musical initiation.
Price: from 3.000 bef/a year

Maison des jeunes Océanique
Rue Delbar, 18
✆ 02 / 354 01 38
ages: 3 - 6: dance tuesdays.
Movement thursdays.
6 - 8: gym thursdays.
Price: 1.400 bef a term.

Créatine
Rue du Gaz, 1
✆ 02 / 351 52 01

Wavre 1300

Créatine ✿
Rue des Brasseries, 10
✆ 010 / 22 82 50
fax 010 / 22 92 74
With range of craft workshops from 5 years old.
Prices 1500 bef for four two-hour sessions.
English spoken.

✿ *indicates holiday activities.*

Sculpture, painting and modelling workshops

Most communes have a Commune Academy running arts courses for children aged 8 and over. Look in the Brussels telephone directory under *"Administrations communales"*.

In addition to the commune academies subsidised by the State, there are other options, including the following:

Genval 1332

Atelier des Jeunes
Le Mahiermont
© 02 / 653 30 16
© 02 / 653 25 76
From the age of 6: ceramics and drawing on Wednesday afternoons. For children from the age of 10: model aircraft making on Saturday mornings. Price: 1,000 bef for 10 sessions.

Limal 1300

Atelier d'Expression Graphique ✿
Scavée de la Carrière, 5
1300 Limal
© 010 / 41 08 76
fax 010 / 410 08 80
From the age of 7 on Tuesdays and 9 on Wednesdays and Fridays. Price: 3,000 bef for 10 sessions.

Rhode-St-Genèse 1640

Atelier de l'Espinette
192 Chssée de Waterloo
© 02 / 358 48 21
Drawing (Martenot method), painting, modelling.
From the age of 7¹/₂.
Wednesdays from 12 noon to 6.30 p.m. and Saturdays from 9 a.m. to 4.30 p.m., other days from 4 p.m. to 8 p.m.
Price: 1,552 bef per month, including materials + 300 bef annual subscription.

Uccle 1180

Ecole des Arts Plastiques Visuels (7 workshops spread over the commune schools in Uccle)
© 02 / 348 65 19
For 6 to 12 year olds: drawing, painting, modelling. Wednesdays from 2 p.m. to 3.40 p.m.: for 6 to 8 year olds. Wednesdays from 4 p.m. to 5.40 p.m.: for 9 to 11 year olds. Registration in September.

Playing ✿
Rue Asselberg, 100
© 02 / 332 08 27
Painting: 6 to 12 year olds. Wednesday afternoons, Saturday mornings and school holidays. Price: 350 bef per 2 hour session (including materials).

Jeunesse et Famille
Place du Chat Botté, 6
© 02 / 380 70 08
© 02 / 374 77 44
Ceramics: from the age of 6. Every Wednesday from 2 p.m. to 4.30 p.m.
Price: 50 bef per session.

Kids' Computer Club ✿
Avenue René Gobert, 31
© 02 / 374 27 08
fax 02 / 374 75 87
http://www.kidscomputer.be
secretariat@kidscomputer.be
Drawing and painting. From the age of 4. Subscription for the year: 3,000 bef. Price per hour: 300 bef.

La Fourmi ✿
Rue Vanderkindere, 211
© 02 / 345 84 65
fax 02 / 343 71 41
Silk painting, handiwork (candles, moulding, flowers, etc.) 6 to 12 year olds. Price: 2,250 bef per week during school holidays.Wednesdays from 2 p.m. to 5 p.m.: 350 bef per session. English spoken.

Woluwé-St-Lambert 1200

Ateliers Malou ✿
Rue Voot, 97
© 02 / 770 92 50
fax 02 / 770 63 07
Drawing and painting. 4 to 14 year olds. Wednesdays at 2 p.m., Saturdays at 10 a.m. Price: 2,900 bef per term.

Woluwé-St-Pierre 1150

Kiddy & Junior Classes ✿
Avenue des Grands Prix, 186
© 02 / 217 23 73
Handicraft courses, cartoon workshop and language classes (**English, French, German, Dutch and Spanish**). For children aged from 6 to 12. During school holidays, from 9 a.m. to 4 p.m.

✿ *indicates holiday activities.*

Les Vacances en couleurs
Sacré-Cœur de Stockel
✆ 02/772 26 32
Water-colours, charcoals,
printing, drawing.
6 to 14 year olds.
Wednesday afternoons.
Price: from 4,150 bef per year
(including materials).

Les ateliers Machri ✿
Avenue des Alouettes, 37
✆ 02/672 18 87
Drawing and painting from
the age of 3.
Theatre skills from the age of 4.
Sculpture from the age of 6.
Cartoons from the age of 7.
Price: 3,400 bef per term.
Holiday courses: 1,800 bef
per week (half days) and
3,000 bef per week (full days).

Waterloo 1410

Poterie Carol Youngner ✿
Rue Mattot, 83
✆ 02/353 05 44
Modelling from the age of 7,
working on the potter's
wheel from the age of 12.
Wednesdays and Thursdays,
in English and French.
Price: 350 bef per session.
Holiday courses.

L'Atelier créatif
Champ du Roussart, 27
✆ 02/648 04 56
Drawing, painting, modelling
and collage. 5 to 12 year olds.
Wednesdays and Saturday
afternoons. Price: from 400 bef
per session.
Italian spoken.

Wavre 1300

Les Ateliers du Beaumont ✿
Rue Ste-Anne, 152
✆ 010/22 77 63
5 to 10 year olds. Wednesdays
from 2 p.m. to 4 p.m.
Price: 2,000 bef for 5 sessions.
Holiday courses.

✿ *indicates holiday activities.*

For all artists and handicraft fans:

Créatine
Rue Longue, 6
1150 Brussels
✆ 772 95 15
Rue des Brasseries, 10
1300 Wavre
✆ 010/22 82 50
Rue du Gaz, 1
1410 Waterloo
✆ 02/351 52 01

Artegra
Chaussée de Bruxelles
1410 Waterloo
✆ 02/354 89 23

La Fourmi
Rue Vanderkindere, 211
1180 Bruxelles
✆ 02/345 84 65

Under 'workshops' we have
included activities, courses and
events for children and teenagers.

We have arranged them into
thematic groups, although
most of them cover more
than one theme.

Take the time to look at several
headings: there's lots
to discover.

NOTE:
Since 1993, a contribution
of 1,500 bef per year has
been required from pupils
aged from 12 to 18 in the
commune academies.

Dance, Musical, Theatre Skills and Mime Workshops

In addition to your commune academy, there are various private options:

Uccle 1180

Les Jeunes Talents ✪
Avenue des 7 Bonniers, 68
✆ 02 / 395 34 70
2¹/₂ to 5 year olds:
introduction to dance,
physical expression,
musicals, fashion parade, etc.
From the age of 6: dance, theatre skills, rhythmics, musical,
singing, basic tap-dancing.
11 to 16 year olds: musical,
dance and theatre skills.
Wednesdays and Saturdays.
Price: 3,000 bef per term or
7,200 bef per year.
Courses: from 4,000 bef.

Catama – Julie Popov
Squash du Fort Jaco
✆ 02 / 358 25 82
From the age of 7.
Theatre skills. Saturdays from
2 p.m. to 4 p.m.
Price: 350 bef per session.

Théâtre qui bouge ✪
✆ 02 / 374 71 16
Classes in theatre skills, story-
telling, improvisation and
puppets.
Price: 4,500 bef per week.
from 10 a.m. to 4.30 p.m.

**Ecole de la Scène –
Studio Tapage**
School:
Rue Verrewinkel, 97
Headquarters:
Avenue de Lancaster, 45
1180 Brussels
✆ 02 / 374 03 85
For children and young people: singing, modern jazz,
theatre skills and improvisation. Price: 9,500 bef for 30
lessons. Super show staged
every two or three years.

Kid's Computer Club ✪
Avenue R. Gobert, 31
✆ 02 / 374 27 08
fax 02 / 374 75 87
secretariat@kidscomputer.be
http://www.kidscomputer.be
From the age of 3:
introduction to music.
Choreography, rhythmics
and elementary musical
theory from the age of 5.
For older children: rhythmic
sporting gymnastics classes.
For children aged from 5 to
12: theatre skills classes
during school holidays.
Price: 3,900 bef for 5 half-
days.

Forest 1190

Théâtre de Millevie ✪
Rue Victor Gambier, 8
✆ 02 / 332 02 35
4 to 12 year olds. Courses in
rhythm, story-telling, singing
and theatre skills during school
holidays.

Woluwé-St-Lambert 1200

**Ateliers du chantier du
Temps Libre**
Avenue Paul Hymans, 251
✆ 02 / 761 27 52
Theatre skills and music for
ages 3 ¹/₂ to 16.
Wednesdays and Saturday
mornings.
Price: 2,400 bef per term.

Waterloo 1410

**Ecole des Arts et du
Spectacle**
Rue J Pastur, 9
✆ 02 / 354 62 74
fax 02 / 351 16 45
http://www.mouvement.be
8 to 13 year olds.
Introduction to theatre skills
and music, improvisation,
mime, clowns. From the age
of 6: flute, guitar, piano, saxophone, drums, etc. Price:
3,300 bef for 12 classes.

Wavre 1300

Musique et Spectacle ✪
Chaussée de Bruxelles, 264
✆ 010 / 22 46 25
From the age of 6.
Musicals.
Price: collective classes:
6,000 bef - registration fee:
4,500 bef per year.

✪ *indicates holiday activities.*

Music Workshops

Contact your commune academy. They often offer very high standards of music teaching, and individual tuition. In these establishments, your child will be required to attend one or more years of music theory, which is not the case in the private schools.

Auderghem 1160

Les Archets Suzuki
Avenue H. Strauven, 62
✆ 02 / 675 44 13
Violin lessons in classes or individually.
English spoken.

Boitsfort 1170

La Note au Bois
Rue des Bégonias, 44
✆ 02 / 672 36 52
From the age of 3.
Introduction to music (Orff method), guitar, piano, recorder, viola, violin, harp, etc. Price: 1,800 bef registration fee per family + 4,000 bef per term for classes and 6,000 bef for individual tuition. **English spoken.**

Etterbeek 1040

Ecole Vasarely
Rue de l'Orient, 92
✆ 02 / 647 19 28
From the age of 4. Individual tuition. Prices to fit every pocket, plus 1 month's free trial! **Multilingual.**

Piano lessons and music classes
18 Avenue Victor Jacobs
✆ 02 / 647 66 27
(Mary Gow)
mary.gow@skynet.be
English, French or Dutch.

Genval 1132

Ecole Internationale de Piano
Avenue Albert Ier, 50
✆ 02 / 653 53 68
From the age of 4.
Introduction to music and piano lessons.
Price: 3,500 bef for half an

hour per week. **English spoken.**

Mums and Youngs Music Group in English
46 rue de Rosières
(Liz Cameron)
elizabethcameron@compuserve.com
a.m. for 2-3 years old
p.m. for 3-4 years old

Ixelles 1050

La Chaise Musicale ✿
Rue du Collège, 24
✆ 02 / 511 04 60
From the age of 9 months: sessions with Mum.
From the age of 3 years: awareness workshop.
From the age of 5 years: piano, flute, guitar, violin, singing, drums and percussion.
Price: between 4,900 bef and 13,500 bef per year.
English spoken.

✿ *indicates holiday activities.*

Les Jeunesses Musicales organise musical awareness workshops, concerts and orchestral events, as well as music courses for children, in Brussels and in the Brabant Wallon area.
✆ 02 / 507 83 31

Overijse 3090

Belgian Music Institute
Tuindelle, 73
✆ 02 / 687 57 98
✆ 010 / 84 58 03
From the age of 4: Piano, flute, cello and violin. Price: 350 bef for 50 minutes in group classes, and 500 bef for 30 minutes of individual tuition, from the age of 7. Registration: 850 bef per family per year. **Courses in English, French and Dutch.**

Rixensart 1330

Ecole Bernadette Jansen ✿
Rue du Baillois, 6
✆ 02 / 653 19 36
fax 02 / 653 84 45
Violin, cello, piano and singing using the Suzuki method for children aged from 2. Organisation of concerts. **English spoken.**

Children's music lessons in English
Avenue Marcel Tilquin 4
✆ 02 / 653 30 41
(Sarah Garner)
From age 3. Also piano lessons.

Rhode-Saint-Genèse 1640

Musicalies
✆ 02 / 387 21 55
From the age of 6. Individual piano lessons, recorder, violin and guitar.

Saint-Gilles 1060

Institut Rythmique Jacques – Dalcroze
Rue H. Wafelaerts, 53
✆ 02 / 534 41 74
From the age of 4. Rhythmics, physical expression, dance, piano and improvisation. Every day from 4.30 p.m., Wednesday afternoons and Saturday mornings.

Uccle 1180

Centre Artisanal La Gaumette
Rue de Linkebeek, 31
✆ 02 / 332 10 58
From the age of 3: musical workshops.
From the age of 8: choir.
From the age of 12: accompanying guitar.

Papagaiesnotes ✿
1483 Chssée de Waterloo
✆ 02 / 332 37 61
fax 02 / 374 76 83
From the age of 4. Recorder, guitar, double bass, choir.

La Musicole ✿
Rue des Carmélites, 173
✆ 02 / 343 24 94
Recorder, piano, violin, brass, guitar, harpsichord, harp, percussion, etc. Price: 3,300 bef (includes: registration fee, use of instruments, insurance). Holiday courses from the age of 7.

Musique à la carte ✿
Vieille rue du Moulin, 237
✆ 02 / 375 44 11
Up to 3 years of age: musical introduction with parents 3 to 6 year olds: music and role playing. From the age of 6: rhythm, singing and instruments (recorder, guitar, saxophone, piano and drums). Price: 3,600 bef per term for classes, 5,000 bef per term for individual half-hour lessons. Holiday courses from 9 a.m. to 5 p.m.
English spoken.

Wezembeek-Oppem 1970

Activités musicales Animer
Espace Franche Cordée
Rue Hard, 37
✆ 02 / 731 95 37
From the age of 4: introduction to music. Price: 3,000 bef per term.

Woluwé-St-Pierre 1150

Art & Santé
Avenue Orban, 227
✆ 02 / 779 06 92
(5 p.m. to 8 p.m.)
From the age of 7: piano lessons without musical theory.

Waterloo 1410

La Scuola
Rue de l'Infante, 21
✆ 02 / 332 50 79
For children aged up to 3. Price: 400 bef per session.

Ecole Amadeus
Place Albert Ier
(Sacré-Coeur building)
✆ 02 / 384 73 60
Individual piano, percussion, woodwind, brass, guitar, violin and cello lessons. Price: 450 bef per half hour.
English spoken

Ecole Redaeli
Avenue des Chasseurs, 112
✆ 02 / 354 31 30 (& fax)
Also in 1150 Woluwe. Collective lessons for beginners and then individual lessons: piano, violin, cello, guitar and percussion. **Multilingual.**

Wavre 1300

Musique et Spectacle
264, Chssée de Bruxelles
✆ 010 / 22 46 25
For children from the age of 5. Violin, cello, recorder, flute, piano, guitar, etc.

For teenagers
An interactive guide for teenagers published DICADO in French in 1996. Lots of still relevant information.
To get one, send a cheque for 500 bef, with your address, to:
Éditions Imaginaction
Avenue Labbé, 69
1310 La Hulpe
We recommend it !

Club des Petits Débrouillards ☼
In Brussels town, Uccle, Woluwe-Saint-Lambert, etc.
For information, call
Nicole Malengreau
Avenue du Roi Albert, 52
1120 Brussels
✆ 02 / 268 40 30
fax 02 / 262 45 29
7 to 12 year olds.
2 days or a week of scientific exploration, from 8.30 a.m. to 4.30 p.m. during school holidays
Price: 1,350 bef for 2 days.

Expérimentarium
Forum du campus de la Plaine
Bld du Triomphe CP 238
1050 Brussels
✆ 02 / 650 56 18
Thirty or so physics experiments, demonstrated and explained by the workshop leaders
Wednesdays from 2 p.m. to 5 p.m.
Price: free of charge for children under 12; 500 bef for 12 pupils for one hour.
English spoken.

Euro Space Centre
6890 Transinne
✆ 061 / 65 01 33
Holiday courses and space camps.
Live the life of an astronaut for 1/2 day to 6 days. For 10 to 18 years old. In **English, French or Dutch.**

Workshops in Museums

An excellent idea from the Brussels museums which are offering workshops and activities based on exhibitions or in the framework of a visit with commentary.

Musées Royaux des Beaux-Arts de Belgique ☼
Rue de la Régence, 3
(Museum of Ancient Art and Museum of Modern Art)
✆ 02 / 508 32 11
From the age of 6.
Discovery tours and creative workshops run by the Schools Service.
Schools Service:
✆ 02 / 508 33 50
educatieve.dienst@fineart-museum.be
English spoken

Centre Culturel du Botanique ☼
Rue Royale, 236
1210 Brussels
✆ 02 / 226 12 18
6 to 12 year olds. Events for children in groups of 15, looking at the subject of the current exhibition.
Flat rate of 1,500 bef for the group + 20 bef entrance charge per child.
English spoken

Royal Army and Military History Museum
Parc du Cinquantenaire, 3
1040 Brussels
✆ 02 / 737 78 11
✆ 02 / 737 78 02
http://www.klm-mra.be
christine.van.everbroeck@klm-mra.be
Open every day except Monday, from 9 a.m. to 12 noon and from 1 p.m. to 4.30 p.m.
Visits with fun explanations, discovery games leading from room to room, 'Hunting the Uniform', 'On the Treasure Trail', 'The Wings of the Wind', etc.
Activities lasting 1½ hour.
For children aged from 6 to 8 or from 9 to 12. Price: 1,500 bef (including the guide, the brochure and the treasure) for a group of from 5 to 15 children.
English spoken

Royal Art and History Museum ☼
Parc du Cinquantenaire, 10
1040 Brussels
Schools Service:
✆ 02 / 741 72 18
fax 02 / 741 72 18
deboeck@kmkg-mrak.be
Secretariat: Madame Delooz
For 6 to 12 year olds.
2 hours exploring some of the objects in the museum and a creative workshop.
Wednesdays from 2 p.m. to 4.30 p.m. and Saturdays from 10 a.m. to 12.30 p.m. Price: 200 bef per session. Dynamusée courses for 6 to 12 year olds during school holidays. Price: 2,500 bef for 4 days from 10 a.m. to 4.30 p.m.

Nature workshops at the Natural Sciences Museum
see p. 95.

☼ *indicates holiday activities.*

Nature Workshops

Workshops to promote discoveries, gardening, animal care or observation, ecology and the environment. In addition to the nature workshop at the Etterbeek museum (see above, p. 76), we would recommend the following addresses:

| Etterbeek 1040 |

Nature workshops at the Natural Sciences Museum ✿
Rue Vautier, 29
1040 Brussels
✆ 02 / 627 42 11
fax 02 / 646 44 66
School service: Mr Héla
✆ 02 / 627 42 26
http://www.kbininsnb.be
atelier-nature@kbininsnb.be
Has set up a nature workshop for 5 to 12 year olds.
Location: Forêt de Soignes or Brussels parks, where the children will learn to observe and collect information 'on the ground'.
Some Wednesdays from 2 p.m. to 4 p.m. and some Saturdays from 10 a.m. to 12 noon.
Price: 200 bef per session or 1,800 bef for 10 sessions.

| Ixelles 1050 |

Kaleidoscope ✿
Avenue E. De Beco 128
✆ 02 / 647 29 10 (& fax)
kaleidoscope@skynet.be

Introduction to the environment, gardening and farmyard animals.
Every day except Sunday.
Holiday courses from 9 a.m. to 4 p.m.: 3,500 bef per week.
English spoken.

| Uccle 1180 |

Kids' Computer Club ✿
Avenue R. Gobert, 31
✆ 02 / 374 27 08
fax 02 / 374 75 87
http://www.kidscomputer.be
5 to 10 year olds.
Price: 3,500 bef for 5 days.
Courses are taught in French but most are suitable for English-speaking children who are learning French. Holiday nature courses can be coupled with artistic, music, language, computing or sports courses to make a full day's programme.

Pom Pom Poney ✿
Chaussée de Waterloo, 1512
1180 Brussels
✆ 02 / 374 84 49

3 to 7 year olds.
Wednesdays from 2 p.m. to 4.30 p.m. and Saturdays from 9.30 a.m. to 12 noon and 2 p.m. to 4.30 p.m. Holiday courses. Price: 750 bef or 500 bef for 5 sessions; 400 bef for a quarterly subscription.

| Watermael-Boitsfort 1170 |

Centre régional d'initiation à l'écologie ✿
Chaussée de la Hulpe, 199
✆ 02 / 675 37 30
fax 02 / 660 53 38
tournesol@skynet.be
http://www.ful.ac.be/hotes/tournesol
Location: the beautiful Parc Solvay
Educational activities organised with the aim of encouraging children to observe and understand the natural environment and fostering a responsible attitude to the environment. Guided tours for families (100 bef for under 12s) and courses during the summer holidays for children aged from 6 to 12.

✿ *indicates holiday activities.*

Story Workshops

| Waterloo 1410 |

Le Contalyre
Avenue Termidor, 3
✆ 02 / 354 17 66
Reading Club, discussions about a book, an author, visit to a printer...
5 to 14 years old. Once a month.

| Wavre 1300 |

Le Chat Pitre ✿
Rue de la Source, 7
✆ 010 / 24 22 64

Stories, theatrical or musical improvisation, puppets.
2 p.m. on Wednesday, Saturdays and school holidays.
Price: 200 bef per session.

| Woluwé-St-Lambert 1200 |

Le Rat Conteur
Rue Saint-Lambert, 116
✆ 02 / 762 66 69
Reading for children from 4 to 5.
Every 1st Saturday of the month from 10.30 to 11.30 a.m.
Reading club for teenagers.

Language Workshops

The aim of these workshops is to teach children languages through fun: with younger children, they use songs, handicrafts or cookery and, with older ones, more 'modern' teaching tools such as computers, videos, slides, etc.

Etterbeek 1040

Call International ☼
Avenue d'Auderghem, 277
✆ 02 / 644 95 95
fax 02 / 644 94 95
callinter@skynet.be
Languages: english, french dutch, german, spanish, italian, portuguese, russian (beginners). Courses during school holidays from 9.30 a.m. to 12.30 p.m.
Price: 6,000 bef per week.

Ixelles 1050

Humpty Dumpty ☼
Rue Van Eyck 37
✆ 02 / 647 03 75
humpty.dumpty@skynet.be
Languages: english, french and dutch. For children from the age of 3.
Price: 3,500 bef per term; 9,000 bef per year.

Anglo-French Kindergarten ☼
Rue Faider, 10
✆ 02 / 537 49 97
For children aged up to 5. The chance of total immersion in English or French every day.
Price: 13,600 bef per month. Courses in July.

Saint-Gilles 1060

Tutti Frutti
Rue Africaine, 27
✆ 02 / 538 37 43
Languages: english, german, spanish, french, italian and dutch. For children aged from 3 to 11. Price: 500 bef per course - annual subscription of 1,500 bef. Every day from 4 p.m. to 7 p.m.; Wednesday afternoons and Saturdays from 10 a.m. to 7 p.m.

Anderlecht 1070

Picky Club ☼
805 rue de Neerpede
✆ 02 / 522 20 84
Courses combined with sport, crafts for 8 to 10 year olds; possibility to board in children's hotel.
4400 Bef/week of full days.

Uccle 1180

Kid's Computer Club ☼
Avenue René Gobert, 31
✆ 02 / 374 27 08
Languages: English, Portuguese, French, German, Spanish and Dutch. For children from the age of 4. Every day from 4 p.m., Wednesday afternoons and Saturdays. Price: 450 bef for 1 hour; 600 bef for 1 1/2 hours. Courses are taught in French, but most are suitable for English-speaking children who are learning French. Holiday language courses can be coupled with artistic, music, nature, computing or sports courses to make a full day's programme.

Woluwé-St-Pierre 1150

Kiddy & Junior Classes ☼
Avenue des Grands Prix, 186
Secrétariat
✆ 02 / 217 23 73
Languages: English, French, German, Spanish and Dutch For children from the age of 3 to 18. Holiday courses in Brussels (Arts Loi), Ixelles, Woluwe, Hoeilaart, Ohain, Wezembeek, Heysel; residential courses at the Euro Space Centre; overseas courses; possibility to combine half-day language sessions with sports, horse riding or computing.
Price 500 BEF per hour, holiday courses from 7000 BEF per week of full days.

Waterloo 1410

Call International ☼
Bld de la Cense, 41
✆ 02 / 353 13 00
fax 02 / 353 08 09
call.woo@skynet.be

Tervuren 3080

The British School
Leuvensesteenweg 19
✆ 02 / 766 04 42
English as a foreign language "Super Summer" programme for 7-16 year olds; prices 2000 Bef half day course for one week.

☼ *indicates holiday activities.*

Website - Le Grand Bruxelles des Enfants: http://www.belkids.com
Website - Expats in Brussels: http://www.expatsinbrussels.com
E.Mail: info@expatsinbrussels.com

Computing Workshops

Auderghem 1160

Shift Club ☼
Bld du Souverain, 53/2
℻ 02/673 19 78
fax 02 / 353 12 00
info@mediaware.org
For children aged from 6 to
12: learning how to use a PC,
educational software
For older children: Word /
Excel / Access and
PowerPoint.Price: 1,500 to
6,000 bef per week. Courses
are run in various communes,
such as Auderghem, Etterbeek.

comicro
aussée Reine Astrid 5
02 / 387 11 09
02 / 387 20 56
ucational and games

Bruxelles 1210

Kiddy & Junior Classes ☼
Rue du Marteau, 8
℻ 02 / 217 23 73

Forest 1190

Futurekids ☼
Avenue Brugmann, 171
℻ 02 / 346 77 90
For children aged from 4 to
14.
Teaching through fun: learn
to surf the Internet, make up a
multimedia composition, lay
out a poster or a newspaper,
etc. Weekdays and Saturdays.
Price: from 500 bef to 575
bef per session.
Courses also given in English!

Ixelles 1050

Humpty Dumpty ☼
Cyber – Jeunes
Rue Van Eyck , 37
℻ 02 / 647 03 75
From the age of 3$^1/_2$: sensory
software, sound and vision.
From 4$^1/_2$ to 6: educational
software: figures and letters,
familiarisation with the
keyboard and mouse.
For 6 to 10 year olds: Logo
programme.
For 10 to 16 year olds: word
processing, tables, databases,
Internet, etc.
Price: from 6,000 bef to
15,000 bef for an annual
subscription.

Uccle 1180

Kids' Computer Club ☼
Avenue René Gobert, 31
℻ 02 / 374 27 08
For 4 to 6 year olds:
Logo using the 'tortoise'
floor computer.
For 7 to 9 year olds:
Logo on computer.
From the age of 10:
practising with Windows,
Internet.
Courses are taught in
French but most are suit-
able for English-speaking
children who are learning
French. Holiday computing
courses can be coupled
with artistic, music, nature,
language or sports courses
to make a full day's pro-
gramme.
Price: 500 bef per hour +
annual subscription of
3,000 bef.

Woluwé-St-Pierre 1150

Vitamômes ☼
Rue au Bois, 369
℻ 02 / 720 87 07
Computing for children
from the age of 4.
Wednesday afternoons from
2 p.m. to 5 p.m. and
Saturday mornings from 10
a.m. to 12 noon.
Price: 180 bef per hour.

Rhode-St-Genèse 1640

Animation Espace Gare
Place de la Station, 18
℻ 02 / 358 17 25
℻ 02 / 358 17 55
Computing for children
aged from 10 to 12.
Price: 400 bef per hour
(by appointment).

Waterloo 1410

**Dynamic language
en computing** ☼
Boulevard H. Rolin, 5
℻ 02 / 354 21 21
fax 02 / 353 03 40
fabienne.penninck@ping.be
(Between 9.30 a.m.
and 12 noon).
From the age of 5: Logo.
From the age of 7: Basic,
Windows and word
processing.
Wednesday afternoons and
all day Saturdays, or after
school during the week.
Price: 4,500 bef for 10 sessions.
English spoken.

☼ *indicates holiday activities.*

Holidays

To help parents to organise their children's holidays here are a few addresses offering varied programmes :

UCPA
✆ 02 / 511 97 83
Sporting activities, mainly in France.

Gulf Stream
✆ 075 / 48 98 40
Sport and languages in Belgium and France.

Children's International Summer Villages
✆ 02 / 426 38 66
Music and sport in Europe and North America.

Tips on Trips and Camps
✆ 02 / 734 67 97
Free service offering advice and addresses for holiday programmes abroad (mainly in the United States) for children, teenagers and youngsters.

Swiss Alps Schools
✆ 02 / 414 15 27
Free service offering advice and addresses for holiday programmes abroad (mainly in Switzerland) for children, teenagers and youngsters.

> Also look up the addresses in the chapters on "workshops" and "sports" with the symbol ✿, which indicates holiday courses are organised.

CAMELEON®

AN ART OF LIVING

Spécialement conçu pour
vous, ce guide de 400 pages
avec + de 3.000 adresses!
apporte une réponse
à toutes vos questions
concernant la santé,
la sécurité, les gardes,
les jouets, la lecture,
la musique, les ateliers,
les vacances, les droits,
les sports, les sorties
insolites..., à faire
avec vos enfants
de 0 à 12 ans.

Parties

Birthdays and Parties at Home

There is a wealth of detail on this theme in 'Le grand Bruxelles des enfants' (see the beginning of this chapter for information), but we have selected some useful addresses for you.

Decoration and accessories

Paper chains, Chinese lanterns, flowers, candles, paper table-cloths, streamers, jokes, make-up, masks, fireworks, bouncy castles, ball pools, etc. While some items may be available in department stores, there are certain businesses which specialise in the materials and requirements for birthdays and parties:

Alain David Show
Winkel, 119
1780 Wemmel
✆ 461 36 90
✆ 075 / 43 35 09
Open on Tuesdays from 9 a.m. to 8 p.m.
Themed decorations: Mickey Mouse, circus, casino, balloons, Western, etc. Helium balloons, bouncy castle, popcorn machine, ball pool, candy floss machine, small roundabout, trampoline, waffle-makers, etc.

Espace Rêve
Rue de la Bruyère, 21
1380 Lasne
✆ 02 / 654 12 38
✆ 075 / 67 13 34
Bouncy castle, giant tunnels, obstacle course, roundabouts, climbing wall, balloon decorations, etc. Clowns, magicians, illusionists, fire-eaters, jugglers, stilt-walkers, pup-

peteers, etc.
Fun with balloon sculpture, face-painting, musical games, mimes, etc.

Palais des Cotillons
Rue du Lombard, 66
1000 Brussels
✆ 512 23 20
Everything for dressing up, plus party accessories: tricks and jokes, fireworks, make-up, etc.
Open from 9.30 a.m. to 6 p.m. from Monday to Saturday

Le Cotillon d'argent
Avenue Albertyn, 70
1200 Brussels
✆ 733 74 27
Party novelties, paper chains, Chinese lanterns, fireworks, make-up, masks, false noses, beards and moustaches, trimmings, etc.
Open from Tuesday to Friday, from 12 noon to 5.30 p.m. and from Monday to Saturday, from 10 a.m. to 6 p.m., in the holiday period.

Cakes

For customised cakes baked in the shape of tennis rackets, dogs, trains, teddies, bunnies or your child's favourite cartoon figures: le rayon «pâtisserie» des **Delhaize,** mais aussi:

Mahieu
Place Dumon, 4
1150 Brussels
✆ 772 72 45
Price: from 110 bef per person.

Espagne
Avenue Georges Henri, 320
1200 Brussels
✆ 02 / 733 63 82 – 734 39 60
Price: 175 bef per person

Patisserie De Pauw
Chaussée de Waterloo, 1472
1180 Brussels
✆ 02 / 374 21 65
Price: 130 bef per child,
or 1,200 bef for 15 children.

Party Entertainment

Why not hire a magician, an
illusionist, a conjurer, a clown
or a witch?

Big Boum
✆ 02 / 384 44 54 – 354 30 20
Two mums will plan a party for your
children from the age of 3, and take
care of everything in your home or
in one of their halls: decorations
with paper chains and balloons, a
customised cake, entertainment with
clowns, magicians, puppets, etc.
For older children, they will handle
the complete organisation of a party
with sound system, hall, caterers
and decorations.
Price: for 12 to 15 children: 5,000
bef all in + hall for 1,500 bef.

Birthy Boum
Rue Général Henry, 2-6
1040 Brussels
✆ 02 / 733 72 19
Complete organisation of birthday
parties for children aged from 4 to
9, at home with two qualified enter-
tainers, face-painting equipment,
piñata, goodies, music, balloons,
birthday tea, etc.
Price: 6,000 bef for 3 hours and 10
children (150 bef per additional
child). Entertainment **in English and
French!**

Abracadabra Manipül
Michaël Katzeff
Rue Vifquin , 45
1030 Brussels
✆ 02 / 245 34 43
Magic show, fantastic stories, musical entertainment, make-up, balloon
sculptures, etc. Entertainment **in
English and French!**

Daniel Adrian
Steenbrugstraat, 23 A
1741 Ternat
✆ 02 / 582 48 61
Magic shows for children aged from
5 to 12 **in English, French or
Dutch!**

**Olivier Klinkenberg et son
Magic Shows**
✆ 02 / 381 06 13
Magician for children and adults,
for all your parties.
Shows performed in **English,
French, German and Dutch!**

Zarathoustra, qualified witch

Avenue du Parc, 83
1060 Brussels
✆ 02 / 534 99 13
A real live pretend witch who loves kids, who will help them make a magic potion and who has the power to transport them into the land of their dreams. For children aged from 5 to 10. Price: for 1 1/2 to 2 hours: 4,500 bef + travel.

Going Out for your Parties

Why not try going to a restaurant, to the pool, to the bowling alley, to a museum, to a playground, to the theatre or to somewhere quite unusual:

Restaurants

To make a change from the GB Quick/McDonalds type of arrangement, which gives you entertainment with a Magic Box, gifts, hats, surprises and a cake, we have found you somewhere delightful:

Le Bonnêt d'Ane

Avenue Brugmann, 518
1180 Brussels
✆ 02 / 346 18 74
In a genuine old schoolroom complete with old-fashioned desks: a special menu, drawing equipment, surprises and gifts ... they think of everything!
Price: 350 bef per child.
Open from 12 noon to 2 p.m. and from 7 p.m. to midnight.

Museums

Some museums offer facilities and staff to organise your child's birthday party:

Two associations organise parties in museums. Everything is included, from personalised invitations to make-up, from the cake to the guided tour. They are:

Club Neptune
✆ 02 / 662 20 43
Musées en fête
✆ 02 / 378 11 52

Note:
Don't forget to look under 'Workshops in the museums' (p. 92) and 'Museums' (p. 111) for some other ideas.

Bowling alleys

Bowling Le Lion

Chaussée de Brussels, 412 D
1410 Waterloo
✆ 02 / 351 10 63
Open every day from 4 p.m. Wednesdays, Saturdays and Sundays from 2 p.m. Price: young person's ticket for children before 6 p.m.: 230 bef including 3 games, shoe rental and one drink. You may bring your own cake.

Most of the indoor play centres offer excellent party facilities and they are a very popular choice with children. Details are listed under "Where to go on a rainy day", pg 109.

At the theatre

See the chapter 'Theatres', p.102.

Swimming pools

Darwin Aqua Club
Rue Darwin, 15
1050 Brussels
✆ 02 / 347 11 51
Rent the pool for a maximum of 12
children on Sunday afternoons
Price: 1,500 bef per hour and 500
bef per hour for the staff member
(optional).

Unusual places

Three associations organise
original birthdays for children:

Club Neptune
Rue du Concours, 15
1170 Brussels
✆ 02 / 662 20 43
Quad-biking in the forest, alpine
skiing at Durbuy, kayaking, treasure
hunts, go-karting at the seaside,
roller-skating and ice-skating, etc.
Wednesdays, Saturdays, Sundays
and public holidays.
For children aged from 6 to 14.
Price for 10 children: 4,000 bef
(organisation + insurance) +
entrance fee if any.
Birthday cake, drinks and invitations: 150 bef per child (optional).

Club Saturne
Rue Kelle, 85
1150 Brussels
✆ 02 / 772 66 61 – 772 11 57
For children aged from 4 to 12.
Mini-cruises at Huy, cave and
cable-car at Dinant, discover
pre-history at Ramioul, golf,
horse-riding, sailing, etc.
Price for one day with 14 children:
4,000 bef (organisation +
insurance).

Musée en Fête
✆ 02 / 378 11 52
For children from the age of 4.
Airport, RTB, treasure hunt at
Beersel castle, etc.
Either a 2 hour brunch (6,000 bef
all in) or a 3 hour afternoon session
(prices vary).

Presents

What is a birthday without a birthday present!
Although you will find toys everywhere, from bazaars to supermarkets (e.g. Maxi Toys in Waterloo and Nosseghem) to specialist shops, there are some places which are outstanding for the way they welcome their customers, the skill of their staff and the quality of their wares.

A few good addresses in Brussels:

Serneels
Avenue Louise, 69
1050 Brussels
✆ 02 / 538 30 66
Open Monday to Saturday from 9.30 a.m. to 6.30 p.m.
A real Ali Baba's cave offering a vast choice of cuddly toys, dolls, board games, dolls' houses, lead soldiers, shops, puppets etc… They have very high quality toys, often made by craftsmen.

Christiaensen
A large chain of shops specialising in toys. Their « Touki Club » offers children a whole host of surprises for a membership fee of 350 bef : welcome gift, free entrance tickets, a magasine etc…

Maxi Toys
supermarkets entirely given over to toys with prices which defy all competition.
A Waterloo
✆ 02 / 387 09 79
A Wavre
✆ 010 / 24 38 88
A Nossegem (à côté d'Ikea)
✆ 02 / 725 58 80

Casse-Noisette
Chaussée d'Alsemberg, 76
1180 Brussels
✆ 02 / 537 83 92
Rue Longue, 15
1150 Brussels
✆ 02/ 731 68 11
More than just a shop, this exceptional place is actually the workshop of a designer of wooden toys: superb trains, bird mobiles, jigsaw puzzles, puppets etc….

Universal Toys Discount
Chaussée de Ruisbroeck, 200
1620 Drogenbos
✆ 02 / 377 15 62
An good place to visit if you are organising a birthday or a party: big name toys at reduced prices and a large choice of little gadgets for 5 or 10 bef each.
Open from 10 a.m. to 6 p.m. and on Saturdays from 10 a.m. to 4 p.m.

Theatre

Théâtre du Perruchet
(puppets)
Avenue de la Forêt , 50
1050 Brussels
✆ 02 / 673 87 30
For children aged from 3 to 15.
Some 40 plays, tales from Perrault,
Grimm and Andersen, La Fontaine
fables, etc.
For birthdays: everything is laid on
(show, table and candles) except the
cake (bring your own).
Price: 3,000 bef rental + 200 bef
entrance fee per child.

Théâtre du Ratinet
(puppets)
Avenue de Fré , 44
1180 Brussels
✆ 02 / 375 15 63
For children aged from 2 to 8.
For birthdays: everything is laid on
(show, decorated table) except the
cake (bring your own).
Price: 4,000 bef rental + 200 bef
entrance fee per child.

Ombres et Silhouettes
(puppets)
Rue F. Haps , 11
1040 Brussels
✆ 02 / 732 11 22
For children from the age of 5.
Price: 200 bef on Wednesdays,
Saturdays and Sundays at 3 p.m.
For birthdays:
Price: 350 bef per child (entrance,
drinks and cake included).

Don't forget: puppet theatre every third Sunday in the month at 3 p.m. at the Toy Museum (supplement of 50 bef)

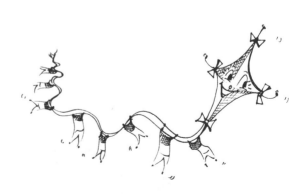

Cinema

We have chosen 4 cinemas that always have children's films in their programme

Kinépolis at Bruparck
✆ 02 / 474 26 00
✆ 0900 / 35 241 (FR)
✆ 0900 /35 240 (NL)
A complex of 23 screens plus a giant 600 square metre Imax screen.

Le Stockel
1150 Brussels
✆ 02 / 779 10 79

Le Wellington
Waterloo
✆ 0900 / 29 678

Le Ciné Centre
Rixensart
✆ 02 / 653 94 95

Imagibraine
Boulevard de France
1420 Braine-l'Alleud
✆ 02 / 389 17 00
10 screens.

Museums

Children's Museum
Le Musée des Enfants
"A Museum like no other"
Rue du Bourgmestre, 15
1050 Brussels
✆ 02 / 640 01 07
For children aged from 4 to 12.
Price: 200 bef per person, or 700 bef for a ticket for 4 people, or 1,500 bef for 10 people. No dusty museum exhibits here but rooms of activities for children to touch, build,act and play, plus cooking painting and more. The theme of the exhibitions changes regularly. Wednesdays, Saturdays and Sunday afternoons from 2.30 p.m. to 5 p.m. For birthdays: Saturdays and Sunday mornings.

Album
Rue des Chartreux, 25
1000 Bruxelles
✆ et fax: 02 / 511 90 55
Didactic museum for the whole family. Interactive exhibitions. Until january 2000:
The spirit of the century:
survey of the 20 th century through Tintin's eyes!
From january 2000:
Europe zig zag
Europe through 17 personnalities from Napoleon to Eddy Merckx...

IMAX at Kinépolis
Marvellous documentaries on a giant screen, shows in french, dutch and english at different times.

Museum for children
see also pp. 111-112

Cartoon festival and animation workshop for children aged from 9 to 13.
When ?
Every year during the February half term.
Where ?
At Auditorium 44, boulevard du Botanique 44, 1000 Brussels
Price: 150 bef (children) and 220 bef (adults)
For further details:
✆ 02 / 534 35 33 – 534 41 25

Cinema «Parents admis»
Films for children aged from 6 to 13 as part of the Brussels International Film Festival every January.
✆ 02 / 534 35 33

Toy Museum
Rue de l'Association, 24
1000 Brussels
✆ 219 61 68
Price: 100 bef (adults), 60 bef (children).
Doll's houses, miniature farm, teddies, electric train sets, etc.
Birthdays: use of all the games, demonstration of the mechanical toys and, on every 3rd Sunday in the month, a puppet show.
Price of birthday tea including entrance, drinks, paper plates and a gift for every child: 295 bef per child.

Belgian Cartoon Centre
Rue des Sables, 20
1000 Brussels
✆ 219 19 80
Birthdays: tour round the museum with a treasure hunt for $1^{1}/_{2}$ hour and a prize. Price: 2,000 bef for the guide and 60 bef per child. You may bring your own meal and eat it in the restaurant.

Brussels Urban Transport Museum
Avenue de Tervuren, 364 bis
1150 Brussels
✆ 513 31 10
✆ 095 / 11 10 92
Price: museum and tram: 150 bef and 50% reduction for children aged 6 to 12.
For birthdays: Celebrate your birthday in an old tram reserved exclusively for you. Take a trip to Tervuren, enjoy a quiz game about the Museum, with cake, drinks, goodies and a present for the birthday child.
Every Saturday and Sunday afternoon from April to the beginning of October.
Price: 350 bef per child under 6, and 400 bef for children aged from 6 to 12.

Children will enjoy the display at the Hôtel de Ville in Brussels, which shows the Manneken Pis in various costumes worn since his creation.

Parks and Playgrounds

Theme Parks

Bellewaerde Park
Meenseweg, 497
8902 Ypres
(A1 motorway, Roncq exit)
☎ 057 / 46 86 86
Lots of attractions: safari train, Wild West village, pirate ship, big wheel, etc.
Open from April to September, 10 a.m. to 6 p.m. and 8 a.m. to 7 p.m. in July and August.
Price: 650 bef (adults) and 590 bef (children).

Walibi et Aqualibi
E 411 motorway, Wavre exit
☎ 010 / 41 44 66
Price: 750 bef
Lucky Luke City, Dalton Terror 78 metre free-fall tower, rafting the Radja River, Sirocco catapult, sharp turns in the Jumbo Jet, mini-cruise to the palace of Ali Baba... thrills and spills galore!
At Aqualibi: water park with giant pool, waves, 140 metre slide, palm trees and tropical atmosphere all year round.

Bobbejaan Land
2460 Lichtaart (Kasterlee) E 39 motorway, Herentals-West exit
☎ 014 / 55 78 11
Over 35 rides and spectacles: cowboy and Indian village, Mississippi boat ride, etc.
Open from Easter to mid-October, from 10 a.m. to 6 p.m.
Price: 330 bef for children aged from 3 to 5; 660 bef for all others.

Boudewijn Park
De Baeckerstraat, 12
8200 Bruges
☎ 050 / 38 38 38
Go-karting, exotic animals, dolphinarium, ice-skating and roller rink, ranch with horses and ponies, etc.
Open from April to the end of September.
Price: free for children under 1 metre tall, 450 bef up to the age of 6, 510 bef up to the age of 12 and 560 bef for adults.

Bruparck
Parc des Expositions
1020 Brussels
☎ 02 / 474 83 77
Fun for all the family:
• **Océade water park**
☎ 02 / 478 49 44
• **Kinépolis**
☎ 02 / 478 05 50
Europe's biggest cinema complex.
• **Mini-Europe**
☎ 02 / 478 05 50
Where kids will be delighted at being able to visit miniatures of 75 monuments or sites in Europe, including the Acropolis, Venice, the Arc de Triomphe, etc.

Océade and Kinépolis are open all year round. Mini-Europe is open from the end of March until the beginning of January.

Zoos and Wildlife Parks

To give you inspiration for outings and holidays, get a copy of the **"Guide to tourist attractions and museums in Belgium"**
✆ 02 / 504 03 90
available free from the Tourist Information Centres; published each year in English, French and Dutch.
It has 80 pages packed with ideas for places to visit and essential information to plan your trip.

Zoo d'Anvers
Koningin Astridplein, 26
2018 Antwerpen
✆ 03 / 202 45 40
A traditional city zoo featuring reptiles amid exotic vegetation, a nocturnal viewing area with a host of nocturnal animals, dolphinarium, monkeys, giraffes and elephants, not to mention a superb aquarium and a pe zoo where the younger kids can get to know little squirrels, rabbits, racoons, mongooses, etc. Open every day from 9 a.m. to 5.30 p.m. Price: 275 bef for children under 12; free for children up to 3.

Planckendael Animal Park
Leuvensesteenweg, 582
2812 Muizen
✆ 015 / 41 49 21
One of the best places in Belgium to take young children. Lots of things to touch, look into and learn about. Plenty of great playgrounds scattered around the park and several cafés. Most of the animals are not in cages, but are housed in a splendid setting, separated from the visitors only by fencing.
Open every day from 9 a.m. to 6.30 p.m. in summer and from 9 a.m. to 5 p.m. in winter.
Price: 250 bef for children aged from 3 to 11; 395 bef for adults.

Zwin Nature Reserve
Ooievaarlaan, 8
8300 Knokke-Heist
✆ 050 / 60 70 86
A wonderful nature reserve which is home to a wide variety of birds, fishes, crustaceans, insects and plants. Open from 9 a.m. to 5 p.m., closed on Wednesdays from 15 November to 1 April.
Price: 150 bef for adults, 90 bef for children aged from 6 to 12.

Parc Paradisio
Domaine de Cambron
7940 Cambron-Casteau
✆ 068 / 45 46 53
A stunning setting with 2,500 birds, a bird garden and botanical garden of 52 hectares, the remains of the Cistercian abbey of Cambron, and a large play area. Open from 10 a.m. to 6 p.m. every day, from Easter to November.
Price: free for children up to 3; 270 bef for those aged from 3 to 14; 395 bef for adults.

Delphinarium de Bruges
Boudewijn park
De Baeckerstraat, 12
8200 Bruges
✆ 050 / 38 38 38
The biggest dolphinarium in Europe, with a fascinating underwater show.
Price: 275 bef for adults, 240 bef for children. Free for children under 1 metre tall.

Domaines provinciaux

The "Domaines provinciaux" are large parks with extensive playgrounds and other attractions for children and are good value places to spend the whole day.

Provinciedomein Huizingen
Torleylaan 100,
1654 Huizingen
✆ 02 /383 00 20
Exit 20 from the Brussels ring; several playgrounds for different ages, woodland walks, beautiful gardens, mini train, boating lake, animals and cafés.

Domaine Provincial du Bois des Rêves
1 allée du Bois des Rêves
1340 Ottignies
✆ 010 / 41 60 72
Follow signs from N25; large playground, nature trail, swimming pool and large paddling pool (summer only), café.

Provinciaal Domein Kessel-Lo
Lentedreef 5 ou
Holsbeeksesteenweg 55,
3010 Kessel-Lo, Louvain
✆ 016 / 25 69 12
From the Leuven ring road take the N2, direction Diest, and look for signs on the left after the railway line. Hands-on water park, playgrounds for different ages, swimming pool, cars, boats, apiary, and newly-opened café.

Bloso-Domein Hofstade,
1981 Hofstade
✆ 015 / 61 78 94
Exit 11 from E19 Brussels-Antwerp; large lake with beaches, playground with adjacent toddler area, cafés

Provinciaal Domein Zoetwaterpark
M Noëstraat 15
3050 Oud-Heverlee
✆ 016 /47 75 55
Take the E40, direction Liege, exit Haasrode; a playground with trampolines, climbing frame, play village, miniature train, children's farm and more.

Provinciaal Domein Bokrijk Park
3600 Genk, Limbourg
✆ 011 / 22 45 75
Further from Brussels than the others but worth a detour; open air living museum with summer entertainment programme, large playground, woods and walks and a mill.

Playgrounds

| Brussels 1000 | Schaerbeek 1030 | Ixelles 1050 |

Bois de la Cambre, 1000 -
On the left after the Avenue Louise entrance, going clockwise round the Bois, a nice playground overlooked by a cafe.

Parc, rue Royale, 1000
Formal park right in the centre of town with a small playground area and fountain.

Josaphat,
boulevard Josaphat
1030 Schaerbeek –
Attractive narrow park with lakes, ducks and lots of paths through flowers and trees, and a bandstand.

Bois de la Cambre
av. Roosevelt, 1050
Take the chain ferry to the island in the lake to find an adventure playground and a puppet theatre in summer.

Rue Camille Lemonnier
1050 Ixelles - Small but pleasant playground close to the back entrance to the Delhaize on the Chaussée de Waterloo near the Bascule.

Rue du Bourgmestre
Small playground in the grounds of Musée de l'Enfant.

Woluwe-St-Pierre 1150

Centre Crousse
rue au Bois 11, 1150
The grounds of an old house with playground; there is an English children's library and toy library on Wednesday afternoons and Saturday mornings.

Uccle 1180

Parc de Wolvendael
Near the entrance on Avenue Wolvendael by the tram terminus - a choice of two playgrounds, one public and free, the other enclosed and with a small entrance charge. An excellent range of equipment for all ages, including one of the few baby swings in Brussels playgrounds.

Woluwe-St-Lambert 1200

Roodebeek
rue de la Charette. Good variety of play equipment and a little zoo.

Château Malou
boulevard de la Woluwe. Excellent playground with great range of equipment. Pleasant café, but areas for older and younger children a bit too far apart to be able to supervise both at once.

Parc régional Georges-Henri, au bas de l'avenue Georges-Henri. A big space to run around in and kick a ball. Play equipment and sand pit.

Waterloo 1410

Set back from the Chausée de Bruxelles between rue Libert F. and rue Dewit R. good range of equipment for young and older children including sandpits.

Parc Jourdain
Small playground behind Château Jordain; chicken runs and café overlooking lake with ducks and geese.

Tervuren 3080

Between the town and the lake; popular park with a good range of equipment for a variety of ages. Café on the lake a short walk away, plus rowing boats, pedalos and animals.

Overijse 3093

Off the N253 south of the crossroads with the N4, the park is tucked away behind the arts centre and swimming pool; play area for small children and more adventurous equipment for older children.

Parks and gardens

Here are some pleasant gardens of interest to grown-ups. These places are not designed specifically for children but there is space to run around.

Tervuren Arboretum
Plantation with good paths for walking, cycling or pushchairs; accessible from Jezus-Eiklaan east of Tervuren or Kapucijnendreef at Jezus Eik.

Parc de Tervuren
Formal gardens leading down from the impressive Royal African Museum to a large park with lakes, very popular place for a Sunday stroll. Long, flat car-free road and an excellent place for children learning to ride a bike. Leuvensesteenweg 13 3080 Tervuren.

National Botanical Gardens
Meise - extensive gardens with trees, ponds and collections of plants, historic castle with exhibition, enormous tropical greenhouse, Domein van Bouchout, Brusselsesteenweg 8-26, 1860 Meise
02 / 269 39 05

Villers la Ville
Abbey ruins– interesting historical site with plenty of corners to explore and some dangerous holes for little children to fall into – take care!

Château de la Hulpe
Beautifully maintained gardens with lakes, woods and lots of open space. Good for kite flying. café; entrances at Ferme du Château signed from av. Reine Astrid and at Chausée de Bruxelles

Beersel Castle
Exciting medieval fortress is great for older children but crumbling steps and dangerous drops make it rather treacherous for toddlers; playground and café.

Gaasbeek Castle, 1682
Gaasbeek– extensive gardens, woods and lakes are recommended, but the chateau full of historical treasures is not really suitable for children.

Where to go on a rainy day

Brussels has an annual rainfall of 72cm, so if you have pre-school-age children you are sure to need some under cover places for outings! There are large shopping precincts at Westland and Woluwe, and, if you are desperate to have somewhere dry for your children to toddle, an enormous new one at Wijnegem near Antwerp, but we hope you will find some far more exciting ideas below.

Many of these suggestions are also suitable for older children on Wednesday afternoons and weekends.

For more ideas on outings for older children see the "Guide to Tourist Attractions and Museums in Belgium" (see box above).

Indoor play centres

Just in case these are new to you, they are real wonderlands for active children – full of climbing challenges and giant inflatable toys to bounce and slide, ball ponds, go-karts, etc and some have outdoor attractions as well.

- They all organise birthday parties.
- Check opening times before you go as most of them are shut during school hours.

Badaboum
Chaussée de Louvain, 491
1300 Wavre
✆ 010 / 22 45 00
Indoor playground for 1 to 11 year olds, café.
Costs 150 BEF per child per hour.

Carré d'As
Rue Walcourt, 110
✆ 02 / 524 33 63
1070 Brussels
Indoor playground for 1 to 10 year olds. Costs 150 BEF per child for first hour and 50 BEF per half hour.

Kid's Fantasy Club Etterbeek
rue de la Grand Haie, 22
1040 Etterbeek
✆ 02 / 735 66 54
Enormous indoor adventure playground; daily mega disco party for 7-14 year olds; café; Cost 250 BEF entrance per child (unlimited time), for 0 to 14 year olds.

Kid's Fantasy Club Etterbeek
New Year's Eve party 2000 and overnight baby-sitting for 4-12 year olds.
Reservations compulsory.

Kid's Fantasy Club Forest
chaussée de Ruisbroek, 81
1190 Forest
02 / 332 16 42
Large indoor adventure playground; Cost 250 BEF entrance per child (unlimited time), for 0 to 14 year olds.

Kid's Factory
chaussée de Bruxelles, 63
1410 Waterloo
✆ 02 / 351 23 45
Giant inflatable obstacle courses and areas for babies and toddlers; café. Cost 250 BEF entrance per child (unlimited time), for 1 to 12 year olds.

Picky Club
rue de Neerpede, 805
1070 Anderlecht
✆ 02 / 522 20 84
Indoor and outdoor playground for 3-8 year olds; pool; café.

Planet Kid's
Grote Geenststraat, 10
1933 Sterrebeek
✆ 02 / 784 28 26
Challenging indoor area for children big enough to climb up the giant steps (about 3 years old); downstairs play area for babies and toddlers; outdoor pedal cars with real road system complete with petrol station and car wash.
Cost 150 BEF per child for the first hour, 100 BEF per extra hour.

Museums and tourist attractions

See also Museums for children listed under "Parties" in this chapter p. 105. Phone for opening times and admission charges or consult the "Guide to Tourist Attractions and Museums in Belgium" (see p. 106)

The African Museum
Leuvensesteenweg 13
3080 Tervuren
✆ 02 / 769 52 11
Free admission on the first Wednesday afternoon of the month.

Atomium at Bruparck
✆ 02 / 474 89 77
Lifts and escalators make this an interesting place to explore and take in the view.

Autoworld
Parc du Cinquantenaire, 10
1040 Brussels
✆ 02 / 736 41 65
A great place for car fans.

Cocoa and Chocolate Museum
Grand Place, 13
1000 Brussels
✆ 02 / 514 20 48
Free chocolate at this interesting museum!

Inclined plane of Ronquières –
This impressive new site of canal engineering has a fascinating walk-through exhibition called "Un bateau Une vie" about life on a canal barge. Children from the age of 5 can wear headphones and hear the commentary in english, french, dutch or german. You can also take the lift to the top of the tower and go on a boat trip. Information Hinaut Tourist Office.
✆ 065 / 36 04 64

Museum of Art and History
Parc du Cinquantenaire, 10
1040 Brussels
✆ 02 / 741 72 11
Miles of corridors full of antiquities to gaze at when it's wet outside.

Museum of Modern Art
Place Royale 1-2
1000 Brussels
✆ 02 / 508 32 11
Its carpeted floors and pictures too-high-to-touch make this a surprisingly good place to take crawling babies and toddlers.

See also children museum p. 103

Natural History Museum
Rue Vautier
1000 Brussels
✆ 02 / 627 42 38
From spiders to dinosaurs, and an interactive exhibition "Living or Surviving"

Royal Army Museum
Parc du Cinquantenaire
1040 Brussels
✆ 02 / 737 78 11
A rather sombre collection but its free and spacious. There is a little outside playground behind the museum.

Scientastic
Métro Bourse, niveau -1
1000 Brussels
✆ 02 / 736 53 35
Experience the fascinating world of science with practical demonstrations and hands-on exhibits; english guide book. Fine for younger children but best for 7 years and older.

The Water and Fountain Museum
Av. Hoover 63
1332 Genval
✆ 02 / 654 19 23
if your children are fascinated by water and you don't mind them getting a bit wet this is a charming little museum. You could also take a stroll around the Lac du Genval.

Other ideas

Swimming pools
Some pools close their children's pools in term time for school lessons so do check to avoid disappointment. We particularly recommend the pools at **Zaventem** (De Motte, Parklaan, 02 / 725 96 96) and **Woluwe-St-Pierre Sports Centre** (2 av. Salomé, 1150, 02 / 762 12 75), as suitable for small children.

Zaventem airport café
watching planes take off.

Go on a tram ride – any tram, anywhere. The Brussels transport network is so good that you can spend a whole afternoon just taking trams, buses and metros.

Art on the Metro: pick up the leaflet available from Metro stations and spend an afternoon visiting different stations to see their artworks.

Head for the coast: sometimes the weather is better there, but if not, wrap up warm and walk by the sea, then take the coastal tram back to the car.

Organised activities for parents and young children

Belgian playgroups

Why not take your child to a Belgian-run mother and toddler group where you can meet the locals, pick up useful local knowledge and have a chance to practice your language skills (see Farandolines p. 80). Enquire at your commune (p. 15-16), ONE clinic, Syndicat d'initiative or the League des Familles (see p. 75) to see if there is a group near you.

Associations for expats v.p. 55
Activities for parents and children are organised by:

The BCT: ℗ *02 / 215 33 77*
• a programme of English-speaking playgroups and activity sessions, mornings and afternoons, at Imagine, 77 chaussée de Malines, 1970 Wezembeek-Oppem.
• 12 local BCT groups spread all over Brussels, each of which arranges a programme of meetings,
• BCT International which brings together members from different countries and organises conversation courses and French-speaking play-afternoons.

The British and Commonwealth Women's Club
Club House in rue au Bois, 509 1150 Brussels
℗ *02 / 772 53 13*
A Mums and Youngs group that meets regularly

The American Women's Club of Brussels
headquarters at av. des Erables, 1 1640 Rhode St Genèse
℗ *02 / 358 47 53*
• playgroup
• story hour
• and a Mothers of Young Children group

Youth Movements

All youth movements, whether Catholic or not, are based on the same principles: team work, action, resourcefulness, responsibility, closeness to nature, solidarity and creativity.

Mouvements belges

The Catholic movements are divided up according to age as follows:

- *Nutons* (ages 5 to 7) for girls, *Balladins,* mixed groups for ages 6 to 8.

- *Brownies* for girls (ages 7 to 11), *Wolf Cubs* for boys (ages 8 to 12).

- *Guides* for girls (from the age of 11) and *Scouts* for boys (from the age of 12).

There are various differences in age brackets and names, depending on the federation.

For further details

Fédération des guides catholiques de Belgique
✆ 538 40 70

Fédération des scouts catholiques de Belgique
✆ 512 46 91
✆ 512 45 77

Les Faucons rouges
(socialist movement)
✆ 085/ 41 24 29

Le Patro
✆ 071 / 41 20 26

Scouts et guides pluralistes de Belgique
✆ 539 23 19

Chiro Jeugd Vlaanderen v.z.w.
Kipdorp, 30
2000 Antwerpen
✆ 03 / 231 07 95

V.V.K.S.M.
Vlaams Verbond van Katholiek Scouts en Meisjes Gidsen v.z.w.
Lange Kievitstraat, 74
2018 Antwerpen
✆ 03 / 231 16 20

English-speaking Movements

Boy Scouts of America
NATO Support Activity
Contact : Vincent Cozzone
℗ *02 / 387 31 83*
vcozzone@compuserve.com
For boys aged 6-18.
Adventure, amusements and
activities to develop a sense of
responsibility.

Also a co-ed venture program
for teens 14 to 20 with an
emphasis on high adventure
activities.

Programs are centred in
Brussels at the Brussels
American School, ISB, and St.
John's. Also programs at
SHAPE and in Antwerp
(Antwerp International School)

British Rainbows, Brownies,
Guides and Rangers and Duke
of Edinburgh Group
• **Rainbows** for girls 5-7 years
old - held at City
International School, British
school of Brussels, British
Primary and St John's School
Waterloo
• **Brownies** for girls 7 - 10 -
held in St Anthony's Church,
Kraainem, British School of
Brussels and St John's School
Waterloo.
• **Guides** for girls from 11 -
meet in the British School
and in St John's School
Waterloo
• **Rangers** for girls of over 14
years
• **The Duke of Edinburgh**
Award for girls over 14;
preparation for expeditions
for the Bronze and Silver
awards.
• Opportunity to go on resi-
dential weekends and camps

Contact Heather Duxbury
(District Commissioner)
℗ 354 20 63(evenings), or
Fax 351 22 62 or
email lxt@compuserve.com.

British Scouts
Some packs are for boys and
girls
•**Beavers**: ages 6-8
•**Cubs**: ages 8-10$^{1}/_{2}$
•**Scouts**: ages 10$^{1}/_{2}$-15

1st Brussels British Scouts:
meet at British School
✆ 02 / 767 26 69
Contact : Mrs Katrina Bromfield
1st Waterloo International

Scouts : meet at St John's
School
✆ 067 / 21 19 49
Contact: Gerard de Vignat

British scouts du SHAPE
✆ 02 / 653 11 35
Contact: Alec Grant

1st St Michael's (International)
Brussels: meet at St Andrews,
chaussée de Vleurgat
Beavers and cubs
✆ 02 / 644.37.08
Contact: Sylvia Howe

Girl Scouts of America
✆ 02 / 358 16 31
Contact : C.J. Wyatt
For girls registered at St John's and
the Brussels American School.

**Jewish Community
of Uccle-Forest**
✆ 02 / 343 29 44
For children from the age of 3 to 12
and 13 to 16.
Hebrew songs and tradition.

Wats
✆ 02 / 353 02 58
A club for Jewish youngsters in
Waterloo.

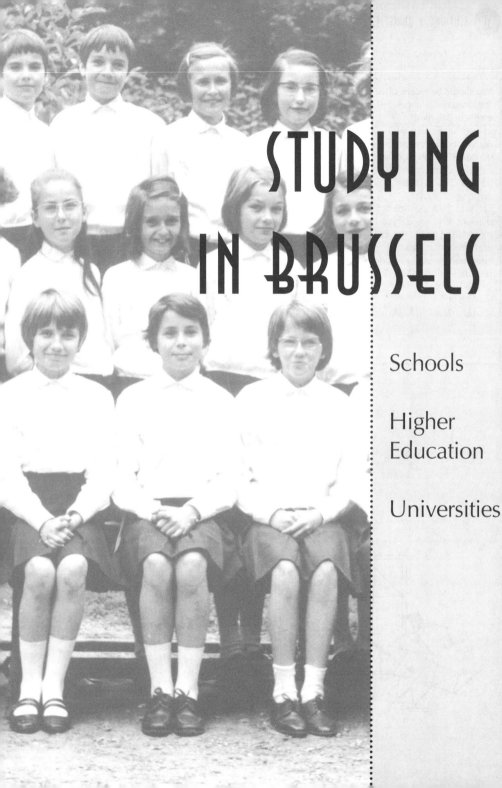

STUDYING

IN BRUSSELS

Schools

Higher
Education

Universities

Schools

Belgian Schools

Three types:

- 'Official education' organised by the State (free).
- Catholic-education, subsidised (free).
- 'Private education', not subsidised by the State (far less common than the other two types).

The system

- Nursery school - from the age of 2 1/2; Not compulsory, but recommended by education experts. This is not a kindergarten, but active preparation for primary school.
- Primary school - from the age of 6 to 12 (a child is supposed to reach his sixth birthday in the course of the calendar year in which he starts primary school). A cycle of 6 years.
- Secondary school - from the age of 12 to 18. There are 4 options: general, technical, artistic secondary and professional secondary.

You should be aware of the language arrangements in Belgium! In the Brussels Capital region, the language of education is Dutch or French, depending on the parents' choice. In the communes around Brussels, the legislation is different. We would therefore advise you to contact the Ministry for National Education (pre-school and primary section) for more details before you register your child.
✆ 02 / 210 55 11 (FR)
✆ 02 / 553 86 11 (NL)

Schools Using New Educational Methods

These schools apply different teaching methods and are experiencing revival of interest following the crisis which has hit education in Belgium.

Freinet method

(Freinet was a French educationalist from the beginning of the century).

The principle: to make the classroom into a miniature society, seeking the promotion and full development of each pupil.

A few schools:
Clair-Vivre
1140 Brussels
✆ 02 / 247 63 65

La Source
1140 Brussels
✆ 02 / 247 63 71

L'autre école
1160 Brussels
✆ 02 / 660 72 38
fax 02 / 660 72 38

Decroly method

(Belgian doctor and psychologist)

The principle: the interest of the child is essential and is the starting point for gaining knowledge.

A few schools:
Ecole Decroly
1180 Brussels
✆ 02 / 374 17 03
fax 02 / 374 02 71

De Zonnnewijzer
3000 Leuven
✆ 016 / 20 29 54
fax 016 / 20 63 87

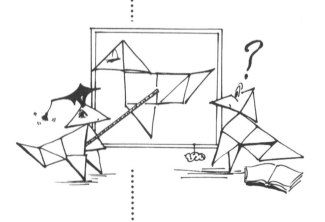

L'Ecole en Couleurs
1180 Brussels
© 02 / 343 86 44
fax 02 / 346 78 67

Ecole Hamaide
1180 Brussels
© 02 / 374 78 90

Ecole St Joseph
1180 Brussels
© 02 / 374 05 35

Montessori method

The principle: Offer the child the opportunity to develop in harmony with his own rhythm, teach him to acquire self-discipline, to be independent and to respect the world around him, starting with himself.

The European Montessori School
1410 Waterloo
© 02 / 354 00 33
fax 02 / 354 51 41
europeanmon@skynet.be
Bilingual French-English school.

The Children's Academy
1410 Waterloo
© 02 / 351 46 52
101737.1752@compuserve.com
Bilingual French-English pre-school for children aged 2 1/2 – 6 years.

Montessori Kids
Route de Renipont, 4
1380 Ohain-Lasne
© 02 / 633 66 52
info@acmontessorikids.com
http://www.acmontessorikids.com

Montessori House Belgium
1420 Braine l'alleud
© & fax 02 / 385 15 03
MHBSabah@hotmail.com
http://www.geocities.com/collegePark/Classroom/6362/
3 classes, crèche, pre-school and primary.

The International Montessori School
3080 Tervuren
© & fax 02 / 767 63 60

La Maison des enfants Montessori
1180 Brussels
© 02 / 375 61 84
fax 02 / 375 12 65
Bilingual French – English Montessori programme. From 18 months to 12 years. Bilingual French – English pre-school. Contact: Catherine Vigreux

Steiner method

(Austrian philosopher)

The principle: consider the child as a being who thinks, acts and feels. Great importance is attached to the child's artistic creativity and his biological rhythms.

Ecole Steiner
1070 Brussels
© 02 / 521 04 92

Libre Ecole Rudolf Steiner
© 010 / 61 20 64

Rogers method

Respect of the child as a whole.
La petite école
1410 Waterloo
© 02 / 353 03 43
From 1 to 6 years of age.

For further details :
French language education:
Ministère de l'éducation,
© 02 / 210 57 14 (primary)
© 02 / 210 55 17
fax 02 / 210 55 61 (secondary)

Dutch language education:
Administratie Onderwijs
© 02 / 553 86 11

Catholic education:
Secrétariat national de l'enseignement catholique/Nationale secretariaat van het katholiek onderwijs
© 02 / 507 06 11
fax 02 / 507 06 21

If you want to find out more about schools:
Three guides :

«L'Enseignement maternel et primaire à Bruxelles»
published by IDJ
☎ 02 / 772 70 20

«Gids voor het Nederlandstalig Onderwijs te Brussel»
published by VOB
☎ 02 / 218 10 10

«Les écoles nouvelles et les écoles en réno-vation»
published by SIEP
☎ 02 / 640 08 32

---

*Plan d'Iena
(Peter Petersen)*

The principle: organisation into 3 stages (3-6 years, 6-9 years and 9-12 years) with no "doubling" during each stage. The child is the 'actor' and the teacher is the 'facilitator'.

A few schools:
**Ecole Catholique
de Boondael St Joseph**
Chaussée de Boondael 621
1050 Brussels
☎ & fax 02 / 672 75 80

**Ecole fondamentale
«Les Sept Bonniers»**
☎ & fax 02 / 343 55 53

Other Schools using their Own Methods

Singelyn
1200 Brussels
☎ 02 / 770 06 22
fax 02 / 770 03 48
Traditional educational structure, but a constant search for new teaching methods. Achieves excellent results.

Le Verseau
60, rue de Wavre
1301 Bierges
☎ & fax 010 / 24 17 00
With 45% of its pupils being English-speaking, this school focuses on the practice of English, creativity, rhythmic and artistic activities.

Jewish Schools

Athénée Ganenou
Rue du Melkriek, 3
1180 Brussels
☎ 02 / 376 11 76
Belgian programme for Jewish children.

Athénée Maïmonide de Bruxelles
Bld Poincaré, 67
1070 Brussels
☎ 02 / 521 26 89
French-speaking Jewish school.

Ecole Beth Aviv
Avenue Molière, 123
1180 Brussels
☎ 02 / 374 37 19
French-speaking nursery and primary school for Jewish children, recognised by the State..

International Schools

These schools do not follow the Belgian programme. Some prepare for the European or the international baccalaureate (IB), giving access to virtually any university in the world.
Tuition fees: between 200,000 and 400,000 bef per year.

English

Pre-school section
See pg 82

Section «School»
See also Montessori schools,
pg 119

**International School
of Brussels (ISB)**
Kattenberg, 19
1170 Bruxelles
℗ 02 / 661 42 11
Admissions
℗ 02 / 661 42 00
admissions@isb.be
Nursery section. French from
the age of 5, possibility of
learning Spanish and German.
American programme and
preparation for the IB. Sports
and artistic activities. Beautiful
setting. Many school trips.

**St John's
International School**
Drève de Richelle, 146
1410 Waterloo
℗ 02 / 352 06 13
fax 02 / 352 06 20 - 30
admissions@stjohns.be
http://www.stjohns.be
Nursery section. French from
the age of 5, Spanish and
German in the higher grades.
American programme.Good
programme of sport and artistic
activities.

**Brussels English Primary
School**
Avenue Fr. Roosevelt, 23
1050 Bruxelles
℗ 02 / 648 43 11
fax 02 / 687 29 68
http://www.beps.com
info@beps.com

Rue Léon Deladrière, 13
1300 Limal
℗ 010/ 41 72 27
fax 010 / 41 75 46
Only nursery and primary
sections.

**International Christian
Academy**
Chaussée de Waterloo, 47
1640 Rhode-Saint-Genèse
℗ 02 / 358 16 64
fax 02 / 358 35 24
ica@xc.org

City International Schools
Bld Louis Schmidt, 103
1040 Bruxelles
℗ 02 / 734 44 13
fax 02 / 733 32 33
American programme.
English curriculum. Possibility
of obtaining an American leaving certificate.

Brussels American School
John F. Kennedylaan, 12
1933 Sterrebeek
℗ 02 / 731 23 35
fax 02 / 782 02 30
ben-berrigs@eu.opedopea.edu
School financed by the
American government -
reserved for the children of US
government and NATO staff.

**The British School of Brussels
(BSB)**
Leuvensesteenweg, 19
3080 Tervuren
℗ 02 / 766 04 30
fax 02 / 767 80 70
English education for children
aged from 3 to 18.
Preparation for GCSE.
Also courses for adults. Cultural
centre and sports centre.

The British Primary School
Stationstraat, 6
3080 Vossem
℗ 02 / 767 30 98
fax 02 / 767 03 51
british.primary@skynet.be
Little English school specialising
in the nursery and primary sections. English programme -
focusing on French, music, creativity and sport.

The British Junior Academy
Boulevard St-Michel, 83
1040 Bruxelles
℗ 02 / 732 53 76
fax 02 / 732 52 76
113302.452@compuserve.com
http://www.ecis.org/bjab
An international school following the English and Welsh curriculum. From 2 to 13 years.
Small classes (max. 14 pupils).
Focuses on French. Science
laboratory, computers, gymna-
sium, music room.

**The 3 European schools are
mainly reserved for the children of the staff of the EU.**
Some sections accept other
children.
Education in the child's mother
tongue + one other language
at primary level + two other
languages at secondary level.
Preparation for the European
baccalaureat

European School Brussels I
Av. du Vert Chasseur, 46
1180 Brussels
℗ 02 / 373 86 11
fax 02 / 375 47 16
www.euronet.be@sceurbs

Brussels Tutor help english-speaking school children and university students with their studies. At
your home or eslsewhere, one-off or long-term support
Hazelaan, 4 - 3080 Tervuren
℗ 02 / 767 06 93
e.mail: 113626.3473@compuserve.com

European School Brussels 2
Avenue Oscar Jespers, 75
1200 Brussels
✆ 02 / 774 22 11
fax 02 / 774 22 60
(primary)
fax 02 / 772 05 30
(secondary)
eu.school1@eeb2.be

European School Brussels 3
Boulevard du Triomphe, 151
1050 Brussels
✆ 02 / 373 88 38

European School
Europa Wijk 24
2400 Mol
✆ 014 / 56 31 85
fax 014 / 56 31 83
smal@eurs.org

Shape International School
Avenue de Rejkjavik, 717
7010 Mons
✆ 065 / 44 57 26
For the children of SHAPE
staff.

German

Deutsche Schule Brussel
Lange Eikstraat, 71
1970 Wezembeek-Oppem
✆ 02 / 785 01 30
fax 02 / 785 01 41
deutsche.schule@a-1.be
German programme.
Pre-school, primary and secondary.

Dutch

De Zonnewijzer
Wedadigsheidstraat, 74
3000 Leuven
✆ 016 / 20 29 54

**Ecole néerlandaise Rudolf
Steiner**
Rue des Millepertuis, 14
1070 Brussels
✆ 02 / 521 04 92

**Ecole Hollandaise Prinses
Juliana**
Rue d'Oultremont, 19
1040 Brussels
✆ 02 / 733 86 16
fax 02 / 736 87 27
bassisschool.princes.juliana@vgc.be
Pre-school and primary .

French

**Lycée français de Belgique
Jean Monnet**
Avenue du Lycée français, 9
1180 Brussels
✆ 02 / 374 58 78
fax 02 / 374 98 43
lycee.francais.j.monnet@skynet.be
Baccalaureat examinations
are organised in Brussels.
Reductions are granted to
families who have more than
one child attending the
school.

Japanese

Japanese School of Brussels
Avenue des Meuniers, 133
1160 Brussels
✆ 02 / 672 10 38
fax 02 / 672 95 27
office@japanese-school-brussels.be

Scandinavian

Ecole Reine Astrid
Square d'Argenteuil, 5
1410 Waterloo
✆ 02 / 357 06 70
fax 02 / 357 06 80
scandinavian.school@ssb.be
http://www.ssb.be

Note: Scholarships are available
for children from French schools
abroad recognised by the French
Ministry of National Education.
This is the case with the Lycée
Français Jean Monnet, the
Collège Français in Ghent and
the European School.
For further details,
✆ 02 / 229 85 32

**For those wishing to follow the French distance learn-
ing programme,** the CNED (Centre National
d'Enseignement à Distance) prepares students for offi-
cial competitions, with 2,750 training products.
A comprehensive catalogue is available from the French
Consulate General in Brussels or by mail:
Tele Accueil du CNED
BP 200
F–89980 FUTURSCOPE CEDEX
✆ 00 33 49 49 94 94

For further details:

CEDIEP
(Centre de Documentation et d'Information sur les Etudes et Professions)
Publishes guides to secondary education and professions.
✆ 02 / 649 14 18 – fax 02 / 649 94 90
cediep@online.be

SIEP (Service d'Information sur les Etudes et les Professions):
Produces a list of French-speaking schools in Belgium and reviews over thirty trades.
✆ 02 / 640 08 32

VOC (Vlaams Onderwijscentrum) for the Dutch-speaking network.
✆ 02 / 218 10 00 – fax 02 / 219 57 00

Infor-Jeunes
Rue du Marché-aux-Herbes, 27
1000 Brussels
✆ 02 / 512 23 74 from 12 noon to 5.45 p.m.

Caw (Centrum Algemeen Welzijnwerk)
rue Grétry, 1
1000 Brussels
✆ 02 / 227 02 00 from 9.30 a.m. to 7 p.m.

Equivalence Rating of Degree Qualifications

Every case is judged on its merits. Applications may be lodged either by the applicant or by the administration in the educational establishment where the foreign student is registered. The 'equivalence' units at the education authorities will explain to you how to complete the formalities.

Note
• All the documents in the application for equivalence rating must be accompanied by a translation made either by a certified translator or by the services at the Belgian embassy or consulate in the countries concerned, except for those written in German, English, Spanish, Italian, French and Dutch.

• Certificates of completion of secondary studies issued by Germany, Spain, France, Italy, Luxembourg, Morocco and the Netherlands give the holder automatic access to certain elements in the Belgian higher education system.

• The 'ratification commission' is also entitled to require foreign students to sit examinations. These students must always provide evidence that they have reached a certain standard in their own country to be admitted to follow, at equivalent levels, options offered to them under the Belgian education system.

For further details:

Service des Équivalences
Cité administrative de l'Etat
Quartier arcade
Bloc D – 5th floor
19 Boulevard Pachéco, bte 0
1010 Brussels
✆ 02/210 56 13

Commission d'homologation
Postal address
rue Marie de Bourgogne, 2
1050 Brussels
✆ 02 / 286 42 10
fax 02 / 286 42 11
Depositing documents and visits
(by appointment)

Jury Central de la Communauté française
rue Montoyer, 57
1000 Brussels
✆ 02/230 15 25

**Bureau de Liaison
Bruxelles-Europe**
Avenue d'Auderghem
1040 Brussels
✆ 02 / 280 00 80
fax 02 / 280 03 86
A particularly well-documented office which provided the information in this paragraph.

**Vlaamse Gemeenschap
Dienst Europese projecten**
Rue Royale, 93 bte 3
1000 Brussels
✆ 02 / 227 14 11

Examencommissie van de Vlaamse Gemeenschap
Rue Royale, 80
1000 Brussels
✆ 02 / 502 60 62 (du 1er au 4ème degré)
✆ 02 / 502 59 22 (pour le 5ème et 6ème degré)

British Council
Information on education and examinations in England.
✆ 02/ 227 08 40
✆ 02/ 227 08 49
http://www.britishcouncil.orj/belgium

For students:
le **Guido** Bruxelles et Louvain-La-Neuve,
published by Editions Guido.
✆ 09 / 233 08 68

The multi-lingual magazine « **Louvain International** » published four times a year aims to inform the international community about the university's academic activities.
For information: *tulkens@reul.ucl.be*

Higher Education and Universities

Brussels has many colleges and universities, accessible to youngsters who have successfully completed a full cycle of general secondary education. They are either state, catholic or private institutions and are too numerous to mention in full.
Here are a few addresses. If you would like to find out more please refer to the "**Useful addresses**" section at the back of the guide.

| English speaking: |

The list of universities in Belgium which offer a full programme in English is given in an invaluable book " **Selected Links: Business and Academia in Belgium**" published jointly by *Focus Career Services*
✆ *02/ 646 65 30*
and the *American Chamber of Commerce*
✆ *02 / 513 67 70*

The Open University
Avenue Emile Duray, 38
1050 Brussels
✆ *02 / 644 33 72*
✆ *02 / 644 33 68*
R.Tuffs@open.ac.uk
http://www.open.ac.uk

International Management Institute
Rue de Livourne 116-120
1000 Brussels
http://www.timi.edu
Business management and public relations.

Vesalius College
Courrier : Pleinlaan,2
1050 Brussels
Site : Boulevard du Triomphe, 32
1160 Brussels
✆ *02 / 629 36 26*
✆ *02 / 629 36 37*
vesalius@vub.ac.be
Summer Web page:
www.vub.ac.be/VECO/summer
An international college which is part of the VUB (Vrije Universiteit Brussel) and works in partnership with Boston University in the USA..

United Business Institutes
Avenue Marnix, 20
1000 Brussels
✆ *02 / 548 04 80*
✆ *02 / 548 04 89*
info@ubi.edu
http://www.ubi.edu
A college which is validated by the University of Wales in Great Britain and affiliated to Mercer University in Atlanta.

Boston University Brussels
Boulevard du Triomphe, 39
1160 Brussels
✆ *02 / 640 74 74*
✆ *02 / 640 65 15*
boston@innet.be
http://www.innet.net/boston/

Solvay Business School
Av. F. Roosevelt, 21 – CP 145
1050 Brussels
✆ *02 / 650 41 83*
✆ *02 / 650 41 99*
mba@ulb.ac.be
http://ulb.ac.be/solvay/mba/index.html

| French speaking: | Dutch speaking |

ULB
(Université Libre de Bruxelles)
Avenue F. Roosevelt
1050 Brussels
✆ 02 / 650 21 11
✆ 02 / 650 28 72
http://www.ulb.ac.be

VUB
(Vrij Universiteit)
Pleinlaan , 2
1050 Brussels
✆ 02 / 629 21 11
✆ 02 / 629 22 82 ·
http://www.vub.ac.be

UCL
(Université Catholique de Louvain)
Information and administrative procedures for foreign students:
In Brussels:
✆ 02 / 764 50 22
In Louvain-La-Neuve:
✆ 010 / 47 40 09
http://www/ucl.ac.be

KUL
(Katholiek Universiteit van Leuven)
Vieux Marché, 13
3000 Leuven
✆ 016 / 32 11 11
✆ 016 / 32 40 22
http://www.kuleuven.ac.be

Registering in your commune:

Students who are non-EU nationals
Nationals can only study in Belgium at a college or university which run, approved or recognised by the state. Some institutions are not recognised but obtain special permission each year to allow the enrolment of foreign students. The temporary residence permit and the Certificate of Registration in the Register of Aliens (C.I.R.E.) are limited to the period of study.

Students who are EU nationals or nationals of equivalent countries
These students can study at all Belgian colleges and universities.
Procedure :
• Registration in the Register of Aliens and temporary residence perm valid for three months on production of the documents required for entering Belgium ;
• Residence card valid for one year on presentation of proof that the necessary requirements are met before the previous document expire
• The residence permit may be extended on a yearly basis if the student still meets all the conditions.

DOC. BUREAU LIAISON BRUXELLES-EUROPE

SHOPPING

Consumer Protection

There is a consumer protection body in Belgium; it is called **Test-Achats**, and its objectives are to inform, defend and represent consumers.

Test-Achats is a member of the BEUC (European Bureau of Consumers' Unions), IT (*International Testing*) and the IOCU (*International Organisation of Consumers' Unions*).

> **For further informations** about the publications:
> Test-Achats
> rue de Hollande, 13
> 1060 Brussels
> ✆ *542 32 11*
> *and for subscriptions:*
> ✆ *542 32 00*
> The offices are open from Monday to Thursday, from 9 a.m. to 5 p.m. and Friday from 9 a.m. to 4 p.m.

Food and household goods

> **To know more:**
> *Petit Futé – Bruxelles*
> Nouvelles Editions
> de l'Université.

> **You can place your order by Internet!**
> Please see « home deliveries» pg 142

Supermarkets / hypermarkets are open from 9 a.m. to 8 p.m. every day (except Sunday) and till 9 p.m. on Friday evenings. You can pay by cash, cheque or Bancontact - Mister Cash card.

GB (Super orMaxi)
the whole range of food and cleaning products. In the Maxi stores: clothes ,books, TV, Hi-FI,Video, toys, car accessories. Own brand GB products and « white products» (cheaper) .

Delhaize
the whole range of food and cleaning products. Own brand Delhaize products and Derby products (cheaper).

Colruyt
Offers bulk-buying in warehouses, low prices, high quality meat department.

Makro
food, household goods, furniture, garden centre, office department … A huge warehouse with good discounts on bulk quantities. Please note ! You must have a compulsory membership card available only to the self-employed, organisations and companies, obtainable from the store on presentation of the appropriate documents
✆ *02 / 251 59 20*

Rob
Luxury foodstuffs : fine groceries, fresh produce all year round, delicatessen/takeout service… More expensive.

Aldi
staple products at very low prices.

Biggs in Waterloo
A large hypermarket in the style of MAXI GB.

DELVAUX

Crée depuis 1829 - Voiles de soie

LUMINAIRES
R I C H O U X

AVENUE DE L'ARMÉE 8 • 1040 BRUXELLES
(02) 734 79 28

Retailers

Retailers

There is a wide choice of small shops in Brussels. Most of them are open from 8 a.m. to 7 p.m. A few, often run by Moroccans or Turks, stay open later in the evening (till 8 p.m.) and on Sundays. We have included some addresses but if you want to find out more refer to the « **Useful addresses** » section at the back of this guide.

Fine grocery stores

Africa

African Asian Food
Chaussée de Wavre, 25
1050 Brussels
✆ 02 / 514 03 86
Open from 9 a.m. to 8 p.m.
Closed on Sundays. Sweet potatoes, plantain bananas, dried fish, henna, etc.

Britain

The English Shop
Rue Stévin, 186
1040 Brussels
✆ 02 / 736 34 88
fax 02 / 735 11 38
Open from 10 a.m. to 6.30 p.m. Closed on Mondays - open on Sundays from 11 a.m. to 4 p.m. Pudding, muffins, teas, candy bars… and even stuffed turkeys at Christmas!

Marks & Spencer
Rue Neuve , 13-15
1000 Brussels
✆ 02 / 209 00 00
fax 02 / 209 00 01
Open from 9.30 a.m. to 6.30 p.m. (Fridays until 8 p.m.) Biscuits, jams, teas and so on, on the ground floor of a big clothes store.

Stonemanor
Steenhofstraat, 28
3078 Everberg
✆ 02 / 759 49 79
British food, books, videos and magazines.
Open from 9 a.m. to 7 p.m. - on Fridays until 9 p.m. and Sundays from 11 a.m. to 4 p.m.

Austria

La Maison d'Autriche
Rue Gérard , 95-97
1040 Brussels
✆ & fax 02 / 734 20 19
Open from 9 a.m. to 7.30 p.m.

Spain

Economato Marisol
Place de la Constitution, 23
1070 Brussels
✆ & fax 02 / 521 47 36
Open from 9.30 a.m. to 7.30 p.m. Closed on Mondays. Opposite the Gare du Midi. Specialises in Spanish products.

España Calidade
Av. de la Porte de Hal, 63
1060 Brussels
✆ & fax 02 / 537 23 87
Spanish specialities. Saturdays from 10 a.m. to 7 p.m. Sundays from 10 a.m. to 2 p.m.

Pakistan/India

Green Pepper
Chaussée de Wavre, 209
1050 Brussels
✆ & fax 02 / 646 02 61
Open from 9 a.m. to 8 p.m. Curry, lentils, masala, chutney, rose-petal jam, spices, etc.

Ireland

The Irish Shop
Rue Archimède, 48
1040 Brussels
✆ 02 / 230 69 11
fax 02 / 230 37 03
Open from 10 a.m. to 7 p.m. Closed on Sundays. Salmon, Guinness, jams, and gifts. Also serves lunch between 12.30 p.m. and 2.30 p.m.

Irish Meal
Rue Le Titien, 30
1000 Brussels
✆ 02 / 732 53 51
Irish butcher

Israel

Bornstein
Rue de Suède, 62a
1060 Brussels
✆ 02 / 537 16 79
Open from 7.30 a.m. to 6.30 p.m. Closed on Saturdays and Sunday afternoons. Authentic Jewish bakery selling delicious specialities: cakes made with nuts and sesame, etc.

Italia

Casa Italiana
rue Archimède, 39
1040 Brussels
✆ 733 40 70
Open from 9 a.m. to 7 p.m. - on Saturdays until 1 p.m. - Closed on Sundays. A good location in the European district, this grocery store will delight expatriate Italians with its authentic pasta, oils, cheeses and cooked meats from their homeland.

Japan

Tagawa
Chaussée de Vleurgat, 119
1050 Brussels
℡ 02 / 648 59 11
fax 02 / 640 10 88
Open from 10 a.m. to 7 p.m.
Closed on Sundays. Fresh
fish, green mustard, pre-
served ginger, ready-made
dishes - but also newspa-
pers.

Miyuki
Chaussée d'Ixelles, 347
1050 Brussels
℡ & fax 02 / 640 56 82
Open from 12 noon to 3
p.m. and from 6 p.m. to
9.30 p.m. Closed on
Sundays and Mondays. Top-
quality fishmongers: sushi,
sashimi, etc. Restaurant at
the back.

Yama Food
Chaussée de Charleroi, 24-26
1060 Brussels
℡ 02 / 538 99 50
fax 02 / 534 25 73
Open from 10 a.m. to 6 p.m.
Closed on Sundays and
Mondays. A small supermarket selling Japanese products: plates of sushi, spices...

Orient

China Co
Rue Van Praet, 16-18
1000 Brussels
℡ 02 / 511 48 31
Open from 10 a.m. to 7 p.m.
Closed on Sundays. 100 %
Asia, from rice to crockery,
even the staff are from the
East!

Ly Chi Minh
Rue Goffart, 79
1050 Brussels
℡ 02 / 647 40 37
fax 02 / 640 29 19
Open daily from 9 a.m. to 7
p.m.
Avenue Fonsny, 3
1060 Brussels
Open daily from 9 a.m. to 6
p.m except Mondays.
℡ & fax 02 / 538 37 83
Wholesalers, suppliers to
Oriental restaurants.

Echo d'Orient
Rue Berkmans, 103
1060 Saint-Gilles
℡ 02 / 537 13 44
Open from 10 a.m. to 9 p.m.
Closed on Mondays. Basmati ,
flavoured rice, dried fruits,
wines from around the world,
fresh dates, Oriental style
gherkins, etc.

Portugal

Casa Portuguesa
Rue van Campenhout, 98
1040 Brussels
℡ & fax 02 / 733 36 30
Open from 9.30 a.m. to 2
p.m., and 3 p.m. to 8 p.m.,
open on Sunday mornings.
Closed on Mondays. This
grocery store imports everything to make the Portuguese
feel at home: dried fish,
cheeses, wines, port, canned
goods, biscuits, frozen
goods... and even newspapers
and washing products made
in Portugal!

Scandinavia

ScanShop
Chaussée de Tervuren, 133
1410 Waterloo
℡ 02 / 351 12 75
Scandinavian specialities.

Ikea
Weiveldlaan, 29
1930 Zaventem
℡ 02 / 719 22 61
fax 02 / 719 23 30
Open Monday to Thursday
from 10 a.m. to 7 p.m.,
Fridays till 8 p.m. and
Saturdays from 9 a.m. to 7
p.m.

If you are looking for a good cellar with wines from all four corners of the globe here is one useful address, if you would like to know more then refer to the « Useful Addresses » sec-tion at the back of this guide pg 205.
Vins De Coninck
Chaussée de Bruxelles, 37
1410 Waterloo
℡ 02 / 353 07 65
One of the oldest wine and spirits shops in Brussels where you will find a huge choice of wines in magnificent surroundings but above all top of the range wines. They offer a whole range of services : making up Christmas/ New Year gift sets, stocking cellars, home deliveries and not for-getting an air-conditioned room containing a collection of cigars which are a connoisseur's dream.

Shops selling organic products

The Belgian network of organic and health food shops has branched out recently into all sectors of the agri-food industry including cosmetics and cleaning products. You can find them everywhere including supermarkets and hypermarkets.
Some of the Belgian quality brands BG (Biogarantie) and NP (Nature et Progrès) are just as good as the European brands (Eco , Bioland ....)

To find out more :
Service d'éco-consommation
✆ 071 / 300 301
can offer you advice and addresses.
Nature et Progrès
✆ 081 / 22 60 65

A few addresses:

Sequoia
av. de Hinnisdael, 14
1150 Woluwé St Pierre
02 / 771 68 38
Chaussée de Saint Job, 532
1180 Uccle
02 / 375 91 91
Supermarket selling organic and natural products – a wide choice of ready-cooked meals.

Le Shanti
Av. Buyl, 63
1050 Ixelles
✆ 02 / 647 88 60
Open Monday to Friday from 9 a.m. to 7 p.m., Saturdays from 9.30 a.m. to 6.30 p.m.
A very wide choice of quality organic food : bread, fruit, vegetables, cereals, wine …
A small delicatessen / take-out counter.

In some areas the fishmonger, milkman or greengrocer pass by every week and sell goods from the back of their van. Ask your neighbours for information.

Organic markets

Day	Time	Place
Saturday	8 a.m. to 1 p.m.	chée de Roodebeek, 300 Woluwé St Lambert
Sunday	8 a.m. to 1.30 p.m.	place Wiener Boitsfort
Wednesday	9 a.m. to 2 p.m.	place de la Monnaie Bruxelles
	4 p.m. to 7 p.m	chée de Roodebeek, 300 Woluwé St Lambert
	1 p.m. to 7 p.m.	place du Châtelain Ixelles

Markets

Market	Where?	When?	What?
Abattoir market	rue Ropsy-Chaudron	Fri, Sat, Sun 7 a.m - 1 p.m	Anything including a chicken or live rabbit!
Midi market	Midi station	Sunday 7 a.m. - 1 p.m.	Le grand souk dans une ambiance orientale
Flower market	Grand Place	Every day 8 a.m. - 6 p.m.	Flowers
Flagey market	place Flagey	Saturday and Sunday 7 a.m. - 1 p.m.	Food and plants
Châtelain market	place du Châtelain	Wednesday 2 p.m. - 7 p.m.	Stylish market in a trendy district
Stockel market	place Dumon	Wed., Fri., Sat. 8 a.m. - 1 p.m.	A variety of goods famous for its nurserymen
Boitsfort market	place communale	Sunday 8 a.m. - 1 p.m.	Very varied. Excellent roast chickens!
Uccle market	place St Job	Monday 7 a.m. - 1 p.m.	Anything and everything
Woluwé market	place St Lambert	Wednesday 7 a.m. - 1.30 p.m.	Food
Auderghem market	Bld du Souverain	Thursday 8 a.m. - 1 p.m.	Food and plants
Etterbeek market	place Jourdan	Sunday 7 a.m. - 2 p.m.	Food and plants

To find out more:
Bruxelles aux 100 marchés on
sale at the TIB
℡ 02 / 513 89 40

Plants: if you are looking for a
reliable address, advice on your
garden from the comfort of your
own home, friendly yet efficient
service and a wonderful choice
of English roses, ask for Jean-
Louis at the Jardin de Clairibel
and mention Expats in Brussels.
℡ 010 / 84 05 53
English spoken.

Shopping districts

If you are looking for high class shops in Brussels these are mostly found on the Boulevard de Waterloo and a section of the Avenue Louise.
There are two symbols to look out for in some shop windows which prove they are high quality establishments :

- The title « **By appointment to the Royal Court of Belgium**» (see illustration opposite). Limited to around a hundred companies ranging from jewellers to interior design by way of chocolates or record shops. Some examples are : **Joaillerie Leysen** in the Sablon district, **Boîte à Musique** rue Ravenstein and **Demeuldre** chaussée de Wavre.

- The label « **Chambre du Haut Commerce de Bruxelles**» (cfr.illustration opposite) Limited to around seventy luxury businesses who all share a respect for tradition, top quality goods, excellent service, impeccable taste and a sense of honour. Some examples are : **Fydjy's** place Stéphanie, **Degand** avenue Louise or **Petites Heure du Matin** , chaussée de Waterloo.

Uptown :
(1000 and 1050 Brussels)

Boulevard de Waterloo

This is the foremost luxury shopping district where you can find some very beautiful shops housing the great international designer labels such as **Hermès, Delvaux, Giorgio Armani, Gucci, Yves St Laurent, Chanel** or **Bulgari** as well as a few lesser known shops.

N° 27 – Delvaux

A Belgian design house which is still one of the jewels in the crown of this country's craftmanship. The elegance and quality of the designs, ladies' handbags together with a range of scarves and small leather goods ensure that Delvaux's reputation has reached beyond the borders of Belgium with branches open in the world's major cities: Monte Carlo, Los Angeles, Tokyo, New York… Open Monday to Saturday 10 a.m. to 6.30 p.m.
If you want to find out their other addresses in Belgium :
✆ *02 / 738 00 40*

Doc. Delvaux

N° 50 – Hermès

Although the most symbolic articles bearing this great designer label are still made of leather or silk, their love of quality is also revealed in the china, crystal, perfumes, clocks, watches and ready-to-wear ranges. Open Monday to Friday from 10 a.m. to 6 p.m., Saturdays from 10.30 a.m.
02 / 511 20 62

N° 37 – Giorgio Armani

A really big name from the Italian fashion scene displayed in splendid surroundings.
Open Monday to Saturday from 10.30 a.m. to 7 p.m.
02 / 513 79 81

N° 9 – Scapa

Quality clothes for men, women and children.Upstairs there is an interior design department along the same lines « Scapa Home ».
Open from 10 a.m. to 6.30 p.m.
02 / 514 26 98

Avenue de la Toison d'Or

The cinema goer's delight! Thanks to the new pedestrian zone this avenue located right opposite the Boulevard de Waterloo is gradually rediscovering its old vitality and brings together the fully renovated UGC cinema, a theatre, a few restaurants and galleries hosting nearly 70 shops, ranging from ready-to-wear fashion to interior design, together with lingerie or leather goods. Easy access thanks to the « deux portes » car park.

The « Galeries Louise » and the cityend of the Avenue Louise

In an extension to the Avenue de la Toison d'Or the Galeries Louise have an even wider variety of shops, essentially offering ready-to-wear clothes.
The finest shops can be found at the city end of the Avenue Louise with jewellers such as **Cartier** and **Holemans.**

N° 4 – Bouvy

A beautiful fashion house with a reputation for elegance and refinement which delights businessmen, ladies or students alike. The clothes are smart yet casual and include one of the biggest collections of shirts and ties in the capital.
Open Monday to Saturday from 10 a.m. to 6.30 p.m.
02 / 513 07 48

Place Stéphanie and surrounds of the Avenue Louise

Place Stéphanie is dominated by the magnificent Hotel **Conrad** together with a new little shopping complex, including the famous chocolate maker **Pierre Marcolini** or the Ali Baba's Cave of a toyshop **Serneels.**

On the opposite side you can also find the jeweller's **Fydjy's,** the interior design shop **Walt** or the famous Belgian fashion designer: **Olivier Strelli.**

N° 56 – Fydjy's

This shop has succeeded in just a few years in forging a fine reputation for itself as a unique jeweller's and art gallery. Clever collection with take-apart or reversible earrings, stones with interchangeable colours and fit-together rings.
Open from 9.40 a.m. to 6 p.m.
✆ 02 / 513 87 17

Doc. Fydjy's

Further along the Avenue Louise towards the Bois de la Cambre the shops are rather few and far between but they are nevertheless worth a detour :

Au n° 415 – La Maison Degand

A temple of classic elegance for men and women.
Fine craftsmanship, all entirely hand-crafted in workshops.
Department « Gifts for Him and Her » : cigar boxes, dressing-table articles, silverware etc.
Adjoining the carpark, « **Degand Sport** » offers a beautiful selection of casual clothes.

.The Town Centre (1000 and 1050 Brussels)

Le Sablon

THE adress for top quality antique shops. Sablon is one of the most fashionable districts in Brussels, with its glittering window displays small bars and restaurants with terraces, where you can both savour a few moments of peace in the Petit Sablon square, or give in to the temptation of a small cake from one of the best cake shops in Brussels: **Wittamer.**

A few addresses on the square itself and in neighbouring streets:

N° 36 – Leysen

A family business which has become a veritable institution in the world of High Class Jewellery. The subtle and harmonious blend of tradition and creativity mark out this designer who was awarded the title « By appointment to the Royal Court of Belgium».
Open Tuesday to Saturday from 10 a.m. to 12.30 p.m. and 2.00 p.m. to 6.30 p.m. Mondays by appointment.
✆ 02 / 513 62 60

N° 37 – Emporio Armani

The full range of clothes for men and women, from jeans to evening gowns, not to mention the vast array of accessories (watches, reading glasses...)in the true « Armani » spirit at very affordable prices. And if you are hunting for gifts, pay a visit to the « Gift Collection ».
Open from 10.30 a.m. to 7 p.m., Sundays from 11 a.m. to 6 p.m. Closed on Tuesdays.

The Sablon Association whose main task is the continual improvement of this district's aesthetic quality. They organise two events per year :
«Les Nocturnes du Sablon» on the last Thursday, Friday and Saturday of November when the whole district celebrates: fairytale atmosphere, horse and carriage rides, all the shops staying open until late at night.
«Les Printemps baroques du Sablon» each spring a series of concerts is given in various private houses or galleries.

✆ 02 / 512 98 41

At the corner of the rue des Minimes :Badi Gadhimi

A permanent member of the Washington Textile Museum, this expert searches above all else for authenticity and quality in old carpets. Collections from the Caucasus, Persia, China, Turkey or India.

✆ 02 / 512 98 41

Open every day from 10 a.m. to 12. noon and from 2 p.m. to 6 p.m.

N° 65 rue Lebeau: Rosalie Pompon

A weird and wonderful shop selling very unexpected items: a water-lily umbrella with dangling frogs or a life-size papier maché soldier.

Open from 10.30 a.m. until 6.30 p.m. including Sundays. Closed on Mondays.

✆ 02 / 512 35 93

DOC. ELVIS POMPELIO

The Grand' Place and the îlot sacré

A tourist high-spot! One of the most beautiful squares in the world where you can admire some outstanding 17th century monuments including the famous Brussels lace shop, Rubbrecht and the equally famous restaurant Le Cygne.

A few addresses on the square itself and in neighbouring streets:

N° 24-26 rue au Beurre : De Greef :

Long-established reputable shop selling beautiful jewellery and an especially large range of exclusive watches: Patek Philippe, Cartier, Jaeger-Lecoultre…

Open from 9h30 à 13h et de 14h15 à 17h45 tous les jours. Le samedi de 9h30 à 17h45.

✆ 02 / 511 95 98

Au n° 60 de la rue du Midi: Elvis Pompelio

Informal, casual, elegant, traditional or trendy, the hats created by this famous Belgian designer will suit any head, any style and any wallet.

Open every day from 10.30 a.m. until 1.30 p.m.

✆ 02 / 511 11 88

The little streets adjoining the Grand'Place form an area known as the Ilot Sacré, a gastronomic paradise.

Useful facts: VAT at 21% may be reimbursed for goods exported to non-EU countries for articles over 7,000 bef. Procedure: When leaving the country, you should go to Belgian Customs at the airport with your passport, your air ticket, the articles concerned and the receipts (indicating the amount of VAT). The procedure must be completed a maximum of 90 days after purchase (you will need dated receipts to validate your claim).

Sales
Summer Sales from 1 July and Winter Sales from 1 January. Credit cards are not taken during the sales.

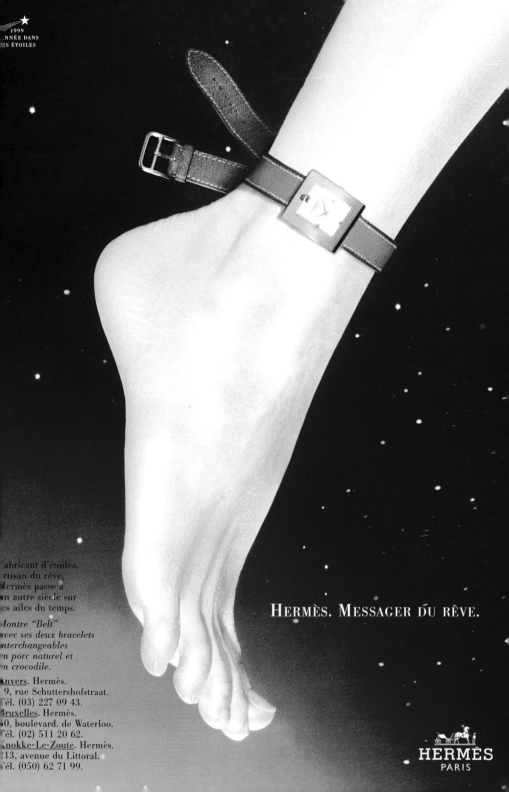

abricant d'étoiles,
rtisan du rêve,
Hermès passe à
n autre siècle sur
es ailes du temps.

Montre "Belt"
vec ses deux bracelets
nterchangeables
n porc naturel et
n crocodile.

nvers. Hermès.
9, rue Schuttershofstraat.
él. (03) 227 09 43.
Bruxelles. Hermès.
0, boulevard. de Waterloo.
él. (02) 511 20 62.
nokke-Le-Zoute. Hermès.
13, avenue du Littoral.
él. (050) 62 71 99.

HERMÈS. MESSAGER DU RÊVE.

HERMÈS
PARIS

GIORGIO ARMANI

**Boulevard de Waterloo 29 Waterloolaan
Bruxelles 1000 Brussel
02-513 79 81**

Daily opened from 10:30 to 19:00
Closed on Sunday

Near the Grand'Place, the **galeries St Hubert** are a very fine example of statue-lined galleries, housing some very beautiful tourist shops.
At the other end of the scale, the **galeries Agora** on the opposite side of the street has small eclectic shops from hippy to porn and ethnic; a good place to look for fancy dress costumes or fake jewellery.

Rue Blaes and rue Haute (lower Sablon)
Go for a Sunday rummage around !
Second-hand dealers , small antique shops, reproduction pieces, traders in « brol »…(a Brussels word for the depths of an attic). If you go on a Sunday the shops are open and you can rummage around the flea market on the Place du Jeu de Balle.

Downtown (1000 Brussels)

Uccle (1180 Brussels)

Bld Adolf Max
A real mix of different styles of shop, including the English bookshop Waterstone's and the Maison du Porte Plume, a must for all your writing requirements: fountain pens, propelling pencils, ball-point pens and office accessories.

Rue Neuve and City 2
Down-to-earth prices!
With shops like **H&M, Marks & Spencer**... and **Fnac** in the heart of the mall.

Rue A. Dansaert
the showpiece for cool Flemish fashion.
Where you can admire the window displays of Belgian designers, most of them from the Antwerp School like **Ann Demeulemeester, Kaat Tilley** etc.

Apart from the long chaussée de Waterloo and Fort Jaco's charming little centre with the shopping mall, this commune has developed 2 flourishing and diverse shopping streets: **chaussée d'Alsemberg** with **rue Xavier de Bue** and **rue Vanderkindere** and **Place St Job** with its bookshop open on Sundays and its Monday-morning market.

The two Woluwé's (1150 et 1200 Brussels)

Stockel Square in Woluwé St Pierre : a small shopping mall in a delightful district worth discovering on market days: Tuesdays, Fridays and Saturdays.

DOC. MAISON DU PORTE PLUME

DOC . OPT

Tintin
Rue de l'Eglise, 96
✆ 02 / 779 38 58
A cult place for all Tintin fans
offering a vast range of T-shirts,
sweaters, jackets, cartoons
books, posters, figurines or
watches all bearing the famous
figure of Tintin .

Avenue Georges Henri in
Woluwé St Lambert where you
can find absolutely everything.

Place St Lambert famous for its
flea market on the 1st Sunday of
the month, and a little further on
the large **Shopping Center** with
its famous shops and department
stores like **C&A, Zara, Inno** and
Habitat.

Etterbeek
(1040 Brussels)

3 districts offering the whole
range of commercial products
from food to ready-to-wear
clothes and all the services you
can imagine : **rue des Tongres**
with the **galerie Linthout** and
galerie Cinquantenaire near the
Cinquantenaire itself and **rue de
La Chasse.**

Caméleon
Very fine collection of ready-to-wear clothes for men,
women and children offering exceptional value for money !
• **Comptoirs Privés**
Exclusive sales organised as an event for which you need
an invitation card (for more information :
✆ 02/ 705 19 41
• **Stores:** shops open all year round.
Two addresses in Brussels
avenue de Tervuren, 109
1040 Etterbeek
✆ 02 / 735 48 50
rue Buchholtz, 8-10
1050 Ixelles
✆ 02 / 644 22 66

Dédale
In the galerie du cinquantenaire.
A treasure trove with games of
every kind : draughts, dice, cards,
memory games, games of strategy,
puzzles, jigsaws, tarots etc.
Open Monday to Saturday from
10.30 a.m. to 6.30 p.m.
✆ 02 / 734 22 55

Ixelles
(1050 Brussels)

The districts around the avenue
Louise are teeming with small
shopping centres : **rue du Bailli,
place Flagey**, but the **place du
Châtelain** has a unique, almost
village, atmosphere with its small
street cafés.

Around Brussels

Of course shopping districts have
sprung up all over the place
around Brussels. Some of them,
like the **rue du Try in Ohain** are
famous for their high quality
shops and charming surroundings, while others like **Waterloo**
with its **galeries Wellington** are
well known for the variety and
choice they offer. Others like the
**avenue des Combattants in la
Hulpe** offer the peace and quiet
of a district far removed from the
hustle and bustle of the city.

Interior Design

please refer to Fittings and Decoration p. 40.

Gifts, Tableware and Crafts

Here are a few addresses if you are looking for gifts. For more addresses, please refer to the « **Useful addresses** » section at the back of the guide pg 205.

Demeuldre
Chaussée de Wavre, 143
1050 Brussels
(customer parking)
✆ 02 / 511 51 44
All the big names in china, earthenware, ceramic art, glassware, silverware and crystal including the magnificent crystal from Val-Saint-Lambert, the jewel of Walloon craftsmanship.
Open from 9.30 a.m. to 6.30 p.m. Tuesday to Saturday.

Cantaria
Rue de Rosières, 10 B
(au coin de l'avenue Albert I)
1332 Genval
✆ + fax: 02 / 652 48 56
Open Monday to Friday from 10 a.m. to 3 p.m. (closed Wednesdays) and Saturdays from 2 p.m. to 6 p.m. A delightful place to go in search of gifts or artisanal tableware: ceramics from Portugal, Sicily and lots more.

Ferramoro
Boulevard de Waterloo, 48
1000 Brussels
✆ 02 / 511 61 80
A ready-to-wear collection for women which also has a wide range of leather goods, scarves and costume jewellery.

Rubbrecht
Grand Place, 23
1000 Brussels
✆ 02 / 512 02 18
Magnificent hand-made antique or modern lace, of such high quality and variety that it is known throughout the world.

Saulaie
✆ 0033 02 41 95 14 55
e-mail: saulaie@wanadoo.fr
htt:// www.saulaie.fr
Interactive shopping on the Internet which offers a whole range of earthenware, china, crystal, household linen or silverware for all your gifts and wedding lists.
Via Internet or a simple phone call to their Brussels agent:
Béatrice Papeians
✆ 0476 / 43 45 34

De Wit Manufacture Royale/ Koninklijke Manufactuur
Schoutetstraat, 7
2800 Mechelen
✆ 015 / 20 29 05
Buying, selling, restoring and cleaning of antique carpets – hand-weaving.

Metrax
Avenue Provinciale, 30
1341 Ottignies
✆ 010 / 61 21 62
Creates cushions and tapestries following traditional designs at excellent prices.

It is a Brussels custom to offer a « ballotin » (box) of chocolates to your host. Chocolate is a Belgian speciality and « pralines » in particular (small bite-sized chocolates with a variety of fillings) :

Godiva
✆ 02 / 422 17 81
Neuhaus
✆ 02 / 568 22 53
Pierre Marcolini
✆ 02 / 216 82 15

DOC. DEMEULDRE

Second-hand shops and discount stores

If you are looking for a designer outfit, furs or a Chanel suit we have chosen some addresses for you:

L'arrière-cour
Beemd, 41
1640 Rhode-St-Genèse
✆ 075/ 81 43 31
Saturdays
from 10 a.m. to 6.30 p.m.
End of series of decorative objects and furniture.
New furniture at between 30 and 60% cheaper.

Les Enfants d'Edouard
175-177 av Louise
1050 Brussels
✆ 02 / 640 42 45
Monday to Saturday from 9.30 a.m. to 6 p.m : An absolute must for second hand clothes!

Michèle Simon
128 Galeries Louise
1050 Brussels
✆ 02 / 512 33 89
Monday to Saturday from 10.00 a.m. to 6.30 p.m. : Sells only designer clothes which have hardly been worn!

Amandine
150 rue Defacqz
1050 Brussels
✆ 02 / 539 17 93
Monday to Saturday from 10.00 a.m. to 6 p.m. Everything a bride could wish for : crinoline petticoats, trains, lace, tulle dresses embroidered with pearls... from as little as 7,000 bef.

Idiz Bogam I
162 rue Blaes
1000 Brussels
✆ 02 / 513 62 11
Monday to Saturday from 10.00 a.m. to 6.30 p.m. – open on Sundays from 10.30 a.m. to 4 p.m. Reconditioned clothes from the 1940's – 1970's.

Discount stores

If you cannot wait for the sales you can still enjoy a discount of up to 50% even on the big name labels:

Dod Homme
Chée de Louvain, 16
1030 Brussels
✆ 02 / 218 04 54
rue du Bailli, 91
1050 Brussels
✆ 02 / 538 02 47

Dod Femme
Chée de Louvain, 44
1030 Brussels
✆ 02 / 218 73 63
rue du Bailli, 64
1050 Brussels
✆ 02 / 538 02 47

Dod Enfant
Chée de Louvain, 41
1030 Brussels
✆ 02 / 217 52 08
Avenue Louise, 179
1050 Brussels
✆ 02 / 640 60 40
Last year's or last season's collections sold in bulk at 50% off.

Degrif
49 rue Simonis
1050 Brussels
✆ 02 / 537 53 04
Monday to Saturday from 10.30 a.m. to 6.30 p.m.
Italian or French designer shoes sold at 50% off all year round!

ZOOM
There is a nice tradition in Belgium on Saint Nicholas's Day (6 December). The children leave their slippers at the bottom of the chimney so that Saint Nicholas can fill them with sweets, mandarins, speculoos biscuits and chocolates (including chocolate coins wrapped in gold and silver paper).

The children also leave the Saint a glass of wine or beer by the chimney, along with a carrot for his donkey!

Home Deliveries

Meals delivered to your home

Italian

Arrivero
✆ 02 / 675 30 00
Real Italian stone-baked pizza. High quality products and rapid delivery.

Moroccan

Allo Medina Couscous
✆ 02 / 644 59 39
Tasty couscous and tajines prepared the traditional way. Ideal if you are organising a Moroccan style dinner.

Chinese

Thai Sun Cocoon
✆ 02 / 346 77 33
An extensive menu offering all the delights of China....

Thai

Tom Yam
✆ 02 / 646 64 04
One of the best Thai restaurants in Brussels. Excellent, high-quality choice.

Vietnamese

La Perle de lune
✆ 02 / 347 50 25
Quality cooking, beautiful presented dishes, lots of choice.

Indian

Le Rana
✆ 02 / 374 40 05
Delicious traditional cooking.

Israeli

Leny & Co
✆ 02 / 539 02 69

Japanese

Shogun
✆ 02 / 512 83 19
The house speciality: Teppan Yaki. Delicate cuisine.

Lebanese

Faraya
✆ 02 / 219 94 16
Mezza, grilled meats. Home catering service.

Portuguese

Saint Adrien
✆ 02 / 647 37 03
Good traditional Portuguese cooking.

Danish

Copenhagen
✆ 02 / 513 50 62
A Danish restaurant that is famous in Brussels. Hot and cold Danish specialities.

Spanish

Casa Manolo
✆ 02 / 513 21 68
Paella, gambas, tapas, tortillas, zarzuela ....
Quality and authenticity.

Greek

Enfants du Pirée
✆ 02 / 345 97 31
A wide choice of meze and kebabs.

Supermarket Home Delivery Services

Rob
The Top Person's supermarket!
Catalogues on request
✆ 02 / 771 20 60

Quick Home Delivery
Home delivery of any product stocked by Colruyt and elsewhere. One of the least expensive. Catalogue on request.
✆ 02 / 332 19 25

Caddy Home
The leader in home supermarket shopping in Brussels. Products from Delhaize
Delivery charge: 245 bef
✆ 02 / 378 22 96

Shop Night & Day
Night-time supermarket (open from 10 a.m. until 1 a.m.)
Delivery charge : 300 bef
✆ 02 / 420 15 57

GB
http://www.ready.be
order via the Internet
Pick up yourself

Frozen Goods and Ice Cream

Ijsboerke
High-quality ice cream and all frozen goods.
✆ 014/ 55 92 11

Wine and alcohol

Two addresses which offer a vast choice of wines delivered to your home:

Le Cellier
✆ 02 / 374 85 33
Vins de Coninck
✆ 02 / 353 07 65

Flowers

Most florists will deliver. For deliveries outside Brussels or abroad, some florists use the Fleurop and Interflora services.

A must read for further information
Home Shopping
free magasine with listing of home services and different menus from restaurants with home delivery.
To receive a free copy:
fax 02 / 675 19 39
info@homeshopping.be

If you can't get out:

Fleurs Anne Duchâteau
☎ 02 / 733 50 82
☎ 0800 / 96 906
3 shops open 7 days a week,
from 8 a.m. to 8 p.m.
Credit cards accepted.
Flowers delivered anywhere in
the world.
English spoken.
http://flowers.duchateau.be

Cleaning and Laundry

De Geest
☎ 02 / 512 59 78

Top of the range dry cleaner's
for all your delicate clothes but
also offers the whole service for
moving in or moving out :
home collection and delivery of
your curtains, sofas and carpets.

Catalogue shopping

Send off for your shopping from a
catalogue and you can avoid the
rush in the shops by sitting calmly
at home choosing the items you
need …

La Redoute
BP 1
7730 Estaimpuis
☎ 02 / 217 43 10
Mainly clothes but also household
linen.

Les 3 Suisses
BP 27
7500 Tournai
☎ 02 / 218 31 60
Mainly clothes but also household
linen, furnishings and electrical goods.

Sunjets Direct
☎ 02 / 250 55 55
Just make one phone call to
receive a very full brochure for
holidays and guided tours in all
four corners of the globe.

Bookshops and Press

It is relatively easy in Brussels to find international magazines and books. International magazines are available in almost all the bigger bookshops in the neighbourhoods popular with foreigners. Foreign-language books are available in a few big bookshops including:

La Fnac – City 2
1000 Brussels
℡ 02 / 209 22 11
«European department» with books in all EU languages.

The European Bookshop
Rue de la loi, 244
1040 Brussels
℡ 02 / 231 04 35
Official agent for the publications of the European Community and the Council of Europe.
Many publications from these two organisations, as well as lots of books about Europe, tourist guides and so on.
In English, French, Dutch, Italian and German.

Press Shops
The only chain of newsagents in Belgium. It has a particularly well-stocked international section and almost all the large European institutions have a Press Shop in the building. In and around Brussels you can find a Press Shop :
• At the **airport in Zaventem** (arrivals and departures)
• In **stations:** Gare Centrale, Gare du Midi, Gare Schuman, Gare du Nord and in the Eurostar, Thalys and Quartier Léopold Stations.
• In **Shopping Centers** : Woluwé, Westland, Basilix, City 2, Cora, galeries Louise and Ottignies.
• In the **metro** : De Brouckère, Louise, Art-Loi, Porte de Namur, Schuman, Delta, Botanique, Hankar etc..
• In the **buildings of international institutions** like NATO or the European institutions in rue Belliard, rue de Beaulieu, avenue d'Auderghem etc…
• And finally in the high street of nearly every commune in and around Brussels.
To find out the address of a Press Shop near you :
℡ 02 / 422 28 11

Photos Éric de Ville

DEGAND
TAILLEUR-CHEMISIER

415, avenue Louise • 1050 Bruxelles
Tél. 02/649 00 73 • Fax 02/640 03 06
Parking privé

Press Shop

Looking for international press ?

Press Shop is the solution:

number 1 for specialist press.

Some international bookshops open on sundays:

Brussels-Ville (1000 Brussels)

Tropismes
Galerie des Princes, 11
✆ 02 / 512 88 52

Etterbeek (1040 Brussels)

Librairie Filigranes
Avenue des Arts , 38
✆ 02 / 511 90 15
Open on Sundays from 10 a.m.
to 6 p.m.

Ixelles (1050 Brussels)

Librairie de Rome
Avenue Louise, 50b
✆ 02 / 511 79 37
Open on Sundays from 8.30 a.m.
to 8.30 p.m.

La Librairie des Etangs
chaussée d'Ixelles, 319
✆ 02 / 646 90 51
Bookshop, literary meeting place,
gallery and tea room.

Candide
Place Brugmann, 1-2
✆ 02 / 344 81 94
Open on Sundays from 8 a.m.
to 7 p.m.

Woluwé (1150 Brussels)

Gavilan
Place Dumon
✆ 02 / 772 78 78
Open on Sundays from 8 a.m.
to 6 p.m.

Uccle (1180 Brussels)

l'Ecrit de St Job
place St Job, 27
✆ 02 / 374 98 16
Open on Sundays from 8.30 a.m.
to 1 p.m.

Rhode-Saint-Genèse

Librairie Centrale
Avenue de la Forêt de Soignes, 363
✆ 02 / 358 43 20
Open on Sundays from 9.30 a.m.
to 1 p.m.

Tervuren

Wittenberge
Brusselsesteenweg, 159 bte 2
✆ 02 / 767 02 07
Open on Sundays from 8.30 a.m.
to 1 p.m.

Some good addresses for second-hand books:

The Book Market
Rue de la Madeleine, 47
1000 Brussels
✆ 02 / 512 92 53

De Sleght
Lievevrouwbroersstraat, 17
1000 Brussels
✆ 02 / 511 61 40
The widest second-hand selection in 4 languages.

Community Help Services Second Hand Bookshop
At ISB
Kattenberg, 19
1170 Brussels
✆ 02 / 647 64 80

Libraries:

You will often find libraries in Consulates, cultural centres, schools, associations and clubs for foreigners. Ask around.
For children:
The Children's Library
at the Centre Crousse in Woluwe.
✆ 672 48 76
Open Wednesdays from 3 p.m. to 5 p.m. and Saturdays from 10 a.m. to 12 noon.

Specialist booksellers

English

Waterstones
Boulevard A. Max, 71
1000 Brussels
☎ 02/219 27 08
From 9 a.m. to 7 p.m.
Sundays from 12 noon
to 6 p.m.

The English Shop
Rue Stevin, 186
1000 Brussels
☎ 02/735 11 38
General store with a small
'bookshop' section.

The Irish Shop
Rue Archimède, 48
1040 Brussels
☎ 02/230 69 11
A general store with an Irish
literature department: fiction,
history, tourist guides, Celtic
art, etc.

Reading Room
Avenue G. Henri, 503
1200 Brussels
☎ 02/734 79 17
New and second-hand
books in English.

Librairie des Galeries
Galerie du Roi, 2
1000 Brussels
☎ 02/511 24 12
Specialises in art books.

Stonemanor
Steenhofstraat 28
3078 Everberg
☎ 02/759 49 79

Posada Art Books
Rue de la Madeleine, 29
1000 Brussels
☎ 02/511 08 34
Many art books in various
languages, including French,
German, Spanish, Italian and
even Chinese. New and second-hand books.

Artemys
Galerie Bortier, 8
1000 Brussels
☎ 02/512 03 47
Feminist bookshop - wide
selection of books written by
and about women.

Schlirf Books
Chaussée de Waterloo, 752
1180 Brussels
☎ 02/648 04 40
Specialises in French, English
and American comic books.

Sterling Books
Rue Fossé-aux-Loups, 38
1000 Brussels
☎ 02/223 62 23

Treasure Trove Books
Tervurenlaan, 1a
3080 Tervuren
☎ & fax 02/767 74 76
Tuesday to Friday 9 a.m. to
12.30 a.m. and 1.30 p.m. to
5.30 p.m. Saturday 9 a.m. to
12.30 a.m.

Spanish

La Tienda Latina
Avenue D. Boon, 19
1160 Brussels
☎ 02/673 34 50

Punto Y Coma
Rue Stevin, 115 a
1000 Bruxelles
☎ 02/648 04 40

Italian

Libro Italiano
Chaussée de Wavre, 354
1040 Brussels
☎ & fax 02/230 06 74
A choice of books in Italian.

Casa della cultura italiana
1st floor of the Italian
consulate
rue de Livourne, 38
1000 Brussels
☎ 02/537 19 34
An active Italian bookshop
which also serves as a meeting
place and arranges lectures.

Dutch

Standaard bookshops.
☎ 03/760 32 11

Russian

Librairie "Du Monde Entier"
Blvd A. Max, 110
1000 Brussels
☎ 02/223 15 21

German

Gutenberg Buchhandlung
Rue de Louvain, 34
1000 Brussels
☎ 02/512 45 10

Lesezeichen
Rue Vander Elst, 38
1950 Kraainem
☎ 02/784 23 34

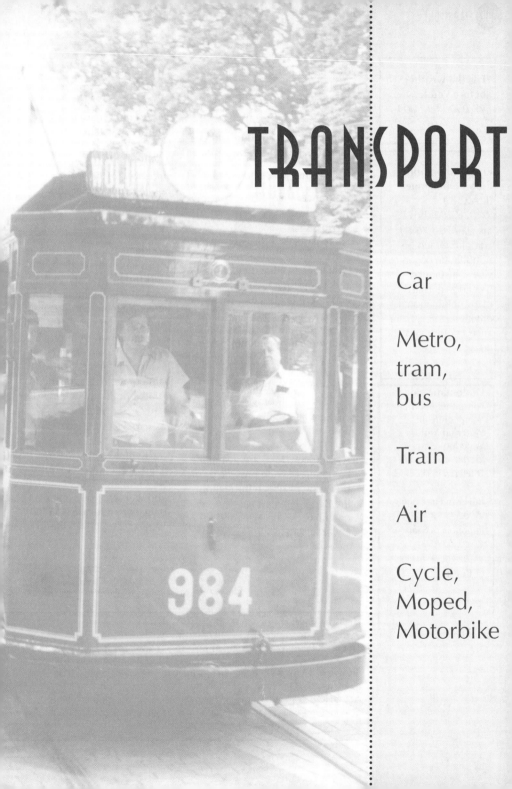

TRANSPORT

Car

Metro,
tram,
bus

Train

Air

Cycle,
Moped,
Motorbike

Car

For the weather before you leave:
℃ 0900 / 27 003

Royal Automobile Club de Belgique (R.A.C.B.)
℃ 02 / 287 09 11
fax 02 / 230 75 84
autoclub@racb.be
A multitude of services : insurance, breakdown, road maps, international driving licence, insurance, motorway stickers...

Diplomatic sales:
For further information enquire at:
Waterloo Motors à Waterloo
℃ 02 / 352 03 10
D'Ieteren in Etterbeek
℃ 02 / 743 21 21
Rover in Etterbeek
℃ 02 / 732 44 00
Importers of **Saab**
℃ 03 / 890 91 11
℃ 02 / 732 44 00
or **Rover**
℃ 02 / 732 99 11

Compared to other European capital cities, traffic is relatively free-flowing in Brussels, provided you avoid the rush hour.

Importing, registration and customs clearance: see pg. 23.

Driving licence: see pg. 24.

Insurance: v. p. 22

Buying a car:
Some garages in Brussels are « licensed for diplomatic sales » which means that they can sell cars under special conditions and at pre-tax prices. These garages act as go-between for the factory and the diplomat and you can sometimes pay in foreign currency, for example in German Marks at BMW. Some of the manufacturers' garages which provide this service are Saab , Rover , BMW and Volkswagen.

Assistance: There are insurance companies which provide a breakdown service throughout the Benelux area, and contracts can be extended to cover all of Europe.

Europe Assistance
℃ 02 / 533 75 75
fax 02 / 537 99 44
help@europ-assistance.be
Touring Assistance
℃ 02 / 233 22 11
fax 02 / 233 23 58
info@touring.be
Service Touring Secours
℃ 070 / 34 47 77
fax 02 / 253 24 35

Accidents
If you have an accident, the most usual approach is the 'constat à l'amiable' or jointly agreed statement for insurance purposes: you simply fill in the accident report form provided by your insurers on the spot. If you and the other driver cannot reach an agreement, call the police switchboard on:
℃ 02 / 517 96 11
fax 02 / 517 98 21

Car Rental
While waiting to get your own car, there are lots of companies who will rent you a car. (Belgacom directory B 6755).

Highway Code:
In Belgium, as in most European countries, you drive on the right. The rule of priority to the right always applies (except on priority roundabouts). Trams always have priority! All passengers must wear seat-belts. Children under the age of 12 must sit in the back of the car. The speed limit is 50 km/hour in town, and 120 km/hour on motorways.
ALCOHOL TEST: After just one beer, one glass of wine or one aperitif, your blood alcohol level will rise to 0.2% for a man weighing 75 kg and 0.3% for a woman weighing 60 kg. The legal limit is 0.5%!

Hertz
✆ 02 / 726 41 80
✆ 02 / 702 05 11
fax 02 / 726 46 80
Avis
✆ 02 / 730 62 11
fax 02 / 726 95 83
Service international
✆ 02 / 726 94 88
fax 02 / 726 94 88
avis@euronet.be
Rent a car
✆ 02 / 640 17 00
fax 02 / 640 82 45
Budget
✆ 02 / 646 51 30
fax 02 / 646 27 21
Keddycar & Truck Rental
✆ 02 / 725 10 40

Taxi Autoluxe
✆ 02 / 411 41 42
(They offer a 25% discount at
Zaventem provided you use the
same firm for your return).
Taxis Verts
✆ 02 / 349 49 49
Taxis Bleus
✆ 02 / 268 00 00
Taxi Orange
✆ 02 / 349 43 43
Taxis Hendriks
✆ 02 / 752 98 00
(Equipped to carry disabled passengers)
Inter Sti
✆ 02 / 736 10 30

CD-Rom of the streets of Belgium

✆ 216 91 00

Taxis

95 bef pick-up charge plus 38
bef per km in central Brussels
and the 19 communes.
Waiting time: 600 bef per hour.
This rate is doubled outside
Brussels.
No surcharge for luggage or
extra night rate.
If you are going to the airport,
remember to ask for the special
airport rate, which will cost
between 900 and 1,000 bef.
In theory, only the official airport taxis are allowed at
Zaventem. These bear an
orange windscreen sticker with
a white aeroplane.

In town, there are not many taxi
ranks, so it is better to book a
taxi by telephone.

Did you know?

Converting kilometers to miles:
60 km   = 37 miles
90 km   = 56 miles
120 km = 75 m

Road signs in Belgium are written in two languages,
French and Dutch, and the place names are often very
different from one language to the other, for instance:

FR	NL
Anvers	Antwerpen
Mons	Bergen
Namur	Namen
Rhode-Saint-Genèse	Sint-Genesius-Rode
Notre-Dame-au-Bois	Jesus-Eik
Braine-le-Château	Kasteelbrakel
Braine-le-Comte	's Gravenbrakel
Braine-l'Alleud	Eigenbrakel
Paris	Parijs
Tournai	Doornik
Lille	Rijsel

Metro, tram, bus

The services run from 5 a.m. to midnight.
The metro does not cover all the Brussels communes to the same extent. The centre is well served by the metro and the pre-metros (trams running in tunnels), but the remaining communes are served by a network of buses and trams. You can pick up a detailed map in any metro station or by telephoning the STIB on 02 / 515 20 00.

Price

- One trip: 50 bef. Tickets are valid for 1 hour and include free transfers (metro-tram-bus)
- 5 trip saver strip: 240 bef
- 10 trip saver strip: 330 bef
- One day ticket: 130 bef
- Season tickets: 1,420 bef (monthly), 14,200 bef (annual).

Reductions

- *Special MTB card*, an interesting scheme for young people (under 25) and senior citizens (over 60), at 1,010 bef per month or 10,100 bef per year. This card is on sale only in 4 metro stations: Bourse, Midi, Porte de Namur and Rogier. It gives you access to the networks of the STIB - TEC - DE LIJN and SNCB in Brussels.
- *School season ticket*
  ✆ 02 / 515 20 00
  fax 02 / 515 32 55
  For school pupils and students aged under 25. It is valid for 12 months, every day, for an unlimited number of journeys on the STIB network only.
  Normal price: 8,350 bef
  Rate for larger families (3 children or more): 4,525 bef

Sales outlets

- At metro stations: only single tickets and 5 trip saver strips.
- Sales offices in the stations at Rogier, Porte de Namur, Gare du Midi and Bourse.
- Bookshops, tobacconists: cards only.

The tickets bear a magnetic strip and must be validated every trip. They are valid for one hour and allow you to make any transfer (metro-tram-bus).

Note:
Public transport is free for children up to the age of 6.

Lost property office:
(Porte de Namur station)
✆ 02 / 515 23 94
From 10 a.m. to 1 p.m. Monday to Friday and also from 2 p.m. to 4 p.m. on Wednesdays.

ZOOM

At the invitation of the city of Brussels, some famous Belgian artists - painters and sculptors - have decorated the metro stations: they include New Fauvists, hyperrealists, action painters, futurists, etc. Why not explore them by taking a trip from Montgomery station (decorated by Folon) to Anneessens (Dotremont), via Thieffry, Botanique and Bourse, with Delvaux, Ghysels, Félix Roulin and many others.

The STIB has published a detailed, practical leaflet, available free of charge, setting out all the art works on the metro system. Also, a beautiful book entitled 'L'Art dans le métro' has been published by the Crédit Communal and can be obtained from the office at the Porte de Namur station or from the Anspach branch at Rue de l'Evêque 31, 1000 Brussels.

For further information:
STIB/ MIVB
(Société des Transports Intercommunaux de Bruxelles)
Av. de la Toison d'Or, 15
1050 Bruxelles
✆ 02 / 515 20 00
From 8 a.m. to 9 p.m. and Saturdays from 8 a.m. to 4 p.m.

If you are the victim of an attack, even a minor one, in the Brussels metro, the following is a good course of action:

- Complain in person to the metro police at the Gare du Nord.
- Report the facts to:
  Capitaine de la gendarmerie du métro station Rogier
  Boulevard Adolphe Max
  1000 Brussels.
- Copy your report to:
  Directeur général STIB
  Av. de la Toison d'or , 15
  1050 Brussels.
  or:
  Surveillance générale STIB
  Av. de la Toison d'Or, 15
  1050 Brussels

If all complaints are sent to the same bodies, they will be more effective than lots of isolated reactions.

Train

The Stations

To leave Brussels, there are four main stations: Gare Centrale, Gare du Nord, Gare du Luxembourg and Gare du Midi, which is where the high-speed trains (TGV) arrive and depart.The number to call for any timetable and ticket information is the same for all the stations:
✆ 02 / 555 25 25
fax 02 / 525 93 13

Eurostar and Thalys

Bookings and sales
✆ 0900 / 10 177
Reductions
- For children under 12.
- For senior citizens.
- Young people's rates.
- Mini rates (a quota is in force, book a month ahead!).
- Reductions for businesses.
- Lys card for frequent travellers (valid for 3 months, 6 months or 1 year). Order on:
✆ 02 / 548 06 00
fax 02 / 511 82 14
Prices are subject to change in the course of the year: for further details, ask for the Thalys or Eurostar brochure on
✆ 02 / 525 45 38
fax 02 / 525 92 57

Réductions sur le réseau SNCB

The SNCB (Belgian railways) offers families various types of special deals: reductions for larger families, weekend tickets, tourist season tickets ('B-Tourrail'), etc. They cannot be used in conjunction with each other!

Card for larger families:
Who? Families who have, or have had, at least 3 children aged under 25 can benefit from a reduction card. This is valid for life for the parents. The children can benefit from it as long as they are 'dependent'.
- Between the ages of 6 and 11, children are entitled to a 75% reduction on the entire Belgian network.
- After the age of 12, and for adults, the reduction is 50%. Children aged from 18 to 25 have to provide a school attendance certificate or a statement from the family allowance office.
How? The larger families card is available in larger stations but, for expatriates, the paperwork should be requested in advance from the Consulate of the country of origin in Brussels, on production of the official family record book.

Billet BIGE
Offers 25% reductions on travel between Belgium and abroad for young people between the ages of 12 to 26 (2nd class travel only). Valid for two months.

B-Tourrail
Tourist season tickets sold throughout the year. Offers 5 days of unlimited travel over a one-month period (Price: 2,600 bef).

Weekend Ticket

A special ticket covering return travel to and from anywhere in Belgium. Reduction of 40% for the first passenger, 60% for the 2nd to the 6th passengers. All those claiming must travel together on both the outbound and return journeys.

ZOOM Card

Preferential rates for international travellers. Travel in a group including at least one young person under the age of 16 and one adult aged over 16.
The reduction is 50% for young people aged under 16 and 25% for any adult.

50% Reduction Card

you can travel for half price for one month anywhere in Belgium (Price: 600 bef).

Ozone Card

10 trips, always between the same two stations, for the price of 6 in the summer, or 8 throughout the year.

Pass 9 +

10 journeys across Belgium for 2100 bef (2nd class). Valid from 9 a.m. in the week - anytime at weekend.

Multi Pass

For 3, 4 or a maximum of 5 people including at least one passenger aged 26 years or more. Valid for 2 months for 2 journeys throughout Belgium.
From 1,260 bef for a maximum of 3 people.

Golden Rail Pass

For senior citizens (those aged over 60) - 6 trips at 1,260 bef (2nd class travel). No restriction on time of travel.
Valid 1 year.

Go-Pass

- For young people aged 12 to 25.
- Price: 1,420 bef for 10 trips in 2nd class throughout Belgium.
- Validity: 6 months.
- Can be used every day from 8 a.m. on Saturdays, Sundays, in July and August at any time.

In the telephone directory:
Trains and stations: See under "Chemin de fer".
Aeroplanes: See in Zaventem, "Régie des Voies aériennes".

Train-Bike special:
A 615 bef ticket automatically entitles you to have a bike waiting for you at the station of your choice. Reservations and informations at stations
☎ 02 / 555 25 25
fax 02 / 525 93 13

Useful to know:
Rail travel is free for children under the age of 6 except on international journeys, when they have to pay from the age of 4.
For further details:
SNCB
(Société Nationale des Chemins de fer Belges)
rue du Progrès, 76
1210 Brussels
☎ 02 / 555 25 25
fax 02 / 525 93 13

Air

The international airport is at Zaventem, 14 km to the north-east of Brussels. The Sabena offices are located
rue du Marché-aux-Herbes, 110
1000 Brussels
© 723 23 23 or at the airport.

Getting from the airport to the centre of town. There are three options:
- Train: The journey to the Gare Centrale takes 20 minutes.There are trains departing every 20 minutes, from 5.30 a.m. to 11.45 p.m., from the station in the basement of the airport terminal.
Tickets may be purchased from 6.30 a.m. to 10 p.m.

Price: 90 bef per journey.
- Bus: The company DE LIJN. The journey to the centre of Brussels takes half an hour. Departures: On weekdays, every hour from 6.20 a.m. to 11 p.m.; at weekends, one departure every odd hour (9, 11, etc.).Price: 70 bef per journey. Tickets may be purchased from the driver.
- Taxi: The fare to the centre of Brussels will be about 1,000 bef. The time taken will depend on the traffic (normally 1 hour to 90 minutes).

Cycles, Mopeds, Motorbikes

Unfortunately, Brussels is not a very cyclist-friendly city. There are few, if any, cycle lanes. On the other hand, there are lovely cycle rides waiting to be explored in the parks on the edge of town, such as the Forêt de Soignes, which is the continuation of the Bois de la Cambre at the end of Avenue Louise, or the Parc de Tervuren, which also abuts the Forêt de Soignes a little further out of Brussels. Some useful addresses in Brussels: see the chapter "Sports", page 192.

Provélo
rue de Londres 15
1050 Brussels
© 02 / 02 73 55
© 075/ 63 11 01
fax 02 / 502 86 41

provelo@skynet.be
http://users.skynet.be/provelo
Organises guided tours both in Brussels and further afield. Theme tours: Brussels across the centuries, Art Nouveau, treasures, cafés and cartoon strips, from castles to abbeys...
Cycle rental from 100 bef per hour.

Vélo Pipette
45-47 rue de l'Hospice communal
1170 Brussels
© 02 / 672 16 98
Bike rental. Minimum 1/2 day: 300 bef
Daily from 9.30 a.m. to 1 p.m. and from 2 p.m. et 6 p.m. Closed Sunday and Monday. Saturday non stop.

Mopeds and Motorbikes

Type A Mopeds: From 16 years old, 25 km/h maximum speed, neither helmet nor licence is obligatory.
Type B Mopeds: From 16 years old, 40 km/h maximum speed, A3 driving licence (with theorical and practical exams), obligatory helmet. Non compliance will incur a fine.
Motorbikes: From 18 years old, A1 or A2 licence depending on the cubic capacity.

For car and motorcycle licences:
Auto-école européenne
Square Ambiorix , 23
1040 Brussels
© 02 / 732 60 60
© 02 / 732 40 49

LEISURE & CULTURE

Theatre

Opera

Concerts

Ballets

Cinema

Festivals

Annual Fairs,
Festivals
and Events

Brussels 200

Theatre

For up to date information on this chapter, see our website:
http://www.culture-news.com

Brussels offers a wide variety of companies and styles, from classical and avant-garde to bourgeois drama and popular farce, including the famous, typically Brussels, play 'Le Mariage de Mademoiselle Beulemans', that absolute masterpiece of Brussels humour.

The Belgian theatre-going public is famous for being a 'good audience': French plays are often tested in Brussels before being put on in Paris.

For the season' 1999-2000, the section on theatre and cinema were written with **Roger Simon's** help.

The theatres

Every theatre tends to focus more or less on one particular style of drama. Some commune theatres are particularly dynamic and present a very varied, high-quality programme. These include **the Auderghem Cultural Centre**, which has had a huge success hosting the 'Paris theatre' (ex Galas Karsenty), always features many French actors including Annie Girardot, Michel Roux, Robert Hirsch ...

This season, **the Woluwe-Saint-Pierre Cultural Centre** will be hosting among others Serge Lama , Michèle Vernier (comedian) , light opera and dance.

The Uccle Cultural Centre is repeating the big successes of the city centre including "Le diner de cons", " Le noir te va si bien " , " Danser à Lughnasa".

Théâtre du Rideau de Bruxelles (3 salles)
rue Ravenstein,23
1000 Brussels
✆ 02 / 507 83 60
fax: 02 / 507 83 63

French versions of " La Chambre Bleue " adapted from "La Ronde " by Schnitzler and " La Nuit de l'Ange" by Furio Bordon. Also includes a new interpretation of "L'Ecume des Jours " by B.Vian and " Les Miroirs

d'Ostende " by P.Willems , " O Vous , Frères Humains " by Albert Cohen and "Mémoire de l'Eau" by Shelagh Stephenson.
http://www.rideaubxl.org

Le Public
rue Braemt, 64-70
1210 Saint-Josse
✆ 0800/944 44
fax 02 / 223 29 98
http://www
The only private theatre in Brussels with 3 auditoria.

A theatre to which its creator, Michel Bogen, has applied in the cultural area all the methods learned in his job as a marketing expert: car service, baby-sitting, special rates for taxis, a restaurant tied in with the theatre (open until 1 a.m.), etc. The trend is towards the big playwrights. This season no fewer than a dozen plays based around games : of love, chess, looks, family, tricks and power -

and the playwrights : Thomas Gunzig, Beckett, Vincent Marganne, Dumas, Valérie Lemaître, Alessandro Baricco, Cormann, Dario Fo, Edward Bond, Edward Albee and Jacques Delcuvellerie . Non-numbered seating. Price: 750 bef (adults), 300 bef (students), 1,300 bef (show plus dinner) Special subscription rates for 3, 5 or 8 shows.

Le Botanique
Rue Royale, 236
1210 Brussels
☎ 02 / 218 37 32
fax 02 / 218 37 32
As well as the Season's programme, an interesting initiative: every Monday, when the other theatres are dark, Marion stages shows which have been highly successful in Brussels.

ADAC ☎ 02 / 218 27 35
The plays are staged at the Palais de Beaux-Arts (Room M), the Auditorium 44 , the Cirque Royal , the Uccle Cultural Centre , Forest National and in Charleroi. Actors include Jérôme Deschamps, Julia Migenes, Belmondo, Francis Huster , Maurice Béjart... and the 3rd Edition of " La Biennale des Francophonies Théâtrales " (Bi-annual festival of French-language theatre) which will take place at the Palais des Beaux-Arts in Brussels from 20th March to 7th April 2000. The theme will be "closeness " and the following are taking part : Switzerland, France, Canada, Réunion, Africa, Martinique and Belgium

---

'**Botanique Monday Theatre**': every Monday at 8.30 p.m. Tickets: 200 bef - reservation At 8 p.m. meet the actors in the bar at the café Théâtre.

Auditorium 44
Bld du Jardin Botanique, 44
1000 Brussels
☎ 02 / 218 27 35
fax 02 / 219 30 40
Stages mostly the productions of the ADAC.

Théâtre Varia
Rue du Sceptre, 78
1050 Brussels
☎ 02 / 640 82 58
fax 02 / 640 88 36
No light comedies, no Marivaux-style comedies of manners, but theatre based on the texts, sometimes even avant-garde. Some repeats : " Sauvés " by E.Bond , "Glenngarry Glen Ross " by D. Mamet and " Les Présidentes " by W. Schwab. Two plays by little-staged French playwrights : Jean-Luc Lagarce and Serge Valletti. New works including : "Enterrer les morts/ Réparer les vivants " (adapted from Platanov and Chekhov - Kunstenfestival des Arts and Théâtre de l'Union in Limoges) not forgetting a contemporary dance performance "Cyberchrist "/ " Pin Up " by Thierry Smits.

Théâtre de Poche
Chemin du gymnase, 1 A
1000 Brussels
☎ 02 / 649 17 27
fax 02 / 647 28 22
(in the Bois de la Cambre) With a new, more spacious hall and a 100 square-metre stage and 240 seats. The repertoire remains very strong and practically avant-garde, with plays derived direct from everyday life and which have already taken a humorous look at most of the 'hot' topics such as violence, drugs and rape. This theatre has the extraordinary advantage of having launched some of the greatest authors (Arabel, Topor, Ginsberg and others) and directors (Derek Goldby) on

the international stage. A tender and terrifying season with "Trainspotting " (repeat), " Les Independan-tristes " by Williams Sassine (a critical, uncompromising text about the daily realities of Central Africa) " Sa Majesté des Mouches" (Lord of the Flies) by William Golding (Nobel Prize for Literature 93).... And of course the eight unmissable shows of the **"Premières Rencontres"** Festival which provides us with new talent each year.

La Samaritaine
Rue de la Samaritaine, 16
1000 Brussels
☎ 02 / 511 33 95
fax 02 / 242 60 53
Featuring among others Boris Vian and Jacques Prévert. Also showing " De Gros Hommes en Jupes " and " Homme Qwet Homme ". There's no risk of getting bored at la Samaritaine thanks to compère Huguette Van Dyck and her "crazy" actors... !

Espace Catastrophe
Rue Glacière, 18
1060 Brussels
☎ 02 / 542 54 15
Spectacles de cirque, danse, musique et théâtre.

Théâtre de la Balsamine
Avenue Félix Marchal , 1
1030 Brussels
℗ 02 / 735 64 68
Concentrates on new
discoveries and explores new
forms. Supports young
companies and new works.
An alternative compared to
the classical repertory theatre. Has discovered new
dance talent (Thierry Smits).

Espace Delvaux
Place Keym
1170 Brussels
℗ 02 / 672 14 39
Basically focuses on comedy
(intelligence of laughter) and
African scenes (music, theatre, concerts, cinema, etc.)

Théâtre 140
Avenue Plasky, 140
1040 Brussels
℗ 02 / 733 97 08
fax 02 / 734 46 31
Avant-garde plays and choreography, high quality singers
and concerts.

Théâtre Poème
Rue d'Ecosse, 30
1060 Brussels
℗ 02 / 538 63 58
fax 02 / 534 58 58
Thanks to the determination
and energy of Monique
Dorsel, this two-auditoria
theatre has a loyal following
heavily into poetry.
In an intimate ambience, share
your passion for beautiful
writing over a drink or even a
meal.

Théâtre Royal de Toone
Petite rue des Bouchers, 6
1000 Brussels
℗ 02 / 513 54 86
fax 02 / 218 55 78
José Géal has taken over this
theatre and made it into one
of the most picturesque
places in Brussels.

It is thanks to him that the
tradition has been maintained
and we have such an irre-
pressibly lively Toone! Géal
selects his authors for their
great poetic qualities and
often focuses on the famous
Ghelderode, who has also
been celebrated at Villers-la-
Ville this summer. The plays
are performed by puppets
who 'speak' French, Flemish
and Brussels dialects.

Espace Senghor
Chaussée de Wavre, 366
1170 Brussels
℗ 02 / 230 29 88
fax 02 / 230 32 45
A cultural centre offering theatre, pocket opera, classical
concerts and world music,
jazz and dance.

Comédie Claude Volter
Av. des Frères Legrain, 98
1150 Brussels
℗ 02 / 762 09 63
fax 02 / 763 29 38
A selection of classical and
historical pieces in a sumptu-
ous setting. Attentive to the
defence of the French language. A contemporary
repertoire often telling of
actors' confrontations. Volter
is welcoming back
Montherlant, Guitry and
Molière and helping us
become better acquainted
with A.R.Gurney and Ira
Levin.

Théâtre La Valette
Place St Remy, 11
1460 Ittre
℗ 067 / 64 81 11
Ex-singer Léonil Mc Cormick
, now director of this
adorable little country theatre
finds himself " in two places
at once ". On stage as an
actor and in the auditorium
championing plays by Guitry,
Brian Phelan, Willy Russel
,Louis Calaferte and the
return of the "Petit Prince " by
Saint-Exupéry .
Most of the audience eat in
one of the two restaurants.

Théâtre National
Place Rogier
1000 Brussels
℗ 02 / 203 53 03
We can celebrate the renewal of director Philippe Van
Kessel's contract as he
announces a glittering season
with 20 or so very varied
shows including a revue featuring the extraordinary
Charlie Degotte ....

Théâtre Royal des Galeries
Galeries du Roi, 32
1000 Brussels
℗ 02 / 512 04 07
fax 02 / 512 60 26
Entertainment based around
comedy. A quite extraordinary satirical political review
celebrating the year 2000 .
Humourous plays by Jean
Marsan and Jean Poiret and
other plays of a very different
kind from the pens of the
prestigious names of Goethe
and Choderlos de Laclos.

Cie Yvan Baudouin-Bunton
Av. d'Auderghem, 219-221
1040 Brussels
℗ 02 / 640 27 60
Concentrates mainly on contemporary creations, with the
highlight " Ay Carmela " by
José Sanchis Sinisterra, a play

which will allow us to see once again the fascinating Lesly Bounton.

Théâtre Royal du Parc
Rue de la Loi, 3
1000 Brussels
℗ 02 / 512 48 23
fax 02 / 512 80 98
Alternates comedies and tragedies. This season: returning to its exquisite bijou residence in the rue de la Loi following the terrible fire of December 98. That is until the end of March. From April 2000 the theatre is due to be completely renovated. Yves Larec, the director is offering 5 plays written by Molière, Feydeau, Jacques De Decker, Crommelynck and Mirbeau.

Théâtre Molière
Square du Bastion, 5
1050 Brussels
℗ 02 / 513 58 00
Concentrates on comedies, amusement and derision, with plays and humorists.

Théâtre des Quat'sous
Rue de la violette, 34
1000 Brussels
℗ 02 / 512 10 22
An intimate theatre showing new works, set up 40 years ago by Roland Ravez, the current director, who also opened the Théâtre de la Poche in his day.

Théâtre Jean Vilar
à Louvain-la-Neuve
℗ 010/ 45 04 00
fax 010 / 45 32 34
Stages foreign plays or puts on his own shows. A beautiful theatre which has built itself a sound reputation beyond our borders. Armand Delcampe is celebrating the 20th anniversary of his theatre in Louvain-la-Neuve with the great success

from Villers-la-Ville " Don Juan" by Molière as well as other theatre greats including T.Williams, Mirbeau, Paul Emond, Claude d'Anna, Willy Russel, A.R.Gurney, Brian Phelan and Philippe Avron " Je suis un Saumon"...
http://europictures.com/jean-vilar

Théâtre de la Place des Martyrs
Place des Martyrs
1000 Brussels
℗ 02 / 223 32 08
fax 02 / 227 50 08
The second season for this splendid new theatre which plays host to Daniel Scahaise and his actors of the "Théâtre en Liberté ". Two venues at the Martyrs where you can applaud both actors and playwrights : L'Atelier with Thierry Debroux, Pinter, Villiers de l'Isle Adam. And the main auditorium : Shakespeare, Marivaux, Chekov, Edgar A. Poe, Labiche and Robin Maugham. A breathtaking programme of great playwrights !

Théâtre Saint-Michel
Rue Père Devroye, 2
(parking au n° 12)
1040 Brussels
℗ 02 / 734 16 65
saintmichel@hotmail.com
An entertainment and cultural venue which is just embarking on its second season. French stars who have made a name for themselves : D.Darrieux and D.Lavanant , R. Lamoureux , J. Piat , Marie-José Nat , B.P.Donnadieu and M. Vlady , M. Boujenah , B. Giraudeau and D. Sandre . And a musical based on " La Belle et la Bête " (Beauty and the Beast) ! This theatre is also staging the shows and

concerts of the Salle Henri Le Boeuf during its renovation.

Théâtre du Méridien
Chaussée de la Hulpe, 200
1170 Brussels
℗ 02 / 672 38 20
A small theatre-cum-exhibition-gallery located in beautifully restored old premises. An intimate theatre concentrating on new works and discovering young writers. An original feature is that, with every play, an artist is invited to show his or her works in the areas around the theatre space, creating a thematic link or simply a harmony between the play and the artist.

Théâtre de la Toison d'Or
Gal. de la Toison d'Or, 396-398
1050 Brussels
℗ 070 / 345 543
http://www.theatredelatoisondor.be
The Hall of Comedy with the humour of Laurence Bibot (Miss B) , Jean-Marc Favorin , Eric De Staercke and Bruno Georis , the " Witloof Cabaret" and "Un Homard , où ça ? " by S. Ministru featuring the director of this theatre , Nathalie Uffner.

Théâtre du Grand Midi
Rue Goffart, 7 A
1050 Brussels
℗ 02 / 513 21 78
fax 02 / 513 40 53
Or the " XL Théâtre " directed
by Bernard Damien who has
kept the "Lettre d'une incon-
nue " by Stefan Zweig and is
hosting a festival of accoustic
music , the Cie Coup de
Théâtre and the Collectif
Pasolini .

Théâtre de la Vie
Rue Traversière, 45
1210 Brussels
℗ 02 / 219 11 86
fax 02 / 219 22 44
Many classical plays.
A « One woman show » and
powerful texts (Brecht , Matéi
Visniec , Gombrowicz ,
P.Emond) back-to-back under
the directorship of Herbert
Rolland who is playing host
to the Théâtre de l'Est
Parisien, Henri Gougaud and
J.Beaucarne. Also featuring 4
musicians in Astor Piazzola

Théâtre du Résidence Palace
Rue de la loi, 155
1040 Brussels
℗ 02 / 231 03 05
fax 02 / 231 07 40
A magnificent theatre staging
splendid shows.

Les Balladins du Miroir
℗ 010/ 88 83 29
fax 010 / 88 03 21
A theatre company with original, high-quality shows, often
performed outdoors.

For other venues, consult the
Yellow Pages, section A 1985.

In English and Dutch

**Koninklijke Vlaamse
Schouwburg**
Rue de Laeken, 146
1000 Bruxelles
℗ 02 / 217 69 37
info@kvs.be
http://www.kvs.be
The Royal Flemish Theatre
aims to bring to Brussels theatre productions from the
Member States of the
European Union, including
some plays in English which
you might have to wait 6
months to see in London!
Plays in various languages,
including English.
Reservations by telephone
from 12 noon to 7 p.m.
Monday to Friday and from 3
p.m. to 7 p.m. Saturday.

**The American Theatre
Company**
Founded 30 years ago for the
American community in
Brussels. Plays by American
playwrights. Staging a musi-
cal in November 99 : "Annie
Get Your Gun".
For further information :
℗ 02 / 734 33 53

Two theatres focusing on ballet and concerts:

Luna Théâtre
Place Sainctelette, 20
1000 Brussels
℗ 02 / 201 09 15
fax 02 / 203 02 26

Studio du Kaaithéâtre
Rue N.-D.-du-Sommeil, 81
1000 Brussels
℗ 02 / 201 59 59

The relevant **cultural
centres** (see pg. 54) will
advise on shows,
concerts and plays.

The European Theatre Convention has launched a new
programme called "**European Theatre Audience**" which
offers all subscription holders of each member theatre a
permanent invitation to the other 31 European institutions.

For example, if you have a subscription to the Théâtre
National or the Koninklijke Vlaamse Schouwburg in
Belgium, both of which are members of this convention
you can see any show free of charge in any other memb
theatre in Paris, Bologna, Madrid, Thessalonika etc...

For further information : ℗ 02 / 223 23 33

Saab vs. Parenthood

The individual becomes a parent. The parent requires a new car to satisfy the needs of the child. The pure joy of driving is sacrificed for space and safety. But what if the car is a Saab 9-5 Estate? With five separate storage compartments for a child's playthings. Antisubmarining seats designed to prevent children from sliding under seat belts. And, what's this? A turbocharged engine. Perhaps one car can accommodate both the child and the individual who becomes a parent.

ase visit our website http://www.saabids.com

EHERMAN BRUSSELS	BEHERMAN WOLUWE	AMBROSIO	GILCON	CLEMENT
avenue Louise 233	Leuvensesteenweg 319	ch. de Nivelles 3	Geldenaaksebaan 454	Lakensestraat 118
1050 Bruxelles	1932 St-Stevens-Woluwe	1420 Braine L'Alleud	3001 Heverlee	1853 Strombeek-Bever
Tel.: 02/640.00.87	Tel.: 02/725.43.50	Tel.: 02/385.05.64	Tel.: 016/40.03.27	Tel.: 02/267.17.75
Fax: 02/640.41.10	Fax: 02/725.41.02	Fax: 02/385.06.17	Fax: 016/40.02.48	Fax: 02/267.47.11

ALREADY IMPRESSED?

BUT YOU'VE SEEN NOTHING YET!

There's no doubt about it. Her line
Sublime. She appears and you're eag
know more. Her interior is charm i
and as for her comfort... words fail
But beneath her seductive exterior,
Rover 75 hides masses of innovatior
that you just wouldn't have imagine
New V6 petrol and common rail tu
diesel engines. 5-speed manual and a
matic transmissions. A revolutionar
Z-axle suspension and unique front v
drive. An extremely high resistance
passenger cabin. One thing is for su
without all this, the Rover 75 woule
just another luxury saloon.

It'll change the way you look at luxury saloons.

R O V E R

Opera

In Belgium, opera lovers can consider themselves spoilt because, for such a relatively small country, it has no less than three companies dedicated to the lyrical arts.

Théâtre de la Monnaie
place de la Monnaie
1000 Brussels
✆ 070 / 233 939
Performances at 12.30 p.m., 3 p.m. and 8 p.m.
This season's event: world creation (10 december 1999), **Wintermärchen** of Philippe Boesmans (music) and Luc Bondy (booklet) from Shakespeare's Wintertale. Also: Mozart's **"The rescue from the Harem"**, Händel's **Agrippina** and Puccini's **Tosca** all three in new productions.

Opéra de Flandre
Frankrijklei 3
2000 Anvers
✆ 03 / 233 66 85
Shouwburgstraat 3
9000 Gand
✆ 09 / 225 24 25
All the performances are presented in rotation at Ghent and Antwerp. Don't forget that this season sees some promising new versions of **Jenufa** by **Janacek** and **Hoffman's Tales** by **Offenbach.**

Opéra Royal de Wallonie
Rue des Dominicains 1
4000 Liège
✆ 04 / 221 47 22
Philippe Sireuil stages **Lulu** by Alban Berg. And for the first time in Belgium, one of Rossini's master piece: **Le Voyage à Reims**.

The sections on opera ands concerts have been produced with **Marcel Croës'** help. Croës presents a daily programme on cinema for Canal + Belgium. He is also the opera critic for the English weekly magazine The Bulletin and a free lance for France Culture and several other french and belgian publications.

How to book?
1. **Telephone** the box office at the venue. You may pay by bank card (Visa, etc.) or by bank transfer. Pick up your tickets when you arrive.
2. **Telephone the FNAC:** ✆ 0900 / 00600 to pay by bank card, and pick up your tickets from the FNAC shop in City 2, Rue Neuve, 1000 Brussels (Monday to Saturday from 10 a.m. to 7 p.m., Friday until 8 p.m.)
3. **Booking Office at the TIB:** on ✆ 0800 / 21 221 at the town hall on the Grand Place (open from 11 a.m. to 5 p.m.). A central booking service for all shows in Brussels, Liège and Antwerp.
4. **Connecticket:** ✆ 070/ 345 543 – central reservation for numerous shows in Belgium.
5. **Internet:** for details of venues with a web page, consult our Internet site: http://www.expats-in-brussels.com.
6. **By subscription.** Most theatres offer subscription arrangements. Call them for details and ask them to send you their annual programme.

Concerts

Jazz:
Jazz lovers who are already familiar with Belgian jazz legends such as Toots Thielemans or Philip Catherine will not be disappointed in Brussels. In addition to the Jazz Marathon, which invades the cafés on the last weekend in May, Brussels hosts two jazz festivals, one in the middle of July at the open-air theatre at the foot of the Atomium, and one in October, the 'Belga Jazz Festival'. To find out the addresses of jazz clubs in Brussels, see the chapter on 'Going out and Having Fun', pg. 67.

For theatre festivals please refer to pg. 166.

Brussels enjoys an exceptionally dynamic life in musical terms. The concerts held here are of high quality, and there are lots of varied festivals as well as prestigious events, such as the Queen Elisabeth competition, which strengthen Belgium's reputation in this field.

The main themes of the season:
- celebration of the 250 th anniversary of Bach's death, including his four most famous religious works and his entire concertos for harpsichord.
- 75 years of Pierre Boulez: 4 concerts conducting the London Symphony Orchestra
- hommage to Olivier Messiaen, which culminates with a version of his only opera, St. Francis of Assisi, never before seen in Belgium.

Ars Musica
A festival known throughout Europe. It's become a must for all lovers of contempory music. 18 days with the unique possibility of hearing the masterpieces of the "greats" of 20th century music as well as those inventing the sounds of the next millenium. The fastival takes place in a variety of locations both traditional and unusual: TRM, Palais des Beaux-Arts, Maison de la Bellone etc.
du 16 mars au 1er avril 2000
✆ 02 / 219 29 60

Not to be missed
Concerts of the Astoria
Every Sunday at 11 o'clock from September to June, music lovers meet in this stunning "belle époque" building to savour chamber music in a warm and friendly atmosphere
Hôtel Astoria
Rue Royale 103 – 1000 Bruxelles
Renseignements à la Boîte à Musique:
✆ 02 / 513 09 65

Where to find the programmes?
- **KIOSQUE**: on sale in bookshops (or write to Avenue Coghen 119, 1180 Brussels) This monthly publication gives good information on all the shows, the 'in' bars and restaurants, the coolest night spots, etc.
- **PARK MAIL POCKET**: on sale in bookshops. Comes out every month, and carries good information on cinemas, theatre, concerts, exhibitions and eating out.
- **MAD** supplement to Le Soir on Wednesdays carries the full programme of all cultural events.
- **Libre Culture**, in La Libre Belgique on Fridays.
- The **WHAT'S ON** supplement in the Bulletin, the English magazine issued every Wednesday. This will provide you with comprehensive details of the week's events.
- The programmes (theatre, concerts, shows and ballets) issued by the **TIB**, the **OPT** and the **VGGT** (adresses pg. 9).

Palais des Beaux-Arts
Rue Ravenstein, 23
1000 Brussels
✆ 02 / 507 82 00
The main hall dedicated to symphonic concerts, is closed for remodeling until April 2000, but the chamber music hall hosts smaller ensembles and recitals.

Théâtre Saint-Michel
Rue Père Eudore Devroye, 2
1040 Brussels
✆ 02 / 507 82 00
A fine theatre in the art deco style, recently restored. Room for 1500 and with impeccable accoustic

Conservatoire Royal de Musique
Rue de la Régence, 30
1000 Brussels
✆ 02 / 511 04 27
A high temple of musical life in Brussels, the Conservatoire was built in the early 19th century. Regular concerts and recitals. Location for the first rounds of the Concours Queen Elisabeth.

Cirque Royal
Rue de l'Enseignement, 81
1000 Brussels
✆ 02 / 218 20 15
A wide program with some musical shows and operas (this season: Carmen)

Halles de Schaerbeek
Rue de la Constitution 20
1030 Brussels
✆ 02 / 227 59 60
In one of the last remnants of industrial architecture are staged opera out the ordinary and contemporary musical shows.

Botanique
Rue Royale , 236
1210 Brussels
✆ 02 / 218 37 32
fax 02 / 219 66 60
A fascinating place located in the greenhouse and halls of the former Botanical gardens. Open to all kinds of music and, among others, some concerts of the Ars Musica Festival.

Lunatheater
Square Sainctelette 20
1000 Brussels
✆ 02 / 201 59 59
A gem of thirties modernist architecture. Concerts held here include light opera and contempory music.

Concerts are also held in some churches. Here are a few of them:

Eglise des Brigittines
Rue des Visitandines, 1
1000 Brussels
✆ 02 / 506 43 00
fax 02 / 503 12 00

Eglise des Minimes
Rue des Minimes, 62
1000 Brussels
✆ 02 / 519 78 99

Cathédrale Saint-Michel et Gudule
Parvis Sainte Gudule
1000 Brussels
✆ 02 / 217 83 45

Ballet

Brussels is an extraordinarily fertile city for dance, and has seen the emergence of directors with an international reputation: Béjart and his Ballet of the 20th Century settled at the Théâtre Royal de la Monnaie back in 1960 and, even then, were the pride of Belgium. Nowadays, the choreographer in residence at the Monnaie is the talented Anna Teresa de Keersmaeker with the company Rosas.

The Cinema

Brussels boasts more cinemas per square metre (and better ones!) than anywhere else in Europe. We inspired the restoration of cinemas in Europe with the construction of the Kinépolis complex of 24 screens up at Bruparck.

The cinemas are basically located in three areas:
• The centre of town, on the Place de Brouckère.
• The uptown area, along the Avenue de la Toison d'Or.
• Kinépolis at Bruparck.

L'Arenberg-Galeries
Galerie de la Reine, 26
1000 Brussels
✆ *0900/27 865*
Features authors as well as new actors and directors to discover for all you movie buffs. Surprise film every Thursday at 9.30 p.m. The 'Ecran Total' festival in summer, showing 57 films often masterpieces, at a rate of 8 films per day for two months. This is Belgium's largest film festival. Publishes a magazine called 'Cinédit' devoted to the cinema.

L'UGC De Brouckère
Place de Brouckère
1000 Brussels
✆ *0900/10 440 (French)*
✆ *0900/10 450 (Dutch)*
10 screens. UGC card offering special rates and benefits. Shows a pre-release. **Midnight Screening'** every Saturday.

Le Vendôme
Chaussée de Wavre, 18
1050 Brussels
✆ *02/502 37 00*
(from 2 p.m.)
A movie devotee's cinema with a high quality programme. All films are shown in their original version, with bilingual sub-titles. Loyalty card entitles you to see one free film for every ten you pay for. Festival of foreign films.

L'UGC Toison d'Or
Avenue de la Toison d'Or
1050 Brussels
✆ *0900/10 440 (French)*
✆ *0900/10 450 (Dutch)*
10 screens. UGC card offering special rates and benefits. The '**Petits déjeuners du cinéma**' at 10 a.m. on Sundays: a recent release plus coffee and croissants for 240 bef.

Le Styx
Rue de l'Arbre Bénit, 72
1050 Brussels
✆ *0900/27 854*
and the **Actor's Studio**
Petite rue des Bouchers, 16
1000 Brussels
✆ *0900/29 969*
Very high-quality programmes. Shows some interesting repeats and retrospectives.

Kinépolis - Bruparck (Heysel)
✆ *0900/35 241 (French)*
✆ *0900/35 240 (Dutch)*
24 screens. Many American blockbusters but also some French films. Imax cinema featuring a giant 22 metre high screen, currently showing the magnificent film 'Everest'.

L'Aventure
Galerie du Centre, 57
1000 Brussels
✆ *219 17 48*
Programme of 16 different major films a week on three screens.

Le Nova
Rue d'Arenberg, 3
1000 Brussels
✆ *02/511 27 74*
Very special showings with, not only films, but also concerts and plays. Read the programme very carefully!

Local cinemas

Le Movy-Club
Rue des Moines, 21
1190 à Brussels
✆ *02/537 69 54*
A lovely cinema dating back to 1934, with one cinema-lover. Shows 9 films a week! Access for the disabled.

Le Stockel
Place Dumon
1150 Brussels
✆ *02/779 10 79*
A nice neighbourhood cinema in Stockel, showing the same films as in the centre of Brussels.

Outskirts of Brussels:

Imagibraine
Boulevard de France
1420 Braine l'Alleud
✆ *02/389 17 17*
A brand new 10-screen complex.

Le Wellington
Chaussée de Bruxelles 135
1410 Waterloo
✆ *02/354 93 59*
Local cinema with a good selection of recent films.

Le Ciné Centre
Avenue de Mérode, 91
1330 Rixensart
✆ *653 94 45*
A cinema in the Brabant Wallon area which offers exclusive screenings and recent releases at the same time as Brussels.

For cinema fans:

At the **Musée du Cinéma** (Palais des Beaux-Arts) you have the chance to see or re-see original subtitled versions of the great classics or films which are rarely shown. Daily presentation of two great 'talkies' and two great 'silent movies'.
Rue Baron Horta, 9
1000 Brussels
✆ 02 / 507 83 70
fax 02 / 513 12 72

At the **Centre Jacques Franck**, you can see retrospectives of contemporary cinema.
Chaussée de Waterloo, 94
1060 Brussels
✆ 02 / 538 90 29
fax 02 / 538 16 48

The Drive-In in summer:
At the Cinquantenaire: films shown on a giant screen (375 square metres) in the open air. Every Friday and Saturday throughout July and August. Doors open at 8 p.m., screenings at 10.30 p.m. in July, 10 p.m. in August Price: 500 bef per car, 150 bef per pedestrian (seating provided) and 250 bef per 'old-timer' cars aged over 25 (don't forget the greycard!)
✆ 0900 / 20 745 (in summer)

La Nuit des publivores
A whole night to admire the year's best advertising films.
Venue: UGC Acropole.
Date: early November.
Price: 850 bef on sale in advance on the door or at the FNAC.

Did you know?

1. Cinema seats are cheaper on Mondays!
2. New films come out on Wednesdays!
3. In Brussels, films are generally shown in their original version (VO) with bilingual subtitles (French and Flemish)
4. There are reductions for students and senior citizens.

Where to find the programmes ?

• In all the dailies, including the supplements in Le Soir (Mad), La Libre Belgique (La Libre Cinéma) on Wednesday and the Bulletin (What's On).
• In the monthly listings magazines on sale in bookshops: Park-Mail Pocket and Kiosque. For reviews: the magazine Première.

For film festivals please refer to pg 164

Useful abbreviations:
VO: original version.
ENA: children not admitted.
EA: children admitted.
S: showing.

Festivals

Theatre festivals

• **Festival of Young Performers** takes place every year from 18th to 28th August at the Samaritaine, rue de la Samaritaine, 16- 1000 Brussels, giving young performers with budding talent the chance to perform in front of a real audience. Song and theatre.

• **Festival of French-language Theatre in Spa** from 4th to 21st August. 120 performances on offer. A good way to see plays from the previous season as well as discovering new ones.
℡ 087 / 79 53 53
fax 087 / 79 53 54

• **«Les Journées du Théâtre» Festival** at the end of May in Ittre.
℡ 067 / 64 81 11

• **Holiday Theatre Festival Stavelot** from 9th to 20th July at the Ancienne Abbaye and the Salle du Versailles . Twenty or more shows from a variety of sources.

• **Impromptu Festival** from 2nd July to 1st August at the Château de Modave (Huy). Theatre and cabaret.

Music Festivals

• **Summer Festival of the City of Brussels** – from 3rd July to 31st August. Classical concerts, jazz, traditional and film music performed at the Grand'Place, the Hôtel de Ville, the Conservatoire, the Solvay Library, the Minimes Church. With the participation of the big symphony orchestras and big name performers.

• **Festival of Minimes Noon Concerts,** from 1st July to 27th August in the Minimes church, 62 rue des Minimes and at the Conservatoire, 30 rue de la Régence. Free concerts of chamber music, foreign music, piano, ancient instruments, XXth century music etc...

• **Light opera at the Château de La Hulpe** at the end of August with the participation of national opera orchestras and a large number of performers.

• **Beloeil Nights** at the beginning of August every year with musical evenings in a charming atmosphere.

• **Festival of Flanders** from April to October in Flanders and Brussels.

• **Festival of Wallonia** from June to October in Wallonia and Brussels.
Two festivals of international fame : concerts and recitals in churches, châteaux and other prestigious sites around the country with the participation of leading orchestras and world-class soloists.
Info : TIB : 02/ 513 89 40.
✆ *02 / 513 89 40*

• **Musical Sundays** from the end of June to the beginning of October in the Saint-Michel Cathedral in Brussels.
Polyphonic masses and motets sung by choirs from Belgium and abroad. Gregorian chants. Music from Burundi. Great composers like Stravinky, Palestrina, Mozart, Bruckner, Lassus...

• **Sunday concerts in the Bois de la Cambre** in July and August on the English Lawn between the skating rink and the restaurant "Les Jardins du Bois ". A programme featuring both classical and jazz music.

• **" Ars Musica " festival** from 16th March to 2nd April 2000 at the Palais des Beaux-Arts, the Maison de la Bellone, the TRM, the Conservatoire and in various churches. Contemporary music with a large number of performers including some of the biggest international names.

• **Rock Festival Lucky Town** in September.

• **" Couleur Café " Festival** in June in the former customs warehouses known as " Tours et Taxis " featuring musicians from all over the world.

• **Festival of Women's Voices** at the Halles de Schaerbeek from 6th to 15th April 2000. Modern folk music.

Dance, Music, Theatre and Circus festivals

• **Festival " C'est du jamais vu "** from 3rd to 12th September at the 'Espace Catastrophe with previews of circus, dance, music and theatre shows.

• **International Festival of Circus Schools** at the Halles de Schaerbeek from 25th May to 4th June 2000 (Brussels, France, Montreal and London).

• **International Festival of Hip Hop Culture and Urban Art** also at the Halles de Schaerbeek from 22nd to 26th March 2000. A multi-discipline festival which aims to highlight the vitality and artistic exhuberance of the Brussels cultural scene offering theatre, dance and music. Part of Brussels 2000.

• **Bellone Brigittines Festival** from 22 nd August to 4th September at the Chapelle des Brigittines, Petite rue des Brigittines in Brussels. A blend of theatre, dance and other forms of contemporary expression with appearances by groups from European countries or, further afield, as was the case in '99 with Hungary and Japan.

Film Festivals

In Brussels

• **Brussels International Film Festival** From 19th to 29th January 2000 in the renovated Pathé-Palace (Bourse) now the Kladaradatsch Palace Cinema as well as in the UGC complex in the place de Brouckère.

• **International Festival of Science Fiction and Fantasy Films** at Auditorium 44 from 29th February to 11th March 2000. A festival which is not to be missed for its film previews.

• **International Festival of Cartoons and Animated Films** from 29th February to 11th March 2000 in Auditorium 44.

• **Summer Festival " Ecran Total "** from 30th June to 14th September at the Arenberg - Galeries cinema in the Galeries Saint-Hubert, near the Grand Place. Fifty or more films, repeats or first-showing with a system of repetitive projection. This festival is for film buffs and anyone who likes cinema.

• **Drive-In Movies** from the beginning of July to the end of August, every Saturday and Sunday in the Parc du Cinquantenaire showing highly successful first rate films.

• The Cinema Museum organises **" Les Cinédécouvertes / Prix de l'Âge d'Or"** every year from 1st to 15th July. Twenty or so new films selected from the recent festivals of Cannes, Rotterdam, Berlin, Toronto etc. It is a way of supporting little known films of considerable interest.

• **Biannual Italian Cinema Festival** in November at the Italian Consulate, rue de Livourne in Brussels.

• **Valvert Nature Film Festival** in October at the Auditorium 44.

• **Spanish Film Festival** at the Cervantes Centre, avenue de Tervuren in Brussels.

• **Iberian Film Festival** in November at the Vendôme cinema, chaussée de Wavre in Brussels.

• **Mediterranean Film Festival** in November at various venues in Brussels.

In the provinces

- **Festival of Love Films**
February in Mons.

- **French-language Film Festival**
September in Namur.

- **International Film Festival**
November in Ghent.

Our cultural web-site :
http://www.culture-news.com

A very pleasant tradition for anyone who has a little time to spare at midday : noon cultural events

Music: Les Midis de la Musique Les Midis de la Musique in Brussels in the auditorium of the Museum of Ancient Art from 12.40 p.m. to 1.30 p.m.
✆ 02 / 512 82 47
Les Midis – Minimes à l'Eglise des Minimes tous les jours en été de 12h45 à 13h30
✆ 02 / 519 78 99
Poetry: Les Midis de la Poésie in the auditorium of the Museum of Ancient Art on Tuesdays from 12.40 p.m. to 1.30 p.m.
✆ 02 / 513 88 26
Cinema: : Midis du cinéma in the auditorium of the Museum of Ancient Art on Thursdays at 12.30 p.m.
✆ 02 / 673 41 07
Jazz: Midis-Jazz at the Charlier Museum from 12.30 p.m. to 1.30 p.m.
✆ 02 / 218 53 82
Literature: Les Coups de midi des Riches Claire one Wednesday in the month at 12.30 p.m.
✆ 02 / 512 95 69

Annual Fairs, Festivals and Events

For precise dates:
MAD supplement in Wednesday's *Le Soir* newspaper or **La Libre Culture** in Friday's *La Libre Belgique* and *«What's on»* in the *"Bulletin"*

The Royal Greenhouses in Laeken
✆ *02 / 504 03 90*
✆ *02 / 513 89 40*
Open for 15 days in May. A veritable town of glass and metal, housing an impressive tropical forest of coconut palms and giant palm trees, with glass-bordered paths, hung with azaleas, hydrangeas and fuchias of every hue.

January	Brussels International Film Festival (Pathé Palace & UGC De Brouckère)
January (every 2nd year)	Motor Show
February	International Festival of Science Fiction and Fantasy Films.
March	Eurantica (Antiques fair), Heisel.
March	International Tourism and Leisure Fair, Heisel.
March	Ars Musica (contemporary music festival), Palais des Beaux-Arts.
March	International Book Fair, Palais des Congrès.
April	Fête de l'Iris (City of Brussels Festival).
April	Opening of the Royal Greenhouses in Laeken.
April (even years)	Artists parade in Saint-Gilles (15 or so workshops open).
End of April	Les printemps baroques du Sablon. Concerts in the district's galleries and houses.
May	Queen Elisabeth Music Competition (alternately piano, violin and singing).
May	The Brussels 20 kilometre Race.
May	Arts Festival all over Brussels.
May	Jazz Marathon.
June (every 5 years)	Reconstruction of the Battle of Waterloo on the actual site.
June	Classical music concerts in the Grand Place.
June	Floral exhibition at the Botanical garden.
July	Ommegang (commemorating the joyful entry of Charles V and his court into Brussels, in costume, on the Grand Place).
July	Jazz festival at the open-air theatre at the foot of the Atomium.
July	Foire du Midi (the biggest funfair in Brussels).
July	Sunday concerts at the Bois de la Cambre (classical concerts).
Summer	Festivals of Flanders and of Wallonia. Information from TIB – ✆ 513 89 40.
August	Floral carpet on the Grand Place.
September	Les Nuits du Botanique (a festival of rock, jazz, rap, etc.)
September	Heritage Day (places normally inaccessible are opened to the public).
16/10/98 to 17/01/99	Europalia: A programme of concerts and exhibitions on a different country every two years. Theme for 1999: Hungary.
October	Belga Jazz Festival.
25th,26th, 27th November	Nocturnes du Sablon.
November	Biennial of Italian Cinema (Italian Consulate).
December	Christmas Market. (stalls from all countries).

Brussels 2000

Brussels is « European City of Culture » for the year 2000. For this highly symbolic year no fewer than nine cities have been chosen: Brussels, Avignon, Bologna, Santiago de Compostela, Prague, Krakow, Bergen, Helsinki and Reykjavik.

The Brussels 2000 team has chosen « The City» as its central theme. A number of development and renovation projects will be completed for the occasion giving both inhabitants and visitors the opportunity to see the city in a new light. A variety of artistic shows will flourish all through the year bathing the city of Brussels in an exceptional light.

We have drawn up a calendar of some of the major events taken from the three hundred or so projects of all kinds organised by more than five hundred cultural partnerships.

From 25th to 27th February 2000
Opening weekend of Brussels 2000
The spotlights will be aimed at a whole range of new or renovated cultural infrastructures and in the evening they will make way for the new creations : the new choreography by William Forsythe performed by the Frankfurt Ballet at the Théâtre de la Monnaie ; the latest Feria-Musica ; the search for the « new Brussels review by Charlie Degotte at the Théâtre National ; the multi-media Opera show from New York company, The Builers

Association, in partnership with the Kaaitheater ; and finally Théâtre 140 inviting the Ballets C de la B with the appearance of Hans Van Den Broeck. Not forgetting the private viewing of the exhibition « The City through Literature » in the Vanderborght building.
On Saturday and Sunday there will be a real urban happening, a mixture of music, new media, dance etc…

23-24th March 2000
Yanus - Twelve world music creations
At the Botannique
Music
The concept of European City of Culture aims among other things to provide a platform for contemporary European culture. Here, four European countries have come together to provide twelve world music creations in the context of Ars Musica. This European project brings together young composers from France, Italy, Spain and Belgium to offer us an early taste of their new compositions.

From March to September 2000
Modern Ball
In each of the 19 communes
Dance
Every Friday evening, one of the 19 communes will put on a new style ball. During a forty-five minute session, three choreographers will teach you a short dance. Everyone can take part, even those who feel that dance is not really their forte.

If you want to find out more :
www.brussels2000.org
✆ 02/214 20 00
Fax : 02/214 20 20

An original way of showing you how choreographers put their work into practice.

From 5th to 15th April 2000
Brussels, City of Africa
Palais des Beaux-Arts Info & reservations : 02/507 82 00
Theatre
This show provides us with a chance to explore the Congo and find out more about the history of its relationship with Belgium in the form of an imaginary guided tour of Brussels through its colonial architecture. The director, Virginie Jortay invites us to "follow a theatrical guided tour through time, space and ideas : from the founding of the Independent State of Congo to the Turkish operation via the exploitation of red rubber and the war effort, a criss-cross route where nothing is either black or white."

From 15th to 18th April 2000
Boulez 2000
Palais des Beaux-Arts & Kuntstencentrum de Siingel Antwerp Info : 02/511 34 33
Music
Pierre Boulez will present two recent works: *Sur Incises and Originel(Explosante-Fixe)* . He will also conduct four concerts at the head of the London Symphony Orchestra..

From 17th May to 15th November 2000
Tour of sculpted retables with painted screens (XVth and XVIth centuries)
Museum of the City of Brussels « Maison du roi » ; cathedral of Saints Michel and Gudule ;

Royal Museums of Art and History; Royal Museums of Fine Arts of Belgium; Museum of the CPAS of Brussels ; Saint–Adrien Church in Ixelles.
Cultural tour
This original tour allows the general public to explore « in situ » Brabançon sculpted retables with painted screens. This heritage owes its artistic success to the great mastery of craftsmanship, the popular taste shown in the details and a rich polychromy which is quite extraordinary. The accent will be placed on the techniques of creating retables and the history of the materials.

From 17th May to 20th September 2000
The golden age of Brussels : tapestries of the Spanish Crown
Cathedral of Saints Michel and Gudule
Exhibition
The art of tapestry reached its height in Brussels from the end of the XVth to the middle of the XVIth century. At the time, tapestries were closely associated with big events and festivals, decorating the most prestigious churches on the days of great celebrations. This exhibition aims to recreate this festive sight by displaying the tapestries of the Spanish crown against the impressive backdrop of the Cathedral of Saints Michel and Gudule, finally restored to its original splendour.

From 25th May 2000 to 7th October 2000
Festina Lente
Erasmus House
Exhibition in a garden
The Erasmus adage " Festina lente" has inspired the Belgian artist Patrick Corillon with the idea of creating a garden of slowness in the Erasmus House Museum. The idea is to create a philosophical garden intended, according to Erasmus, to make the visitor « humaniores » more human. As he strolls around he comes across a sculpture, a painting, a poem which makes him stop and think. Next to this philosophical garden a « sickness garden » has been created where all the plants used by Erasmus' doctors have been identified and compared. The idea is to build up a botanical portrait of the illnesses he suffered from or thought he suffered from. The medicinal plants are grouped together in squares, each one devoted to a specific illness. The two sections aim to reflect the intimate being of Erasmus, body and soul.

27th May
La Zinneke
All over Brussels
Parade
At first "zinneke" was simply another word for « Brussels-born » as well as meaning a mongrel dog. Over time this typically Brussels word has become to mean more generally anything which is « bastard, hybrid, from Brussels ». With its carnival-style parade and artistic procession, the parade will symbolise the culturally mixed blood of

Brussels life, both cosmopolitan and different.
Trained by choreographers, musicians and scenographers, five processions of floats will pass through five imaginary gates and converge on the city centre.

From 4th to 10th June 2000
The Great Sablon Carousel
Caserne Albert, rue du Pépin
Open air show
The Great Sablon Carousel is a « genuine baroque piece». The show, comprising traditional equestrian games integrated into an original scenario with the theme of « Europe at peace » will unite horses and riders, jugglers, acrobats, falconers and people on stilts. Inspired by the formal way equestrian carousels of the XVIIth and XVIIIth centuries were organised, the show is based on Zeus' mythological abductions and traces the quest for a Europe at peace. The music is taken from the operas and motets of Jean-Philippe Rameau.

From 4th July to 30th September 2000
« We are so happy »
Public areas around Brussels
Photography
One hundred images of happiness from the archives of, among others, the Magnum agency, will take over the city. These snaps will cover the façades of public or private buildings and transform the city into a gigantic open air museum of photography during summer 2000.

September 2000
The Invention of Brussels
In cinemas and on television
Cinema
A number of foreign film-makers –from a whole variety of cinema cultures – will each tell of how they discovered the city in a 10 minute long fictional film. One way for us to rediscover Brussels through the eyes of outsiders.

From 16th to 23rd September 2000
Heritage day / Metamorphoses
Various Brussels heritage sites
For the first time this already very popular event will put on a whole range of new contemporary creations in the fields of dance, music, plastic arts and theatre at twenty or so sites. A contrast which will help the general public see Brussels architecture in a new light.

18th October 2000 to 18th October 2001
Hidden Friends
Royal Institute of Natural Science of Belgium
Interactive Exhibition. Aimed at the young.
This educational exhibition shows how the city, despite being highly urbanised, harbours a surprising range of animal life. Like a huge interactive space for discovery and games it will combine imagination, fantasy and theory. A « sound landscape » based on the sounds of the city will be created by composers and musicians.

From the Fables of La Fontaine to the poems of Robert Desnos via Indian legends, fairy tales and animal stories will greet the visitors through the voices of professional storytellers. Guided tours given by young people from the area, audio guide and catalogue.

From 21st to 29th October 2000
Science Festival
ULB-VUB
Interactive exhibition
A science pavilion will be open to the public, dominating the XIXth century ice-houses on the VUB campus in Etterbeek. Interactive and multimedia displays will allow visitors to discover through games and experiments the impact of science on (city) life.

From 23rd November 2000 to 28th January 2001
Voici - 100 years of contemporary art
Palais des Beaux-Arts
Exhibition
The Voici exhibition is devoted to modern and contemporary art. It invites us to view over one hundred and fifty works chosen for their quality and the way they interact with each other.

ART AND THE ART MARKET

Museums

Antiques

Art galleries

Salerooms

Art Experts

Restoration

Second-hand
Dealers

Museums

Brussels has over one hundred museums dealing with every subject imaginable, from the classics, like paintings and antiques to folklore, not forgetting beer and comic strips.

The main ones are the **Museum of Central Africa in Tervuren**, the **Museum of Ancient Art**, rue de la Régence, the **Museum of Modern Art**, the **Museum of Art and History**, at the Cinquantenaire, the **Maison du Roi**, on the Grand-Place, the **Army Museum**, at the Cinquantenaire, the **Planetarium** in Uccle and **the Albertine**, on the Mont des Arts, which groups together the National Archives, the Nassau Chapel and other institutions linked to the world of paper. Information on all these museums can easily be found in newspapers or tourist guides.

However it is more difficult to find out about local museums, run by the smaller communes in the Brussels Region, devoted to one specialist subject or one individual. We aim to tell you about some of them.

This chapter was written with the help of **Philippe Fancy**, a specialist of the art world and a journalist with *La Libre Belgique*.

Guidebook
Muser à Bruxelles,
published by Le Cri
✆ 010 / 42 03 20
which contains
a full list

Guillaume Charlier Museum
avenue des Arts, 16
1040 Saint-Josse
✆ 02 / 218 53 82
Superb collections of works of art from the end of the XIXth and beginning of the XXth centuries.

Saint-Gilles Town Hall
place van Meenen
1060 Saint-Gilles
✆ 02 / 536 02 23
In the same vein as the previous museum, this local town hall offers a wealth of 'fin de siècle' surprises in its pictures, sculptures and furniture.

Erasmus Museum
rue du Chapitre, 31
1070 Brussels
✆ 02 / 521 13 83
This is one of the most delightful places in the capital where the town of Anderlecht has gathered together assorted collections from the XVIth century full of high renaissance flavour.

Wittockiana Library
rue du Bémel, 21
1150 Brussels
✆ 02 / 770 53 33
In this private collection you enter a world of books and fantasy where book-bindings are venerated like the silver plates of antique missals. Fine architecture.

Les Nocturnes du Sablon

Each year in November.
25, 26, 27 November 1999
23, 24, 25 November 2000
Information: 02 / 502 16 31

ANNE DE BEAUJEU
ARC LINEA
ARNUMIS
ART THEMA GALLERY
ARTA
ATMOSPHERE
BERKO
BISHOP TAILORS
BOLENS ROBERT
BONS ENFANTS (AUX)
CABINET DE L'AMATEUR
(LE)
CAP SABLON
CARPE DIEM & L'AUTHEN-
TIQUE
CARRETTE (GALERIE)
CASTELLO BANFI
CENTO ANNI
CESAR ET ROSALIE
CHARLIER
CHARLOTTE AUX POMMES
CHERCHE MIDI (AU)
CHINTZ SHOP
CLAEYS GALLERY
CLAUDE-NOELLE SPRL
CLE DES CHAMPS (LA)
CONTRAST GALLERY
COSTERMANS SPRL
COUDENBERG
CROISBIEN DE VRIES
DE GEEST
DE LEYE SPRL
DE MAERE
DENYS PHILIPPE
DESMET TOM
DETRY
DEWART GALLERY
DOMINIQUE SPRL
DREES
DUFRASNE PHILIPPE
DUVIVIER
ECAILLER DU PALAIS
ROYAL (L')
EGIDE,L' SPRL
EMPORIO ARMANI
ENTREE DES ARTISTES, L'
FEUILLE D'ARMOISE (LA)
FINE ARTS
FLAMANT
FORMANOIR
FUTUR ANTERIEUR
GHADIMI
GHADIMI CATHERINE
GODIVA
GRAND MAYEUR, LE
GRANERO, GALERIE D'ART
HERBE ROUGE (L')
ISABELLE DE BORGHRAVE

ISADORA
JANSSENS VAN DER MAELEN FR
JUAN PACIFICO
KESSELER PAUL
KESTELOOT FILIP
KUDLIK
KYOTO GALLERY
LA PIPE
LAGRAND
LAMBRECHT MICHEL
LANCZ PATRICK
LEMAIRE SPRL
LEYSEN JOAILLIER
LINEN HOUSE (THE)
LOLA
LORELEI (GALERIE D'ART)
M&N UZAL
MARCOLINI
MILSTAIN, GALLERY
MINIMES (GALERIE DES)
MODERN STUDIO
NELIS
NOUVELLE GALERIE
OLIVIER, L'
PAIN QUOTIDIEN
PAREYN&SPEYBROUCK
PASSE TEMPS (LE)
PHILIPPE SAINT, GALERIE
PIC VERRE (LE)
PUCCI
RICHARD SA
RITTER CHRISTINE
ROBERT
SALOME ANTIQUE 26
SANTOURI
SENSES
SHAMBLEAU
ST JACQUES, GALERIE
ST LOUIS, GALERIE
ST MICHEL, GALERIE
ST NICOLAS
THEUNISSEN
T'KINT DE RODENBEKE
TORTUE DU ZOUTE (LA)
TOUR D'Y VOIR
TRENTE RUE DE LA PAILLE
VAISSELLE AU KILO (LA)
VAN HOVE FRANCOIS
VERSCHUEREN SA
VIEUX ST MARTIN (LE)
VILLARS
WARCHE & ZÜRCHER
WECKMANS
WITTAMER
YANNICK DAVID, GALERIE
ZABIA DAVIDOFF
ZADA
ZAVEL SPRL

D'Ieteren Etterbeek

SERVICE VENTE
SALES SERVICE
Avenue de l'Armée 61
1040 Brussels
Tel. 743 21 21 • Fax 743 21 32

SERVICE APRÈS-VENTE
AFTER SALES SERVICE
Rue des Bataves 17
1040 Brussels
Tel. 743 21 11 • Fax 743 21 31

Horta Museum
rue Américaine, 25
1060 Brussels
℡ 02 / 537 16 92
This is a highly symbolic place in Brussels' heritage. Horta is THE symbol of Art nouveau. His house is a manifesto, a public statement of the innovative ideas from around 1890-1910. Not to be missed.

Van Buuren Museum
avenue Errera, 41
1180 Brussels
℡ 02 / 343 48 51
Another place you should not miss. The Van Buurens bequeathed their house to the nation as a parting gift for eternity, with all the Art déco furnishings they lived with. Worth a look.

The Comic Strip Museum
rue des Sables, 20
1000 Brussels
A vast warehouse designed by Victor Horta, houses a very dynamic museum covering one of the major arts of Belgian cultural heritage : the comic strip. From Tintin to Buck Danny, from Michel Vaillant to the Smurfs, the collections are vast and there are a large number of exhibitions.

Camille Lemonnier House
chaussée de Wavre, 150
1050 Ixelles
℡ 02 / 512 29 68
Yet another little-known place hidden away, where you can breathe in the fin de siècle atmosphere of a century ago. In this large and beautiful house there is a museum devoted to the Belgian literature of the Art nouveau period with, as focal point, the documents connected to C. Lemonnier, the Belgian Zola, father of modern Belgian literature.

Museum of the Grand Lodge of Belgium
rue de Laeken, 79
1000 Brussels
For information call
Mr. Somville
℡ 02 / 354 14 80
This surprising place does open on request. The museum contains important pictures by Belgian artists of the XIXth century and a large number of 'objets d'art'. The temples are worth going out of your way to see.

Dynasty Museum
Hôtel Bellevue
place des Palais, 7
1000 Brussels
℡ 02 / 511 55 78
If you want to learn about the history of the Belgian dynasty this museum is the perfect medium. Recently enriched by the addition of objects used by the late King Baudouin, the museum traces the history of the five kings who have ruled Belgium since 1831 with a thousand endearing memories.

DOC. OPT

Antiques

Brussels is a true hub of antique markets. You really must do the tour of the Brussels antique shops as the asking prices for objets d'art and some paintings are much lower than in the other European capitals. The Sablon district mentioned earlier remains the number one art market in Brussels but it is not the only one. You can find good antique shops almost everywhere in the districts of Saint-Gilles, Uccle, Ixelles and Etterbeek.

Silversmiths

Francis Janssens van der Maelen
rue Allard, 5
1000 Brussels
✆ 02 / 502 71 80
✆ 075 / 48 62 00
Antique Belgian, English and French silver from the XVIIIth and XIXth centuries.

Bernard De Leye
rue Lebeau, 16
1000 Brussels
✆ 02 / 514 34 77
✆ 075 / 46 54 51
The number one specialist in antique Belgian silver.

Philippe d'Arschot Schoonhoven
avenue Louise
1050 Brussels
✆ 02 / 649 56 21
✆ 075 / 78 35 05
This young dealer has some very fine antique Belgian and foreign pieces tucked away.

Henri Vanhoenacker
rue des Minimes, 25
1000 Brussels
Recently moved to Brussels from Courtrai, this young dealer has stock at very affordable prices. He has good taste and works hard.

Le Poinçon
Jost zu Stolberg-Stolberg
rue Thérésienne, 3
(Porte de Namur)
1000 Bruxelles
✆ 02 / 512 09 30
Specialised for over 80 years in 19th century silver tableware. Buys, sells and restores.

Oriental art

Zen Gallery
rue E. Allard, 23
1000 Brussels
✆ 02 / 511 95 10
✆ 075 / 43 37 33
Art from the Far East, Japanese screens, Chinese High-Period. This gallery, presided over by André Cnudde and Luc Van Mulders is one of the best in Europe. It is famous for the high quality of ancient bronzes and Chinese terracotta.

Gisèle Croës
boulevard de Waterloo, 54
1000 Brussels
✆ 02 / 511 82 16
Very high quality art from China and the Far East with an international reputation. Gisèle Croës is the diva of the profession, and internationally known .

Primitive Art

Bernard de Grunne
rue de la Paille, 26
1000 Brussels
℘ 02 / 502 31 71
℘ 075 / 61 62 14
Former department head for Sotheby's
in New York, Bernard de Grunne is one
of the great specialists in African and
Native American art in Brussels.

The Sablon district is the hub of the
world market in primitive art, just as
Antwerp is for precious stones. There
are more than sixty galleries specialising in this field in and around Sablon,
some of which are : **Martial Bronsin**
(Impasse Saint-Jacques), **Pierre Loze**
(Ambre Congo, Impasse Saint-Jacques),
the Grusenmeyers (rue Lebeau, 14, à
1000 Bruxelles), **Alain Naoum, Bert
Garrebbeek.**

Philippe Guimiot
avenue Llyod Georges, 16
1000 Brussels
℘ 02 / 640 69 48
In the same way as Gisèle Croës for
Chinese art, Philippe Guimiot is the
leading light in his specialist field of
African art. One address you should
not miss.

Lin et Emile Deletaille
rue aux Laines, 31
1000 Brussels
℘ 02 / 511 69 73
This antique dealer couple are also
leading lights in the field of Central and
South American art. Yet another place
not to be missed by antique lovers.

French furniture and articles of the XVIIth, XVIIIth and XIXth centuries

Formanoir et Launoit
rue Stevens, 35
1000 Brussels
℘ 02 / 512 08 18
℘ 075 / 52 46 47
Two young antique dealers combine
their eclectic tastes to offer high quality
objets d'art and furniture.
Formanoir has opened a second shop
at the corner of the place Brugman and
the avenue Lepoutre in Ixelles, together
with *François d'Ansembourg*.
You can also enjoy the *Gaston Renard*
antiques at the back of the gallery in
rue Stevens.

Zurcher et Warche
rue des Minimes, 59 bis
1000 Brussels
(opposite the church of the same name)
℘ 02 / 502 53 04
This dealer offers the best French furniture available in the Sablon, as well as
china, silverware and clocks.

André Legot and Olivier Thisse
rue Simonis, 55
1050 Brussels
℘ 02 / 537 31 78
℘ 075 / 90 82 51
This beautiful gallery can be found near
the place du Châtelain where you will
appreciate the French furniture from the
end of the XVIIIth century and especially
the Empire and Charles X furniture.

Costermans
place du Grand Sablon, 5
1000 Brussels
℘ 02 / 512 21 33
In the most beautiful town house on
the square, with its incredible Louis
XVI staircase and its salons of infinite
charm, you can find fine French furniture and objets d'art from the XVIIIth
century and antique marble fireplaces.
This building is also a centre for
wrought iron craftsmanship

ZOOM
Each year during
the second week
in June four open
days are held in
the various primi-
tive art shops,
under the name of
« BADNEA »
This is a world-
class gathering.
Collectors and
dealers even
come from the
USA for the occa-
sion.
Administrative
office : at Pierre
Loze's call
℘ 02 / 514 02 09

René and Francine Richard
drève du Duc, 102
1170 Brussels
✆ 02 / 660 83 44
✆ 075 / 32 64 12
This treasure-trove of a house opens
its doors twice a year for about a
week, otherwise by appointment
only. French or Belgian marquetry
and painted wood furniture.
Consoles, seats, paintings and objets
d'art are arranged in the dealers' own
private house (which only adds to the
temptation).

Percy's Antiques
rue des Minimes, 27
1000 Brussels
✆ 02 / 513 47 69
✆ 075 / 74 69 31
Hans, the master of the house, is a
young antique dealer full of talent and
good taste. Hidden beneath the confu-
sion of the shop lurk many fine, decorative items, often dating from the
XVIIIth century.

Antique paintings

Jan De Maere
rue des Minimes, 9
1000 Brussels
✆ 02 / 502 24 00
✆ 075 / 73 34 00
With *Francis Devaux* (16, rue Marie
Lepage à Uccle: (✆ 02 / 347 47 48),
Jan De Maere is the last dealer of
antique Flemish paintings in Brussels.
He also sells a lot of antique drawings, particularly Italian ones.

Old books

Eric Speeckaert
boulevard Saint-Michel, 53
1040 Brussels
✆ 02 / 736 43 29
✆ 075 / 70 72 16
Rare books from the XVth to the XXth
centuries. Eric Speeckaert specialises
in genealogy, history and literature.
He organises public sales once or
twice a year.

Tulkens
rue du Chêne, 21
1000 Brussels
✆ 02 / 513 05 25
High quality antique books.

Posada
rue de la Madeleine, 29
1000 Brussels
✆ 02 / 511 08 34
The best place in town to buy new or
second hand exhibition catalogues
and art books.

Van Loock
rue Saint Jean, 51
1000 Brussels
✆ 02 / 512 74 65
They have autographs, manuscripts,
antique prints, rare books.

There is a special district for
books. It is between rue Saint-
Jean, rue de la Madeleine,
Galerie Bortier, rue des
Eperonniers, near the Grand
Place and the Gare Centrale.
There are also a number of book-
shops along the Chaussée de
Charleroi.

Oriental rugs, Kilims and some tapestries

Zada
place du Grand Sablon
1000 Brussels
(opposite the entrance to the
church of the same name)
✆ 02 / 513 78 55

Sadrae
boulevard de Waterloo, 20
1000 Brussels
✆ 02 / 502 24 77
✆ 075 / 26 50 05

Badi Ghadimi
rue des Minimes, 1
1000 Brussels
✆ 02 / 512 98 41
With 30 years' experience in antique
Oriental rugs, he is the most influen-
tial man in this field in Sablon.

Philippe and Michel Antoine
rue des Echevins, 169
1050 Brussels
✆ 02 / 647 60 89
✆ 02 / 649 65 34
Rugs and objets d'art.

China and porcelain

Guy Charlier
Grande rue au Bois, 158
1030 Brussels
✆ 02 / 736 68 58
✆ 075 / 84 20 50
Big specialist in Tournai china but that
is not all. His lair, located in a very
discreet district, is well worth a visit.

Famille Lemaire
place du Petit Sablon
1000 Brussels
✆ 02 / 511 05 13
Now settled into their new home since
the middle of June 1999 the Lemaire
family are once again slaving over a hot
kiln with their customary taste and
good-nature in an idyllic, tranquil setting
hidden from view, just next to the Palais
d'Arenberg, known as "Egmont". The
Lemaires specialise in Tournai china and
are branching out into the French manufacturers of the XVIIIth century.

Camille Lagrand
rue de la Paille, 28
1000 Brussels
✆ 02 / 512 60 11
Collectors' items, silverware, china,
glassware, miniatures and gilded
bronzes are the preserve of this
antiques dealer of proverbial frankness
who has inherited a long tradition in
this business.

N. Ikodinovic
rue Stevens, 37
1000 Brussels
✆ 02 / 514 04 77
A specialist in French, German and
English china from the first half of the
XIXth century.

Glassware

Le Pic Verre
rue E. Allard, 18
1000 Brussels
✆ 02 / 513 70 19
Old glassware (Val-Saint-Lambert,
Vonêche, Baccarat...) old decorative
silver including numerous table set-
tings, table china and small furniture.

Bronzes, sculptures

Au fil du Temps
rue Lebeau, 41
1000 Brussels
✆ 02 / 513 34 87
High quality bronzes from the XIXth
century (Carpeaux, Rodin...)

Biedermeier furniture

Jacques de Caters
rue Watteuw, 19
1000 Bruxelles
✆ 075 / 830 635
He shares the gallery with Yves
Macau, who runs the Art nouveau
and Art déco "department".

Libermann
Avenue des celtes, 22
1040 Brussels
✆ 02 /732 48 65
✆ 075 / 541 848
Open Monday and Wednesday
evenings from 6 p.m. to 8 p.m. and
Saturday afternoons from 4 p.m. to
6 p.m. or by appointment.

Art nouveau and Art déco

Philippe Denys
rue des Sablons, 1
1000 Brussels
✆ 02 / 512 36 07
Art déco, Art nouveau , paintings,
silverware, sculptures and bronzes
(1880-1940). Together with his
neighbours from over the road
(**Galerie Cento Anni**, **Galerie Futur
Antérieur**) and **Yves Macau** mentioned above, Philippe is the main
player on the Sablon in his field.

English furniture and items

Nicholson
rue Franz Merjay, 131
1050 Brussels
✆ 02 / 343 86 82
Specialises in Victorian furniture and
antique nautical items and boats.

Paintings and drawings of the XIXth and early XXth centuries

Galerie Patrick Berko
Grand Sablon, 36
Shopping Garden
1000 Brussels
✆ 02 / 511 15 76
✆ 075 / 85 00 61
Belgian, Dutch, French and German
paintings of the XIXth and occasionally early XXth centuries. Editions of art
books which are the reference works.
It is noteworthy that the Berkos have
saved hundreds of scorned Belgian
artists from oblivion.

Deliveries
Most antique dealers
will deliver free or for a
small charge. If you
wish to have an object
or a piece of furniture
delivered abroad we
would advise you to
contact specialist trans-
porters.

Mocla Express
specialists in transporting
works of art by road or
air.
✆ 02 / 268 05 612
Art on the Move
deliveries, storage,
packaging, price by
volume
✆ 02 / 538 82 79
Farin
✆ 02 / 216 83 84
The mover preferred by
the antique dealers.

Galerie Patrick Derom
rue aux Laines, 1
1000 Brussels
✆ 02 / 514 08 82
✆ 075 / 27 96 32
This gallery is a reference point for the big names in Belgian art, *Khnopff, Ensor, Delvaux, Mellery, Delville*

Galerie Patrick Lancz
rue des Minimes, 38
1000 Brussels
✆ 075 / 24 82 65

Galerie Jean Nélis
rue Van Moer
1000 Brussels
Situated opposite the offices of the Antique Traders' Federation since June 1999
✆ 075 / 82 91 81

Contemporary Art

see later in the Art Galleries section.

If you want to find out more:

Chambre royale des Antiquaires de Belgique
rue Van Moer
1000 Brussels
✆ 02 / 513 48 31
President: Christian de Bruyn

Guilde des Antiquaires flamands
✆ 02 / 569 03 18

Union Professionnelle des Antiquaires et des Brocanteurs
✆ 02 / 511 50 56

Customs formalities

For EU nationals there are no longer any customs formalities, the invoice proves that the goods have been duty-paid in Belgium. There are no special rules for antiques, as long as you have the invoice and a certificate of authenticity from the antique dealer. However you should note that the maximum value imposed on goods for export outside the EU allows the authorities to check up on works of art leaving the country.

Antique shows

«**Portes-Ouvertes du Sablon**» the last weekend in November and the first weekend in December ; place: Sablon
For all information call✆ 02 / 512 98 41
Mr Badhi Ghadimi (also a specialist in antique rugs).

Antique Fair
generally the last two weeks in January
Palais des Beaux-Arts de Bruxelles
✆ 02 / 513 48 31
This is the best quality fair in the country with fifty or so Belgian and foreign antique dealers.

Eurantica
towards the middle of March, just after the Maestricht fair (TEFAF) at the Parc des Expositions in Heysel: ✆ 041 / 84 50 52
✆ 02 / 501 27 80
A huge gathering of Belgian and foreign art dealers. The quality is variable (from the very best to decent junk) in comparison with the Beaux-Arts fair but that is part of its charm and the 25,000 visitors can make a lot of good finds at reasonable prices.

Art Galleries

Contemporary Art Fair:
Art*Brussels*
In April at the Parc des Expositions in Heysel Information:
Albert Baronian:
✆ 02 / 734 68 28

Chekhov said: « *Works of art can be divided into two categories: the ones I like and the ones I don't like. I know of no other criteria*».
Firm in this knowledge, we shall limit ourselves to a few interesting addresses, leaving you the pleasure of going off in search of the places and genres you like.
These are listed in alphabetic order and are all beyond reproach when it comes to quality.

You can find the following in bookshops to help you :

L'Evènement lists the antique dealers, art galleries, salerooms, experts and art professions. It is an excellent tool full of addresses published each year.
Arts Antiques Auctions
A monthly illustrated magazine with very full information on sales and art exhibitions. It is the leader in its field.
De Facto - Art Magazine
A very beautiful magazine on art history and archaeology with articles on the big exhibitions.
Le Marché de l'Art in La Libre Belgique, by Baudouin van Steenberghe Editions de l'Octogone.
& 02 / 673 87 56
«Guide du Sablon» published by the Association « Sablon Quartier des Arts et du Commerce », every year around October just before the Open Day.
Brochure Art-Expo on sale in bookshops features the exhibitions, private viewings and public sales each month.
Le Guide Artistes et Galeries published by S.I. Belgium
& 02 / 736 69 99

http://www.artexpo.be

Avant-garde galleries

Albert Baronian
Boulevard Barthélemy, 20
1000 Brussels
✆ 02 / 512 92 95
Baronian has set up his gallery downtown near the canal. In just two years this boulevard has become the main centre of contemporary art in Brussels.

J. Bastien Art:
rue de la Madeleine, 61
1000 Brussels
✆ 02 / 513 25 63

Damasquine
rue de l'Aurore, 62
1000 Brussels
✆ 02 / 646 31 53

Dorothée De Pauw
rue De Hennin, 70
1050 Brussels
✆ 02 / 649 43 80.

Pierre Hallet
rue E. Allard, 33
1000 Brussels
✆ 02 / 512 25 23

Xavier Hufkens
rue Saint-Georges, 6
1000 Brussels
✆ 02 / 646 63 30

Willy D'Huysser
place du Grand Sablon, 35
1000 Brussels
✆ 02 / 511 37 04

Rodolphe Janssen
rue de Livourne, 35
1050 Brussels
✆ 02 / 538 08 18

Maurice Keitelman
rue de la Paille, 9
1000 Brussels
✆ 02 / 511 35 80

Fred Lanzenberg
avenue des Klauwaerts, 9
1050 Brussels
✆ 02 / 647 30 15

Meert Rihoux
rue du Canal, 13
1000 Brussels
✆ 02 / 219 14 22

Vedovi
boulevard de Waterloo, 11
1000 Brussels
✆ 02 / 513 38 38

Velge et Noirhomme
rue de la Régence, 17
1000 Brussels
✆ 02 / 512 50 10

Sabine Wachters
avenue de Stalingrad, 26
1000 Brussels
✆ 02 / 502 39 93

Traditional galleries

Contrast Gallery
rue E. Allard, 21
1000 Brussels
✆ 02 / 512 98 59
Essentially geared towards figurative contemporary art with a majority of Belgian artists of the expressionist and realist movements.

Galerie St. Jacques
Impasse Saint Jacques , 5
1000 Brussels
✆ 02 / 502 64 21
Organises exhibitions of established talents.

Every two months the jeweller's **Fydjy's** at 56 Avenue Louise welcomes young artists. The juxtaposition of the works displayed in glass cubes and the jewels can create surprising effects.

A tip:
As soon as you are settled in Brussels give your name and address to the big Brussels galleries. You will then be included on their mailing lists and will receive invitations to their private viewings.

Born in Antwerp, 15 January 1923, **Nat Neujean**, is the sculptor of the Tintin statue on the cover of this guide. Internationally known, he has done portraits of famous people around the world and many sculptures, including this one "the watching soul" in front of the administrative centre in Brussels. Nat Neujean takes part in many exhibitions in Europe, the USA and Canada. His work can be found in the greatest public and private collections in the world. The Tintin sculpture can be seen in the hall of the cartoon Museum at the moment where it is on loan from a private collector.
Atelier de Nat Neujean
15 Avenue du Gui – 1180 Brussels
✆ 02 / 374 73 68

Photo: Bertrand Neuman

Salerooms

The salerooms, a dozen of which are well worth a look, are regularly visited by foreign buyers, living in or coming from a radius of 400 km around the capital, including Holland, Great Britain, France and Germany. You can find out the dates from the AAA (Art Antiques Auctions call 09/ 269 10 10), bookshops, or directly from the salerooms. Brussels has a dozen salrooms scattered around the various districts of the capital. Generally they organise one session per month. The most famous are :

Ventes Publiques au Palais des Beaux- Arts, Servaerts S.A.,
managed by François De Jonckeere et Philippe Serck
rue Royale, 10
1000 Brussels
✆ 02 / 513 60 80

Hôtel des ventes Horta
Avenue de Roodebeek, 70
1030 Brussels
✆ 02 / 741 60 60
Managed by Messieurs Julien et Van Hamme

Hôtel des ventes Vanderkindere
chaussée d'Alsemberg, 685
1180 Brussels
✆ 02 / 344 54 46
Managed by Stéphane Nicais

Galerie Moderne
rue Caroly et rue du Parnasse, 3
1050 Brussels
✆ 02 / 513 90 10
Managed by Marcel Devadder

Hôtel de Ventes Ferrer
Rue Vanderkindere
1180 Brussels
✆ 02 / 346 78 72
Managed by Ferrer Ugguccioni

Hôtel de Ventes Flagey
rue du Nid, 4
1050 Brussels
✆ 02 / 644 97 67
Managed by Michel Pinckaerts

Other salerooms:

Thémis (furniture and objects)
✆ 02 / 512 26 10

Godts-Moorthamer (books)
✆ 02 / 647 85 48

Speeckaert (books)
✆ 02 / 736 43 29

Romantic Agony (books)
✆ 02 / 544 10 55

de Sadeleer (books)
✆ 02 / 513 26 48

A good tip :

• If you cannot attend the sale, ask for a phone line or place a purchase order. However, to be on the safe side you should attend in person to avoid any nasty surprises or breakdowns in communication.
• You must add 20% costs to theauction price.
• Internet subscribers can zoom in on the digital photo of the object they desire. The main Belgian site is « antiques-world.com », obtainable on ✆ 02 / 511 31 61 61 from Patrick van der Stichelen-Rogier

Art Experts

In addition to the services offered free of charge by the salerooms, you can call on private experts specialising in jewellery, antique or modern paintings, engravings or silverware.
For help, look in the art directory published by
L'Evènement magazine
✆ *02 / 332 04 05*

If you would like to find out more :
Chambre belge des Experts en oeuvres d'art
✆ *02 / 346 57 09*
The list of members can be obtained on request.

Restoration

Restoration of antique furniture:

Bert Declerck
Ganzemanstraat, 19
3040 Huldenberg
✆ *02 / 768 20 90*
Specialist in marquetry of a very high level.

Patrice Stinghlambert
1160 Brussels
✆ *02 / 672 07 54*
Restoration and advice on buying.

Jean-François d'Oultremont
rue St Georges, 58
1050 Brussels
✆ *02 / 649 58 59*
Restoration, buying and selling.

Copet et le Grelle
rue Philippe Baucq, 155
1040 Brussels
✆ *02 / 640 53 75*

Adragante
rue des Béguinettes 26
1170 Brussels
✆ *02 / 672 69 42*

Restoration of antique Japanese furniture:

Stefan Geyns
cabinet-maker-restorer in Uccle
✆ *02 / 376 89 12*

Restoration of antique and modern pictures:

Salv'Artes, a team which works for the museums, antique dealers and collectors, in Leefdaal
✆ *02 / 767 97 80*

Jean Nélis
rue de la Luzerne, 38
1030 Brussels
✆ *02 / 732 12 51*

Restoration of clocks:

An-Hor, established 20 years in Brussels
✆ *02 / 502 18 94 – 95*

Restoration of earthenware or china:

Atelier Roanne
in Brussels
✆ *02 / 648 81 53*

A good tip:

Every year in February, the Woluwé Shopping Center organises the Foire des Métiers d'Art (Art Professions' Fair) where you can discover a whole host of small designers, craftsmen and restorers.
To find out:
Devimo
✆ *02 / 771 20 45*

Second-hand dealers

Hunting for bric-a-brac or doing the flea-markets is one of the best ways to spend a Brussels weekend.
Although the *Sablon* is given over mainly to antique dealers you should also go there for the weekend market held in tents by the church. The district of *rue Blaes* and *rue Haute*, further down, as far as the *Place du jeu de balle* will round off your visit to the second-hand dealers. An excellent address:

Au Siffleur
rue des Tanneurs, 141
1000 Brussels
✆ 02 / 511 05 26
Door knobs, keys, handles, candelabra arms and all kinds of things you can't find elsewhere.

Half-way between junk and antique, these two "depots" are like true Ali-Baba caves:

Rue des Minimes,23
1000 Brussels
✆ 02 / 511 28 25

Chée St-Pierre, 371
1040 Brussels
✆ 02 / 735 20 08

Flea markets

Place du Jeu de Balle
every day from 5 a.m. to 1 p.m.

Place du Grand Sablon
Saturdays from 10 a.m. to 6 p.m.
Sundays from 10 a.m. to 2 p.m.

Tram Museum
in Woluwé Saint-Lambert
first Saturday of the month from 9 a.m. to 4 p.m.

Auderghem-Viaduc Debroux
last Sunday in the month from 7 a.m. to 1 p.m.

Place St Lambert in Woluwé Saint-Lambert
first Sunday in the month from 7 a.m. to 1.30 p.m.

In September and March:
Antiques Fair in the Woluwé Shopping Center

October: Antiques Fair in the Royal Army Museum
✆ 02 / 733 63 05

November : Antique dealers' fair on Bigg's car park
✆ 02 / 345 01 82

To find out other flea markets in the area:

Daily newspapers
(including *le Soir* on Saturdays and *la Libre Belgique*, *Libre Culture*, on Wednesdays)

Le Journal du Collectionneur et de l'Antiquaire
on sale in bookshops

Le Carnet, monthly collectors' publication
on sale in bookshops

SPORT

Venues

All kinds
of sport

Venues

If you are interested in practising a sport, the following may help you to find the right place to go.

Commune Sports Complexes:
These offer a wide range of sports and are open to all, including non-residents, at reasonable prices. Telephone the commune sports centre to find out the times, prices and sports available (see in the telephone directory under 'Administration communale').

Independent Sports Centres:
There are lots of sports clubs and leisure centres in Brussels.

◇ *Look in the Yellow Pages under 'Centres sportifs' or 'Clubs de sports' (Section A 2080).*

Clubs:
Payment of a joining fee and/or an annual subscription gives you membership of a club and entitles you to use its facilities.

Sporting Federations
The sporting federations bring together the clubs in the country or in certain regions. There is one for almost every sporting discipline.

They can give you information on how and where to play the sport you are interested in (see Yellow Pages, Section A 2083).

ADEPS
Boulevard Léopold II
1040 Brussels
✆ 02 / 413 23 11
fax 02 / 413 28 25
Information on sporting and outdoor activities in the French-speaking part of the country.

BLOSO
Koloniënstraat, 29-31
1000 Brussel
✆ 02 / 209 45 11
Information on sporting and outdoor activities in the Dutch-speaking part of the country.

SPORTA
Geneide, 2
2260 Tongerloo
✆ 014 / 54 10 48
fax 014 / 54 12 48
Information on sporting outdoor activities in the Dutch-speaking part of the country.

BSA (Brussels Sports Association)
Boulevard Henri Rolin, 2
1410 Waterloo
✆ 02 / 354 11 14
fax 02 / 354 46 24
English-speaking voluntary organisation bringing together the sporting activities of various international schools. Open to all. Organises seasonal team games for children aged 7 to 15. Coaching and training several times a week. Competitions at weekends.

British School of Brussels (BSB)
Leuvensesteenweg, 19
3080 Tervuren
✆ 02 / 766 04 30
fax 02 / 767 80 70
Very active in many fields, including sports.

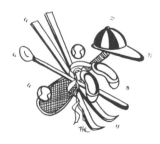

Multi-sport Centres

For young children, this is a practical and versatile solution.
Here are some addresses for children, listed by commune:

Auderghem

Club Neptune
Centre sportif de la forêt
de Soignes
rue du Concours, 15
1170 Brussels
✆ 02 / 662 20 43
    0477 / 38 61 61

Ixelles

Kid's Winners ✿
Rue Général Thys, 12
1050 Brussels
✆ 02 / 644 55 44

Action Sport ✿
✆ 02 / 734 94 16
Ixelles, Etterbeek,
Woluwé-Saint-Pierre

Rhode-Saint-Genèse

Les ateliers de la Gare ✿
Place de la Station, 18
1640 Rhode-Saint-Genèse
✆ 02 / 358 17 25
    02 / 358 17 55

Tervuren

K.R.T. Kultuuraad Tervuren
De Steenberg
Spechtenlaan
3080 Tervuren
✆ 02 / 767 15 31
Training in Dutch: tennis,
judo , badminton, swim-
ming...

For further details:
This is a must-have: **Le Grand Bruxelles des Enfants**,
published by Clair de Lettre, on sale in all good book-
shops or by mail from the following address:
Editions Clair de Lettre
Avenue des Combattants, 140 - 1332 Genval

Uccle

Kids Computer Club ✿
Avenue René Gobert, 31
1180 Brussels
✆ 02 / 374 27 08
fax 02 / 374 75 87
This club offers masses of
sporting activities, as its name
doesn't indicate!

Watermael-Boitsfort

Parc Sportif des 3 Tilleuls ✿
Avenue L. Wiener, 60
1170 Brussels
✆ 02 / 675 48 99
fax 02 / 675 42 42

Wezembeek-Oppem

Animer
Wezembeek-Oppem ✿
Chemin au Bois, 91
1970 Wezembeek-Oppem
✆ & fax 02 / 731 95 37

Toboggan ✿
✆ & fax 02 / 731 11 96
(from 10 a.m. to 4 p.m.)
Activities held in:
Schaerbeek, Wezembeek-
Oppem, Rixensart et
Etterbeek.

Imagine
Chaussée de Malines, 77
1970 Wezembeek-Oppem
✆ & fax 02 / 731 11 96
Circus skills, swimming,
dance, tap-dancing, etc.

Woluwé-Saint-Lambert

JJJY ✿
Service de la Jeunesse
Place du Tomberg, 6A
1200 Brussels
✆ 02 / 761 28 80
fax 02 / 772 50 41

Woluwé-Saint-Pierre

Vitamômes ✿
Courses: rue au Bois, 369
1150 Brussels
✆ 02 / 720 87 07
(after 4 p.m.)
Computing and sports.

**Centre de Formation
Sportive** ✿
✆ 010 / 22 73 96
(from 9 a.m. to 5 p.m.)
fax 010 / 24 38 42
Activities held in:
Auderghem, Evere, Jette,
Laeken, Uccle, Woluwe-
Saint-Lambert, Woluwe-
Saint-Pierre, Wavre,
Rixensart, Chaumont
Gistoux, Walhain, Braine-
l'Alleud, Ottignies.

Waterloo

Waterloo Tennis ✿
Blvd H. Rolin, 5
1410 Waterloo
✆ 02 / 354 58 17
fax 02 / 353 03 40
Tennis, karate, gymnastics.

✿ *indicates holiday activities.*

All kinds of sport

Aérobics, keep-fit and gymnastics

Available in most communes and sports centres.
See Yellow pages:
Section A 2080.

Some useful addresses:

Physical Center
Avenue E. Vandervelde, 55
1200 Brussels (near the Woluwe Shopping Centre)
℡ 02 / 762 91 80
fax 02 / 770 56 22

Studio Jacaranda
Rue Blockmans, 10
1150 Woluwe-St-Pierre
℡ et fax 02 / 779 23 19

John Harris Fitness
Avenue du Lac, 87
1332 Genval
℡ 02 / 655 74 66
fax 02 / 655 74 49
rue Fossé aux Loups, 47
(at the SAS hotel)
1000 Brussels
A high-powered sports club.
The membership card is valid for all the John Harris centres (Genval, Brussels, Vienna and London).

Centre sportif de Woluwé-Saint-Pierre
Rue Salomé, 2
1150 Brussels
℡ 02 / 773 18 20
classes with English-speaking teacher.
℡ 02 / 762 12 75

For further details:
Fédération royale belge de gymnastique
Boulevard E. Machtens, 143
1080 Brussels
℡ 02 / 414 90 58
fax 02 / 414 90 62

Athletics

Available in most commune sports centres.
You can train individually in the stadia of sports centres with the appropriate facilities.

Some useful addresses:

British School of Brussels
℡ 02 / 767 77 80

For further details:
Ligue Royale Belge d'Athlétisme
Avenue du Marathon, 119b
1020 Brussels
℡ 02 / 474 72 10
fax 02 / 474 72 12

Badminton

Ligue Francophone Belge de Badminton
Rue de Moorslede 139
1020 Brussels
℡ 02 / 425 54 87
fax 02 / 425 09 81

Brussels British Badminton Club
Avenue du Saphir, 16
1640 Rhode Saint Genèse
℡ 02 / 380 70 84

Baseball and Softball

Vlaamse Baseball en Softball Liga
Boomgaardstraat 22 bus 30
2100 Antwerpen
℡ 03 / 286 07 87

Ligue Francophone de Baseball
Rue Val Notre-Dame
4520 Moha
℡ 085 / 21 53 02

BSA (Brussels Sports Association)
Boulevard Henri Rolin, 2
1410 Waterloo
℡ 02 / 354 11 14
fax 02 / 354 46 24
Also runs training sessions for children from 5 to 18 years.

Basketball

Féderation Royale Belge des Sociétés de Basketball
27 Avenue P.H.Spaak
1060 Brussels
℡ 02 / 521 48 79
fax 02 / 522 18 15

Féderation Belge de Mini-Basketball
Rue de Chièvres 451
7332 Neufmaison
℡ 065 / 52 06 31

BSA (Brussels Sports Association)
Boulevard Henri Rolin, 2
1410 Waterloo
℡ 02 / 354 11 14
fax 02 / 354 46 24
also runs training sessions for children from 5 to 18 years.

Basket Ball in Brussels
℡ & fax 02 / 767 83 68

Bowling

Fédération de Bowling de Belgique
Chaussée de Louvain, 550
1030 Brussels
℡ 02 / 732 48 08

Bowling The Lion
Chaussée de Bruxelles, 412
1410 Waterloo
℡ 02 / 351 10 63
An English-speaking club plays here (among others).
For further information
℡ 016 / 47 38 31

If you would like to find out more addresses of sports clubs, please refer to the « **Useful Addresses** » section at the back of the guide.

LAND ROVER MONTGOMERY
RUE DE L'ESCADRON 41-43
1040 BRUSSELS
TEL. 02 / 742 26 62 • FAX 02 / 742 26 76

Nice kitchens for your home.

LIEDSSEN

Wingepark 16
3110 **Rotselaar**
Tel. : 016/44 01 64
Fax : 016/44 01 80
e-mail : info@liedssen.be

Cricket

Antwerp Cricket Club
✆ 03 / 239 74 03
✆ 03 / 202 32 11

Royal Brussels Cricket Club
✆ & fax 02 / 384 73 93

Cross Bow

There are 60 Cross Bow clubs in Belgium.

Fédération de Cross Bow
✆ 02 / 241 31 77

Cycling

Belgium's national sport. Causes detours to be put in place on roads over the weekend! There are lots of cycling clubs, which organise rides and other bike-related activities. Helmets are not compulsory but you are strongly advised to wear one.

Pro- Vélo
Avenue Ernest Solvay, 32A
1050 Brussels
✆ 02 / 502 73 55
✆ 075 / 631 101
fax 02 / 502 86 41

En septembre:
«De Gordel»:
promenade en vélo autour de Bruxelles

The Bike Market
In summer on Sunday mornings between the Gare du Midi and the Porte de Hal.
New and secondhand bikes, spare parts, tyres, ...

Reading tips:

Cyclotourisme en Belgique – published by La Renaissance du livre. Ideas for cycle rides. Over 1,500 km of rides: practical aspects, advice, train + bike deals, etc.
Les plus belles ballades à vélo en pays de Brabant – Édition Alice. Practical advice, maps, photos, etc. Vélodécouverte de Bruxelles and **Le guide des balades à vélo en pays de Brabant**, published by Pro Vélo

If you are looking for ideas for cycle rides, cycle routes, meetings for cycling enthusiasts :
Royale Ligue Vélopédique Belge
Avenue du Globe, 49
1190 Forest
✆ 02 / 349 19 11
fax 02 / 343 12 56
Pour vous donner des idées de ballades, itinéraires, rassemblements de fans de vélo:

Fédération Belge de Cyclotourisme
✆ 02 / 521 86 40
Publishes a calendar which comes out in January each year showing the events and cycle rides organised by all the clubs.

Les Cyclistes bruxellois
(an amateur group)
✆ 02 / 223 01 01

't Greun Veloske
Dutch-speaking organisation. Provides information on routes in Brussels.
✆ 02 / 646 80 88

Dance

Most communes have dance schools open to all. Ask your commune administration for details. Many private dance and ballet schools in Brussels.
See Yellow Pages, section A 2015.

Classes in some schools, both international and others

Ballet School
✆ 095 / 20 03 70

Balletomania
Avenue des Volontaires, 140
1040 Brussels
✆ 02 / 734 26 56

Académie Karys
Rue Louis Hap, 58
1040 Brussels
✆ 02 / 647 50 23

Studio Tapage
Avenue de Lancaster, 45
✆ & fax 02 / 374 03 85
School address:
Rue de Verrewinkel, 97
1180 Brussels

Rock Climbing

Many sports centres have a climbing wall. Some rock climbing centres in Brussels provide professional coaching for individuals or groups aimed at tackling the famous rocks at Marche-les-Dames.

Some useful addresses:

Salle d'escalade New Rock
Chssée de Watermael, 136
1160 Auderghem
✆ *02 / 675 17 60*
fax 02 / 672 52 84

Top Rock Sippelberg
Rue de Sippelberg, 1
1180 Brussels
✆ *02 / 414 43 45*

Horse Riding

Many riding clubs and centres in and around Brussels. Lessons are available. For riding out, look for a club in the countryside or on the edge of the forest.

Some useful addresses:
American Horseriding
La Ferme du Parc
Parc 2
7830 Silly-Hoves
✆ *02 / 395 83 58*

Les Drags
Chaussée de Bruxelles, 197
1560 Hoeilaart
✆ *02 / 654 00 25*

L'Eperon d'Or
Streekstraat, 38
1980 Tervuren
✆ *02 / 767 94 92*
fax 02 / 767 23 69

La Chevalerie
Avenue Brassine, 38
1640 Rhode-St Genèse
✆ *& fax 02 / 358 37 64*

Pom Pom Poney
Chaussée de Waterloo, 1512
1180 Brussels
✆ *02 / 374 84 49*

For further details:
Fédération Royale Belge des Sports Equestres
Avenue H. de Strooper, 156
1020 Brussels
✆ *02 / 478 50 56*
fax 02 / 478 11 26

Poney Club de Belgique
Chaussée de Nivelles, 62
1420 Braine-l'Alleud
✆ *02 / 385 20 80*

Football

There are so many football clubs that you are bound to find one whose closeness, language, players, etc. suit you.

In English:
Royal Brussels British Football Club
Avenue Boetendael 65
1180 Uccle
✆ *02 / 287 83 20*
fax 02 / 287 83 33

For ladies:
International Ladies Soccer Team
✆ *02 / 282 32 75*
fax 02 / 230 53 60

For further details:

Union Royale des Sociétés de Football
Avenue H. De Strooper, 146
1020 Brussels
✆ *02 / 477 12 11*

Union Royale Brabançonne des Sports Corporatifs-Football
c/o OTAN
1110 Brussels
O.T.A.N.- N.A.T.O.
✆ *02 / 728 50 56*
fax 02 / 702 42 01

BSA (Brussels Sports Association)
Boulevard Henri Rolin, 2
1410 Waterloo
✆ *354 11 14*
fax 354 46 24

American Football

Played very little in Belgium. Even the BSA does not run American Football training.
For further details:
American Football League
A. Vanheestraat, 58
8470 Moere
✆ *059 / 27 38 50*

Golf

Many golf courses close to Brussels. In all clubs you must be a member in order to play at the weekend. Some are open to non-members on weekdays. Visitors must declare an official handicap in order to be allowed on to the course. Classes for adults and children in most clubs.

Some useful addresses:

Golf Château de la Bawette
1300 Wavre
✆ 010 / 22 33 32
27 holes.

Golf du Bercuit
1390 Grez Doiceau
✆ 010 / 84 15 01
18 holes.

Brussels Golf Club
1180 Brussels
✆ 02 / 672 22 22
9 holes.
Excellent for beginners

Royal Golf Club de Belgique
3080 Tervuren
✆ 02 / 767 58 01
27 holes.
Membership full.

Golf de Sept Fontaines
1420 Braine l'Alleud
✆ 02 / 352 02 46
45 holes.

Royal Waterloo Golf Club
1380 Ohain
✆ 02 / 633 18 50
45 holes.

For further details:

Fédération Royale Belge de Golf
Chaussée de la Hulpe, 110
1050 Brussels
✆ 02 / 672 23 89
fax 02 / 672 08 97

Hockey

Indoor hockey is played in many sports centres..

Hockey & Tennis Oranje
Joseph Kumpsstraat, 83
1560 Hoeilaart
✆ 657 11 82

There is only one place in Brussels where you can learn and play ice hockey:

Forest National Ice Hockey Club
Patinoire de Forest National
Avenue du Globe, 36
1190 Brussels
✆ 02 / 345 16 11

For further details:
Association Royale Belge de Hockey
Gossetlaan, 8
1702 Groot-Bijgaarden
✆ 02 / 466 92 40
fax 02 / 466 92 97

Fédération Royale Belge de Hockey sur Glace
Avenue Reine Elisabeth, 61
5000 Namur
✆ 081 / 22 74 72

Jogging

There are joggers everywhere in Brussels.
Brussels Hash House Harriers
✆ 02 / 734 45 60
✆ 02 / 771 88 33
Jogging every Saturday afternoon at 3 p.m. in the countryside around Brussels. Very informal English-speaking group. All welcome.

Karate and Judo

Bois de la Cambre closed to traffic: paradise for joggers, skaters, cyclists and walkers.

Closed:
From 7 a.m. to 7 a.m. the next day
• from 1 March to 31 December: Sunday to Monday,
• during the Easter holidays: Saturday to Monday,
• Easter weekend: Saturday to Tuesday,
• from 1 July to 31 August: Saturday to Monday.

Walks guide.
Les Chemins du Rail de G. Perrin, Éditions Labor
Vol. 1: *Bruxelles, Wallonnie, Grand-Duché de Luxembourg;*
Vol. 2: *Bruxelles et Flandre.*

Ligue Belge de Judo
Rue Général Thys, 12
1050 Brussels
✆ 02 / 648 76 52
fax 02 / 640 34 69

Fédération Belge de Karaté
Steendam,61
9000 Gent
✆ 09 / 225 05 13

Fédération Francophone de Karaté
Bld Léopold III, 17 Bte 41
1030 Schaerbeek
✆ 02 / 705 78 05

Hiking and Walking

The Sunday afternoon family walk is one of the Belgian's favourite activities. This means that the parks in Brussels are very busy at weekends, particularly in good weather. You can always get in the car and drive out of town a bit: in Brussels, you have the Forêt de Soignes virtually on your doorstep.

Swimming

• Commune and public swimming pools.
• Private pools.
• Hotel pools.

If you want to swim lengths, try to go when the school children are not there. Check that at least one lane is set aside for individual swimmers. Competitions: training sessions are organised by various clubs after public opening hours, mainly in the evenings.

Note: swimming caps **must** be worn in all public pools. Men, and even boys, can under no circumstances wear 'boxer' type swimming

shorts. Only mini trunks may be worn.

Some useful addresses:

Centre sportif de Woluwé St-Pierre
Rue Salomé, 2
1150 Brussels
✆ 02 / 773 18 20
fax 02 / 773 18 15
Private lessons
✆ 02 / 773 18 39
Collective lessons and training:
CNB Atalante
✆ 02 / 771 93 58

Piscine Longchamp
Square De Fré, 1
1180 Uccle
✆ 02 / 374 90 05
fax 02 / 374 28 88
Training on Mondays and Thursdays at 7 p.m.:
Longchamps Swimming Club and *Les Nageurs Ucclois*
✆ 02 / 378 17 14

Pools recommended for children, see page 112.

For further details:
Féderation Royale Belge de Natation
Rue du Chevreuil, 28
1000 Brussels
✆ 02 / 513 87 08
✆ 075 / 87 34 18

Skating

Ice-skating:

Patinoire de Forest National
Avenue du Globe, 36
1190 Brussels
✆ 02 / 345 16 11
Poseidon
Avenue des Vaillants, 4
1200 Brussels
✆ 02 / 771 66 55

Ice-skating rink on the Grand Place at Christmas.

Roller skating

Watch out for people skating in the street! Parks, the Bois de la Cambre on the days when it is closed to cars (see above, 'Jogging') and skater lanes are safer than the street!

A useful address is:
Le gymnase Bois de la Cambre
Chemin du gymnase,1
1000 Brussels
✆ 02 / 649 70 02
fax 02 / 649 63 35

For further details:
Féderation Belge Francophone de Patinage
Rue des Sept Etoiles, 90
1082 Berchem-Ste-Agathe
✆ 02 / 465 91 18

Fédération Royale Belge de Patinage Artistique
Avenue Elisabeth, 61
5000 Namur
✆ 081 / 22 74 72

Fédération Royale Belge de Patinage de Vitesse
Muilemstraat 263
1770 Liedekerke
✆ 053 / 67 17 79

Fédération Belge de Roller Skating
Langeveld, 180
3220 Holsbeek
✆ 016 / 44 91 53
fax 016 / 32 79 80

• To find out the snow conditions:
Royal Touring Club
✆ 02 / 233 22 11
Royal Automobile Club
✆ 02 / 287 09 11

• For a map of the ski runs « Ski Ardennes »
OPT
✆ 02 / 504 02 00

Squash

Most tennis clubs also have squash courts.

For further details:
Fédération Belge de Squash Rackets
Boomgaerdstraat, 22 bte 49
2600 Berchem
✆ 03 / 286 58 03
fax 03 / 331 60 32

Tennis

Very popular in Belgium with adults and children alike. If you are looking for partners, join a club. Some are very dynamic and organise masses of activities such as courses, training sessions, tournaments, etc. for adults and for children.

Polo

Antwerp Polo Club
Moortstraat, 12
2530 Ranst
✆ 03 / 485 64 46

Rugby

Fédération Belge de Rugby
Rue Timmermans, 13
1190 Forest
✆ 02 / 343 38 31
fax 02 / 346 64 70

Brussels British Rugby Club
15 Specktenstraat
3078 Everberg
✆ 02 / 759 23 78
    02 / 759 74 02
fax 02 / 759 62 22

Skiing

When it snows you can ski in the Belgian Ardennes.

If you do have partners, all you need to do is hire a court on an ad hoc basis or for the season (September to April) in a centre or club close to home.

Classes for children are organised in sports centres, clubs, the sports halls of some schools, etc.

Inter-clubs tournaments during the summer season.

Inter-school tournaments: some schools have a team and coaches for tournaments. These include Le Verseau, St Johns, ISB, BSB, the European School, the Scandinavian School, and so on.

Some useful addresses:

Brussels
Chaussée de Waterloo, 890
1000 Brussels
✆ 02 / 374 92 59
fax 02 / 372 21 74

European Club
Av. Paul Hymans, 123 bte 1
1200 Brussels
✆ 02 / 770 08 44
fax 02 / 771 35 37

Some useful addresses:

Brussels
Chaussée de Waterloo, 890
1000 Brussels
✆ 02 / 374 92 59
fax 02 / 372 21 74

European Club
Av.Paul Hymans, 123 bte 1
1200 Brussels
✆ 02 / 770 08 44
fax 02 / 771 35 37

Davis Tennis Club
Rue Frans Landrain, 26
1970 Wezembeek-Oppem
✆ 02 / 731 77 07
   02 / 731 81 34
fax 02 / 731 81 34

Royal Léopold Club Tennis
Avenue J. et P. Carsoel, 52
1180 Uccle
✆ 02 / 374 32 27
fax 02 / 374 32 27

Tennis Club de Belgique
Rue du Beau-Site, 26
1000 Brussels
✆ 02 / 648 80 35
fax 02 / 648 48 24

**Wimbeldon Tennis
et Squash**
Chaussée de Waterloo, 220
1640 Rhode St Genèse
✆ 02 / 358 35 23
fax 02 / 358 14 61

Hockey & Tennis Oranje
Jozeph Kumpsstraat, 83
1560 Hoeilaart
✆ 02 / 657 15 64

Waterloo Tennis
Blvd Rolin, 5
1410 Waterloo
✆ 02 / 354 58 18
fax 02 / 353 03 40

For further details:

**Fédération Royale Belge
de Tennis**
Gal. de la Porte Louise, 203
1050 Brussels
✆ 02 / 513 29 27
fax 02 / 513 79 50

**Région du Brabant de
l'Association Francophone
de Tennis**
Chaussée de Wavre, 2057
1160 Auderghem
✆ 02 / 675 11 40
fax 02 / 675 12 10

Table Tennis

For further details:
**Fédération Royale Belge de
Tennis de Table (Bruxelles et
Brabant Wallon)**
Rue de l'Aigle, 7
1480 Tubize
✆ 02 / 355 88 96
fax 02 / 355 29 01

Volleyball

**Association Interprovinciale
Francophone de Volleyball**
278 Boulevard Lambermont
1030 Brussels
✆ 02 / 242 95 04
fax 02 / 241 56 45

Vlaamse Volleybalbond
22 Beneluxlaan
1800 Vilvoorde
✆ 02 / 257 16 00
fax 02 / 257 16 02

Two official Belgian magazines:
Play Tennis
Play Golf
✆ 02 / 647 17 50

Competitions and Tournaments
In order to participate in sporting competitions, you normally need
to be a member of a club: the club will train you and keep you
informed about competitions organised in your sporting discipline.
Some schools organise inter-school competitions.

HEALTH CARE

Doctors

Reimbursement

Chemists

Clinics
and Hospitals

Duty Services

After-hours
chemists:
✆ 0900 / 10 500

For pregnancy and
childbirth please
see the
« Children »
chapter on pg 74

Belgium is very well equipped
from the medical angle, and has
a health care network which is
among the best and most modern in the world, with over 380
hospitals and 30,000 doctors.

Sickness Insurance

See the chapter entitled
'Insurance', p. 21.

Choice of a Doctor

Unlike some other countries, in
Belgium you have complete
freedom to choose your own
doctor.

A list of doctors in Brussels, both
GPs and specialists, is given in
the telephone directory under
'Professions libérales - docteurs
en médecine'.

Prices

So-called 'fund doctors' generally apply a price close to the
amount which the mutual insurance association will cover. But
with the amount of medical fees
being unfixed in Belgium, some
doctors, and especially some
specialists, apply significantly
higher rates.
We would therefore advise you
to make enquiries before making
an appointment.

Reimbursement

All fund doctors must, at the end
of your consultation, issue you
with a care certificate
('attestation des soins') which
you should send or take to the
mutual association in order to
claim your reimbursement.
Some international bodies or
companies operate their own
reimbursement schemes. You
should therefore check with your
employer.

Chemists

Opening hours vary, although most close for lunch.
On Saturday afternoons and Sundays, the local chemists take it in turns to provide a duty service.
The addresses are posted every month in the windows of all the chemists, with a telephone number:

Useful facts:

In hospitals, the fees of the doctors, the room rate and the cost of the various services provided are charged and then reimbursed almost completely by the mutual association, provided that you are in a shared ward.
If you are in a single or two-bed room, you will be asked to pay a supplement for the occupation of the room and the nursing services, as well as for the doctors.
The expenses will be reimbursed if you are covered by a hospitalisation insurance (see p. 21).

Medicines

Most medicines available on the international market can be obtained in Belgium, although they may have a different name than in your home country. In this case, ask your doctor to draw you up a prescription setting out the chemical composition of the medicine you usually have, so that an equivalent can be found in Belgium.

Most chemists have a homeopathic section although, unlike in other countries, no reimbursement for homeopathic preparations is currently provided for by mutual associations in Belgium.

Duty Doctors

Doctors usually hold their surgery only on weekdays, so at weekends you will need to call a duty doctor:

- either the local GP making house calls (ask at your commune);
- or the duty doctor service at major hospitals (see Map)

After-hours Service

Chemists' duty service	0900 / 10500
Doctors	02 / 513 02 02
Dentists	02 / 426 10 26
Vets	02 / 538 16 99

Clinics and Hospitals

Hospitals, university clinics and private general hospitals ('polycliniques'), a full list of which is given under 'Cliniques et hôpitaux' in the telephone directory (Yellow pages 990 A).

Emergencies

Accidents, injuries or sickness	100
Fire	100
Road accidents	100
Emergency police and gendarmes	101
Fire station	219 49 90
Ambulance	649 11 22
Anti-poison centre	345 45 45
Burns centre	268 62 00

cf: Emergency page 6.

Institut Jules **Bordet**	Rue Heger Bordet, 1 1000 Bruxelles	✆ 02 / 541 31 11
Hôpital Universitaire **Brugmann**	Place A. Van Gehuchten, 4 1020 Brussels	✆ 02 / 477 21 11
Centre Hospitalier **César de Paepe**	Rue des Alexiens, 11 1000 Brussels	✆ 02 / 506 71 11
Institut Médical **Edith Cavell**	Rue Edith Cavell, 32 1180 Brussels	✆ 02 / 340 40 01
Hôpital Universitaire des **Enfants–Reine Fabiola**	Avenue J.J. Crocq, 15 1020 Brussels	✆ 02 / 477 31 00
Hôpital **Erasme**	route de Lennik, 808 1070 Brussels	✆ 02 / 555 34 05
Centre Hospitalier d'**Etterbeek**	Rue D. Huet, 79 1050 Brussels	✆ 02 / 641 41 11
Hôpital **Molière Longchamp**	Rue Arconi, 142 1180 Brussels	✆ 02 / 348 51 11
Clinique du **Parc Léopold**	Rue Froissart, 38 1040 Brussels	✆ 02 / 287 51 11
Clinique **Ste Elisabeth**	Avenue De Fré, 206 1180 Brussels	✆ 02 / 373 16 11
Clinique **St Jean**	Rue du Marais , 104 1000 Brussels	✆ 02 / 221 91 11
Cliniques Universitaires **St Luc**	Avenue Hippocrate, 10 1200 Brussels	✆ 02 / 764 16 02
Hôpital Universitaire **St Pierre**	Rue Haute, 332 1000 Brussels	✆ 02 / 535 40 51
Clinique Universitaire **VUB**	Avenue Laerbeek, 101 1090 Brussels	

Did you know? Normal body temperature: 98.4° F, 37° C

Useful Address

Brussels Child Birth Trust
✆ 02 / 215 33 77
A group of English-speaking families in Belgium which provides information on pregnancy, childbirth and the early years.

Paediatric Clinic
the War Memorial in the Baron Lambert clinic
rue Baron Lambert, 38
1040 Brussels
✆ 02 / 739 84 11

Useful Reading Matter

The Guide du Mieux-Être (psychology, health and environment) by Benoît Dumont, published by Parcours Éditions. This is a very well-written guide which will give you full information and a list of addresses for organic shops, plus techniques such as yoga, relaxation therapy, Reiki, Tai Chi Chuan, Tantra, etc., as well as centres specialising in therapies such as herbal medicine, meditation, hypnosis, thalassotherapy, etc.

This is a real classic on the subject of complementary therapies to promote holistic well-being, relaxation and personal development.

INDEX

Editors: Anne-Claire de Liedekerke and Claire de Crayencour
Illustrations: Philippine de Laroussilhe
Photographs: Patrick Rittweger
Cover photograph: Sculpture of Nat Neujan – document OPT
Color Map: de rouck
Layout & prepress: (e)**media**
Printing: Imprimerie Enschedé Van Muysewinkel

Thank you to Marie-Christine de Wasseige of Editions Clair de Lettre
with Le Grand Bruxelles des Enfants for her support in the production of this guide.

Published by:
Promart asbl
Avenue Parmentier, 92
1150 Brussels
© 763 11 46
info@expatsinbrussels.com

ART GALLERIES

Zen Gallery
Rue E. Allard, 23
1000 Bruxelles
✆ 02 / 511 95 10
fax: 02 / 511 80 80
Open from Tuesday to Saturday
from 2.00 PM to 6.30 PM. Closed
on Sunday and Monday.

APARTHOTELS

your Home in Brussels TREVI

Immocom
31 Rue Croix de Pierre
1060 Bruxelles
✆ 02 / 534 86 11
fax 02 / 534 86 44
immocom@immocom.be
http://www.immocom.be
Furnished apartments and
studios, short or long term.
Locations: Louise, EU,
Cinquantenaire, Mérode, NATO

BRUSSELS COCOONS

Place Stéphanie, 10
1050 Bruxelles
✆ 02 / 534 76 88
fax 02 / 537 43 22

Studios and apartments with
1, 2 or 3 bedrooms
Fully furnished, fully serviced
Tastefully decorated, weekly
service, Louise and Stock
Exchange neighbourhood.
http://www.brusselscocoons.com

New Continental
rue Defacqz, 33
1050 Bruxelles
✆ 02 / 536 10 00
fax 02 / 536 10 15
e-mail: info@ncf.be
http://www.ncf.be

Hilton Brussels Residence
square Ambiorix, 28 B
1000 Bruxelles
✆ 02 / 743 51 11
fax 02 / 743 51 12

Arcotrade
Rue du Page, 11-13
1050 Bruxelles
✆ 02 / 538 35 85
fax 02 / 538 36 11
http://www.expatsinbrussels.com/arcotrade

BELGIAN SPECIALITIES

La Maison du Diamant
House of Diamonds
Member of the Antwerp
Diamond Exchange
Bd de Waterloo, 10
1000 Bruxelles
✆ 02 / 512 38 63 & 64
fax 02 / 511 82 73
diamonds@europe-internet.com
http://infodiamond.com
Purity and Elegance brought
together with a large selection
of the finest Belgian-cut
diamonds. Representative of
O.L. PERRIN in Brussels.
Purchase of fine gems.

BOWLING

Reservation and booking
available - special price for
youngster before 6.00 PM.
Open from 4 PM. Monday to
Friday - from 2 PM wednesday
and week-end.

CAR- RENTAL

Keddy Car & Truck Rental
Hermesstraat, 3
1930 Zaventem
✆ 02 / 725 10 40
fax 02 / 725 11 15
Car, minibus, truck and
lorries renting.

CAR - SECOND-HAND

Transautomobile sa
Second Hand Cars
Departement
Chssée de Waterloo, 1595
1180 Bruxelles
✆ 02 / 375 66 00
fax: 02 / 375 62 79
quality cars «vendeurs
agréés» – «transit» –
registration documents.

CAR - NEW PURCHASES

Transautomobile sa
Chaussée de Bruxelles, 41
1410 Waterloo
✆ 02 / 352 01 31
fax: 02 / 352 01 52
transauto@skynet.be
taxe Free Cars Sales- new
cars all makes

CAFES & RESTAURANTS

The Thea House
Rue de Rollebeek, 5
1000 Bruxelles
✆ & fax 02 / 511 81 17
Wide choice of teas. Open
from Tuesday to Sunday.

DECORATION

The new decorators
20.000 m of fabric in stock
from 350 BF/m

Furnishing fabrics
Les Tissus Colbert®
Widths from 1,40 m to 2,80 m

Welcome to
32, Avenue d'Oppem
1950 Stockel
✆ 02 / 731 31 27
1383, Chéé de Waterloo
1180 Uccle
✆ 02 / 375 88 13

NICOLE COOREMANS
DÉCORATRICE
ARCHITECTE D'INTÉRIEUR
ASSOCIÉE HONORAIRE DE
DAVID HICKS

FOURNISSEUR BREVETÉ
DE LA COUR DE BELGIQUE
62 RUE DE LA CONCORDE
1050 BRUXELLES (PL. STÉPHANIE)
TEL. (02) 511 31 86 - (02) 511 20 55
FAX (02) 514 08 28

DECORATION – CROCKERY

la vaisselle au kilo

Rue Bodenbroek, 8 A
1000 Bruxelles
(Grand Sablon)
✆ 02 / 513 49 84
fax: 02 / 512 22 27
Earthenware, porcelain,
glassware, cutlery. Open from
Monday to Saturday inclusive
from 10.00 AM to 6.00 PM and
Sunday from 10 AM to 5.30 PM

The House of
Villeroy & Boch
Since 1748

New decoration dept.
Avenue Louise, 37
1050 Bruxelles
✆ 02 / 533 10 51
fax 02 / 533 10 52

Open from 10 AM to 6 PM
Monday to Saturday

FITNESS

John Harris Fitness
Avenue du Lac, 87
1332 Genval
Rue Fossé-aux-Loups, 47
1000 Bruxelles
See announcement on
following page.

GIFTS

Easy Living
Avenue de l'Armée, 20
1040 Bruxelles
✆ 02 / 733 33 11
fax: 02/ 733 11 00

Le Poinçon
Rue Thérésienne, 3
(Porte de Namur)
1000 Bruxelles
Mme Stolberg
✆ 02 / 512 09 30
Silverware
Restoration
Resilvering
Cutlery
Antiques

HOTELS

Alfa Sablon Hotel ★★★★
Strostraat 2-8 Rue de la Paille
Brussel 1000 Bruxelles
Tel. + 32(0)2/513.60.40
Fax + 32(0)2/511.81.41
alfa.sablon@alfahotels.com
SUPRANATIONAL — HOTELS —

In the heart of Brussels near
the worldfamous «Sablon».
32 standard rooms all
equipped with 4 star ameni-
ties. 4 suites with TV, fax,
minibar, safe, telephone
24h roomservice. Non
smoking floor – sauna –
meeting-rooms…
Rue de la Paille, 2-8
1000 Bruxelles
✆ 02 / 513 60 40
fax: 02 / 511 81 41
alfa.sablon@alfahotels.com

INTERNET

Europe Internet.com
info@europe-internet.com
http://www.europe-internet.com
Internet meeting for quality hunters.

JEWELLERY

Avenue Louise, 56
1050 Bruxelles
© & fax: 02 / 513 87 17
Fine collection of modular, interchangeable jewellery.

Berlitz
Avenue Louise, 306
1050 Bruxelles
© 02 / 649 61 75
fax: 02/ 640 11 37

PROPERTY AGENCIES

LANGUAGE COURSES

HRV

Rittweger - Verger
Av. Guillaume Gilbert, 45
1050 Bruxelles
© & fax: 02 / 648 01 91
Original, exclusive creations of traditional and contemporary jewellery. Transformation, restoration and valuation of jewellery. Choice of precious and semi-precious stones. Creation of objets d'art and sculptures in stone, gold, silver and bronze.

**CD-Rom des
rues de Belgique**
© 02 / 216 91 00

FRENCH COURSES

ACTIVE FRENCH SCHOOL
YOUR SPECIALIST IN FRENCH

Groups & private lessons for adults, teenagers & children
daytime – evening – weekend –
at school – at home – at the office.
small groups (max. 7) - friendly atmosphere. once or twice weekly groups.
private lessons: same price for 1 or 2 p.

Brusselsesteenweg, 416
3090 Overijse
© & fax 02 / 657 20 44
email: active-french-school@online.be

Victoire
PROPERTIES
*Residentials Real Estate
Sales – Rentals.
Ground – Villas – Town House.
Apartments furnished or unfurnished*
*Sales: 02 / 772 15 30
Rentals: 02 / 771 12 40
www.publisite.be/victoire
Avenue de Tervuren, 418
1150 Bruxelles*

**CD-Rom des
rues de Belgique**
© 02 / 216 91 00

RELOCATION OFFICES

Brussels Relocation
Bld Henri Rolin, 3
1410 Waterloo
℡ **02 / 353 21 01**
fax 02 / 353 06 42
Professionnal relocation,
services: housing, education...

ROOMS

Rooms to let
+ Bed & Breakfast.
Fully furnished flat.
Rue Martin Lindekens, 59
1150 Bruxelles
℡ 02 / 771 72 45

PETS & GARDENING

Stock L. Garden
Rue d'Argile, 16
1950 Kraainem
℡ 02 / 731 45 58
Everything for the garden, decorating
supplies and articles for pets.

UNIVERSITIES

Where else can you
study with student
from 60 different
countries? Choose
from a wide
variety of Bachelor
degrees.

Vrije Universiteit Brussel
in association with Boston University

RELOCATION
Expatriate Service + Housing Service
Bruxelles – Brabant wallon – Hainaut
LET US DO FOR YOU WHAT WE WOULD LIKE
SOMEONE TO DO FOR US
Tel. +32 / (0)65 / 84 74 05
Fax: +32 / (0)065 / 84 70 17 • e-mail: 4s@pronet.be • URL: www.quatress.com

Vesalius College - VUB
Admissions Dept. 30/0
Boulevard du Triomphe, 2
1050 Bruxelles
℡ 02 / 629 36 26
fax: 02 / 629 36 37
email: vesalius@vub.ac.be
http://www.vub.ac.be/VECO

REMOVALS

ZIEGLER
INTERNATIONAL MOVING

Ziegler
Rue Dieudonné Lefèvre, 160
1020 Bruxelles
℡ 02 / 422 21 10
fax: 02 / 422 21 51

Gosselin Worldwide Moving
Keesinglaan, 28
2100 Deurne
℡ 03 / 360 55 00
fax: 03 / 360 55 79
http://www.gosselin.be

TRAVEL AND TOURISM

V.I.P. Travel
Avenue Louise, 365 bte 26
1050 Bruxelles
℡ 02 / 639 00 35
fax 02 / 646 92 49

CD-Rom des
rues de Belgique
℡ 02 / 216 91 00

UNITED
BUSINESS
INSTITUTES

BBA
Bachelor of Business
Administration
MBA
Master of Business
Administration
UBI
United Business Institutes
Avenue Marnix 20
1000 Brussels
℡ 02 / 548 04 80
Fax 02 / 548 04 89
e.mail: info@ubi.edu
http://www.ubi.edu